ROBERT WEDDERBURN, ABOLITION, AND THE COMMONS

Building on scholarship in Romanticism, Black studies, and environmental humanities, this book follows the political thought of Robert Wedderburn, a Black Romantic-era writer. Wedderburn was deeply influenced by his enslaved mother and grandmother, who raised him in Jamaica. After migrating to London, he became a key figure in ultraradical circles and was prosecuted by the British government for blasphemous libel. Wedderburn's vision for abolition from below sought to forge a transatlantic alliance between English agrarian radicals and enslaved people in the Caribbean. Instead of emancipation administered by British colonial and commercial interests, Wedderburn championed the ecological projects of enslaved and Maroon communities in the Caribbean as models for liberation. His stories of Black, place-based opposition to slavery provide an innovative lens for rereading significant aspects of the Romantic period, including the abolition of slavery, landscape aesthetics, and nineteenth-century radical politics.

KATEY CASTELLANO is Professor of English at James Madison University and author of *The Ecology of British Romantic Conservatism* (2013).

CAMBRIDGE STUDIES IN ROMANTICISM

This series aims to foster the best new work in one of the most challenging fields within English literary studies. From the early 1780s to the early 1830s, a formidable array of talented men and women took to literary composition, not just in poetry, which some of them famously transformed, but in many modes of writing. The expansion of publishing created new opportunities for writers, and the political stakes of what they wrote were raised again by what Wordsworth called those 'great national events' that were 'almost daily taking place': the French Revolution, the Napoleonic and American wars, urbanization, industrialization, religious revival, an expanded empire abroad, and the reform movement at home. This was an enormous ambition, even when it pretended otherwise. The relations between science, philosophy, religion, and literature were reworked in texts such as *Frankenstein* and *Biographia Literaria*; gender relations in *A Vindication of the Rights of Woman* and *Don Juan*; journalism by Cobbett and Hazlitt; and poetic form, content, and style by the Lake School and the Cockney School. Outside Shakespeare studies, probably no body of writing has produced such a wealth of commentary or done so much to shape the responses of modern criticism. This indeed is the period that saw the emergence of those notions of literature and of literary history, especially national literary history, on which modern scholarship in English has been founded.

The categories produced by Romanticism have also been challenged by recent historicist arguments. The task of the series is to engage both with a challenging corpus of Romantic writings and with the changing field of criticism they have helped to shape. As with other literary series published by Cambridge University Press, this one will represent the work of both younger and more established scholars on either side of the Atlantic and elsewhere.

See the end of the book for a complete list of published titles.

ROBERT WEDDERBURN, ABOLITION, AND THE COMMONS

Romanticism's Black Geographies

KATEY CASTELLANO
James Madison University

CAMBRIDGE
UNIVERSITY PRESS

CAMBRIDGE
UNIVERSITY PRESS

Shaftesbury Road, Cambridge CB2 8EA, United Kingdom

One Liberty Plaza, 20th Floor, New York, NY 10006, USA

477 Williamstown Road, Port Melbourne, VIC 3207, Australia

314–321, 3rd Floor, Plot 3, Splendor Forum, Jasola District Centre, New Delhi – 110025, India

103 Penang Road, #05-06/07, Visioncrest Commercial, Singapore 238467

Cambridge University Press is part of Cambridge University Press & Assessment, a department of the University of Cambridge.

We share the University's mission to contribute to society through the pursuit of education, learning and research at the highest international levels of excellence.

www.cambridge.org
Information on this title: www.cambridge.org/9781009523905

DOI: 10.1017/9781009523875

First published 2024

A catalogue record for this publication is available from the British Library.

Library of Congress Cataloging-in-Publication Data
NAMES: Castellano, Katey, 1971- author.
TITLE: Robert Wedderburn, abolition, and the commons : romanticism's Black geographies / Katey Castellano, James Madison University, Virginia.
DESCRIPTION: New York : Cambridge University Press, 2024. | Series: Cambridge studies in romanticism | Includes bibliographical references and index.
IDENTIFIERS: LCCN 2024013536 (print) | LCCN 2024013537 (ebook) | ISBN 9781009523905 (hardback) | ISBN 9781009523868 (paperback) | ISBN 9781009523875 (ebook)
SUBJECTS: LCSH: Slavery–West Indies–History–19th century. | Wedderburn, R. (Robert)–Criticism and interpretation. | Abolitionists–England–London. | Politics and literature–Great Britain–History–19th century. | Romanticism–Great Britain.
CLASSIFICATION: LCC HT1071 .C37 2024 (print) | LCC HT1071 (ebook) | DDC 306.3/62–dc23/eng/20240402
LC record available at https://lccn.loc.gov/2024013536
LC ebook record available at https://lccn.loc.gov/2024013537

ISBN 978-1-009-52390-5 Hardback

Contents

Figures

Acknowledgments

Conceived a few years before the pandemic, much of this book was written without the support of regular in-person conferences that facilitate constructive feedback from other scholars. However, in the early stages, two conference meetings encouraged this new research direction. In 2019, Regina Hewitt and Michael Demson organized a panel commemorating Peterloo at the North American Society for the Study of Romanticism (NASSR) where I presented a paper making tentative connections between William Cobbett and Robert Wedderburn. I remain grateful for the encouraging response from the audience and other panelists. At the same conference, Fran Botkin, a scholar who has long been dedicated to drawing the connections between Romanticism and the Caribbean, was kind enough to have lunch with me to discuss this project. I presented early work on Wedderburn's abolitionist geographies at my home institution's African, African American, and Diaspora Studies (AAAD) conference the following year.

During the pandemic, Kate Singer and Chris Washington organized a virtual Romanticism and Black Studies conference where I gave a presentation about Wedderburn and *The History of Mary Prince*. I learned so much from the presentations at that conference and received encouragement from other Romanticists, including Joseph Albernaz, Allison Dushane, Shelby Johnson, Eric Lindstrom, and Matthew Rowney. Eric Lindstrom invited me to give a talk about Wedderburn via Zoom to his lively undergraduate Romanticism class. Thanks are also due to Sonja Lawrenson and Emma Liggins, organizers of the North West Long 19C Research Seminar where I spoke about the life narratives of Mary Prince and Wedderburn. I noticed Matthew Lewis's war against pigs after reading Ron Broglio's *Animal Revolution*, which taught me to acknowledge the natural world's hawkish energies. A brilliant scholar I met in graduate school, Nihad Farooq, provided feedback about the book's overall trajectory. Alex A. Moulton, a scholar of Black Geographies in Jamaica, generously read and commented on an early version of the manuscript.

My first essay about Wedderburn's work was published in *Small Axe* instead of a Romanticism journal because I wanted the research to be vetted by Black and Caribbean Studies scholars. I am grateful for the work of the anonymous readers, the managing editor Vanessa Pérez-Rosario, and editor David Scott, all of whom provided rigorous and encouraging feedback. That essay initiated this book project. Deidre Lynch emailed after reading the *Small Axe* article to say she had decided to add Wedderburn to the *Norton Anthology of English Literature: The Romantic Period*. This is arguably the most important outcome of this project: More students and scholars will read and engage with Wedderburn's texts. My decision to shift this book project to centering Black freedom practices instead of consigning them to a chapter took place at the British Library during an Eccles Centre Fellowship in American Studies. The fellowship provided much-needed time at the British Library to think, read, and access research materials. I especially thank Polly Russell, Philip Abraham, Jean Petrovic, Chantelle Richardson, Kate Mulry, and the British Library reference team in the Humanities and Rare Books reading room.

Curator Sara W. Duke and the reference team in the Library of Congress Prints and Photographs Division provided additional research support. James Madison University's Carrier library, the English library liaison, Brian Flota, and the tenacious and unflappable interlibrary loan department supported this research. At my home institution, I received funding from the College of Arts and Letters Alumni Award, the JMU Emeriti Award, and the Roop Distinguished Professorship of English. Current and former English department colleagues, including Robert Aguirre, Lauren Alleyne, Dabney Bankert, Annette Federico, Mollie Godfrey, Dawn Goode, Laurie Kutchins, and Mark Rankin, offered insightful feedback at various stages of the project. The current English department head, Becky Childs, supported my research through its final phases. Thanks are also due to the upper-level undergraduate and graduate students in my "Romantic Literature and the Caribbean" seminars over the past five years, where I tested many of the ideas in this book. Of these students, I would especially like to thank Morgan Aderton, Edana Colegrove, Austyn Haywood, Colleen Moran, and Grace Thomsen.

I would also like to thank the Cambridge University Press commissioning editor Bethany Thomas and Cambridge Studies in Romanticism series editor James Chandler for guiding this book through its final stages. The insightful anonymous readers returned generously detailed reports that helped me to write a much better book. Earlier versions of parts of Chapters 1 and 3 appeared in the following journals: "Provision

Grounds against the Plantation: Robert Wedderburn's *Axe Laid to the Root*," in *Small Axe: A Caribbean Journal of Criticism* 25.1 (2021), republished by permission of Duke University Press; "'She Trafficked on Her Own Account': Black Women's Abolitionist Geographies in Robert Wedderburn's *Horrors of Slavery* (1824) and *History of Mary Prince* (1831)," in *European Romantic Review* 35.2 (2024). The insightful suggestions from *ERR*'s anonymous readers and the editors, Benjamin Colbert and Lucy Morrison, improved Chapter 3. Special thanks are also due to Paul Lewin, who generously allowed the reproduction of his painting *Nanny and the Pumpkin Seeds*.

Finally, I want to thank my children and their partners, Faith Castellano, Jake Castellano, Stephen Simmons, and Hanna Frye; and my grandchildren, Adalyn, Savanah, and Wyatt Castellano, for their energetic companionship and humor. My partner, Pete Bsumek, cheered me on at every stage of this project. For six years, many dinners and hikes included lengthy discussions about Wedderburn's writing. His expertise in rhetoric and environmental advocacy helped me think more clearly about Wedderburn's land-based politics, and his belief in the project gave me the courage to put it forward.

Introduction
Robert Wedderburn, Romanticism, and Black Geographies

Is not the system of private property in land chargeable with murder?
—Robert Wedderburn, *The Forlorn Hope*

How does a scholar of British Romanticism end up writing a book about Black Caribbean geographies? The project began by exploring how Romantic-era working-class class writers, such as William Cobbett and John Clare, were writing against the enclosure of the commons by imagining new ways to develop commons in Great Britain. Places where ordinary people farmed and lived communally, commons have been described by Peter Linebaugh, whose materialist approach to the topic emphasizes that commons were created "*through* labor *with* other resources; it does not make a division between 'labor' and 'natural resources.'"[1] Inspired by his ecological reading of the commons, I initially decided to add a chapter on the critically neglected Black British writer Robert Wedderburn. Accustomed to grappling with working-class periodicals, particularly Cobbett's *Register*, my attention was drawn to a line in the last issue of Wedderburn's *Axe Laid to the Root*, in which he prophesied a growing movement toward abolition in Kingston, Jamaica: "The free Mulattoes are reading Cobbett's *Register*, and talking about St. Domingo" (6.90).[2] Wedderburn's vision of a transatlantic alliance between Cobbett's agrarian radicalism and West Indian slave revolts gestured toward a global, transracial solidarity absent from Cobbett's politics. Moreover, since Wedderburn's imagined transatlantic collaboration was a performance for his primarily white, working-class audience in London, Wedderburn was – beyond aligning interests – *championing* Black, West-Indian resistance against slavery as a *model* for his white audience. In the turbulent and repressive era of the 1810s, just before the Peterloo Massacre, Wedderburn imagined new ways of creating commons, like William Cobbett and John Clare. Yet Wedderburn's commons were based quite differently on long-established African-Jamaican land use and food sovereignty practices. To explore Wedderburn's vision fully, I put aside the first project. *Robert Wedderburn, Abolition, and the Commons* follows the political thought of Robert Wedderburn, whose advocacy for Black, place-based opposition to slavery provides an innovative lens for reading Romantic-era political prose, slave narratives, and travel writing.

Robert Wedderburn was born in 1762, and his mother, Rosanna, was his father's enslaved house manager (Figure I.1). His father, the Scots planter James Wedderburn, owned several large sugar plantations in the Westmoreland parish of Jamaica. When Rosanna was pregnant with Robert, James Wedderburn sold her to another enslaver. Throughout the rest of his life, he refused to acknowledge or support Robert, except to manumit him and his brother James for £200.[3] Although he was not enslaved, Wedderburn was raised by his enslaved mother and grandmother. He further witnessed the violence of slavery as he matured into adulthood as a jobbing millwright who traveled to many parts of Jamaica. Wedderburn joined the Royal Navy at age sixteen and migrated to London, where he united with other African, Irish, and lower-class English people in London's ultra-radical networks. In 1817, he became the de facto leader of the Spencean Philanthropists, a group dedicated to achieving social equality by ending private property in land, after the former leader was jailed for his political activities under the suspension of habeas corpus.[4] Wedderburn's significant publications were written after this moment: his working-class periodical of 1817, *Axe Laid to the Root,* and his 1824 life narrative, *The Horrors of Slavery.*

As a leader of the Spencean Philanthropists, Wedderburn became well known for his preaching and public debates at his Hopkins Street Chapel in Soho, London.[5] In many ways, Wedderburn's debates followed ultra-radical traditions. As Iain McCalman points out, "the Spenceans' preference for the tavern debating club as a radical organisation and strategy linked them with long-established popular traditions."[6] Wedderburn's topics for debate, however, were anything but traditional. For example, his topic "Can It Be Murder to Kill a Tyrant?" and "Has a Slave an Inherent Right to Slay His Master, Who Refuses Him His Liberty?" evoked slave rebellion as an ethical model of liberation for his white audience (Figure I.2). In an intellectual milieu when proslavery writers resisted the end of slavery, and antislavery activists desired an "emancipation from above" that was administered and controlled by British colonial and commercial interests, Wedderburn's championing of abolition from below through slave revolt marked a startling departure from mainstream politics.

Wedderburn's debate about slave revolts occurred at a significant moment, just one week before the Peterloo Massacre. Like Henry Hunt

Figure I.1 Portrait of Robert Wedderburn. Frontispiece from *Horrors of Slavery*, London, 1824.

and other working-class activists, Wedderburn escalated his rhetoric precisely then, establishing his participation in this quasi-revolutionary cusp in British working-class history. A handbill for Wedderburn's next debate, scheduled on the same day as the Peterloo massacre, August 16, 1819,

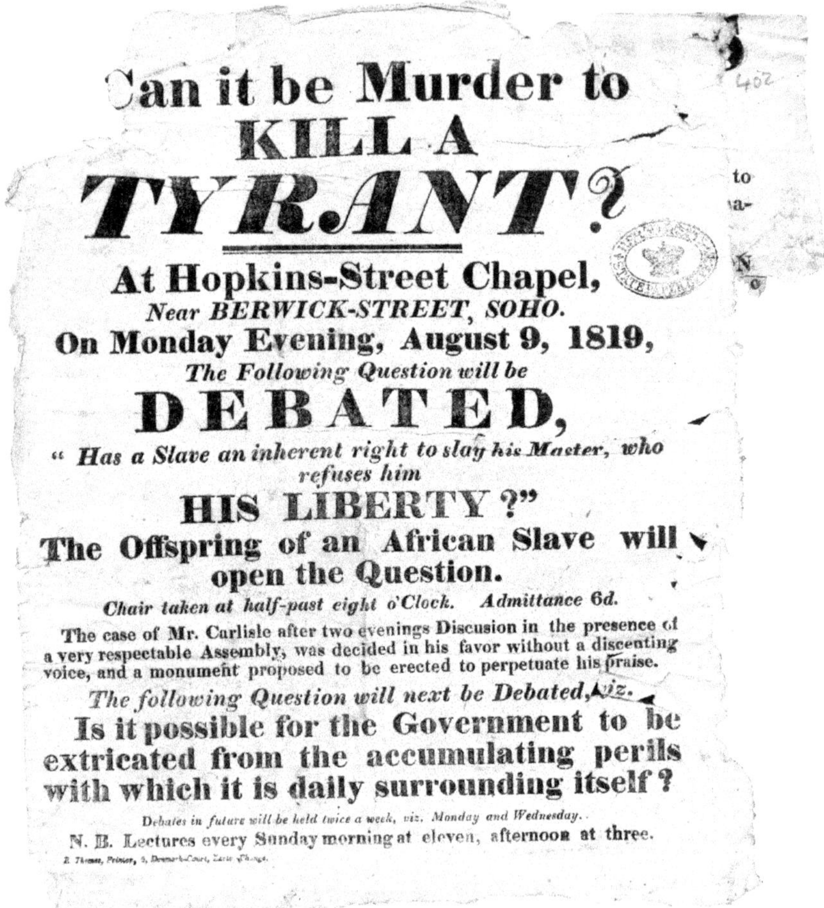

Can it be Murder to
KILL A
TYRANT?

At Hopkins-Street Chapel,
Near BERWICK-STREET, SOHO.
On Monday Evening, August 9, 1819,
The Following Question will be
DEBATED,
" Has a Slave an inherent right to slay his Master, who refuses him
HIS LIBERTY ?"
The Offspring of an African Slave will open the Question.
Chair taken at half-past eight o'Clock. *Admittance 6d.*

The case of Mr. Carlisle after two evenings Discusion in the presence of a very respectable Assembly, was decided in his favor without a discenting voice, and a monument proposed to be erected to perpetuate his praise.

The following Question will next be Debated, viz.
Is it possible for the Government to be extricated from the accumulating perils with which it is daily surrounding itself ?

Debates in future will be held twice a week, viz. Monday and Wednesday.
N. B. Lectures every Sunday morning at eleven, afternoon at three.

Figure I.2 Handbill advertising a debate on August 9, 1819, "Can It Be Murder to Kill a Tyrant?"
Courtesy of the National Archives of the UK.

reported that at the previous week's debate, the assembly gathered at his Hopkins Street Chapel decided in favor of slave revolt (Figure I.3). Wedderburn's summary of the debate alluded to the Haitian Revolution, boasting that the assembly of working-class men "expressed their Desire of hearing of another sable Nation freeing itself by the Dagger from the base Tyranny of their Christian masters." By calling for another Haitian Revolution, this time in the British West Indies, Wedderburn expressed moral outrage against the British system at home and slavery in the

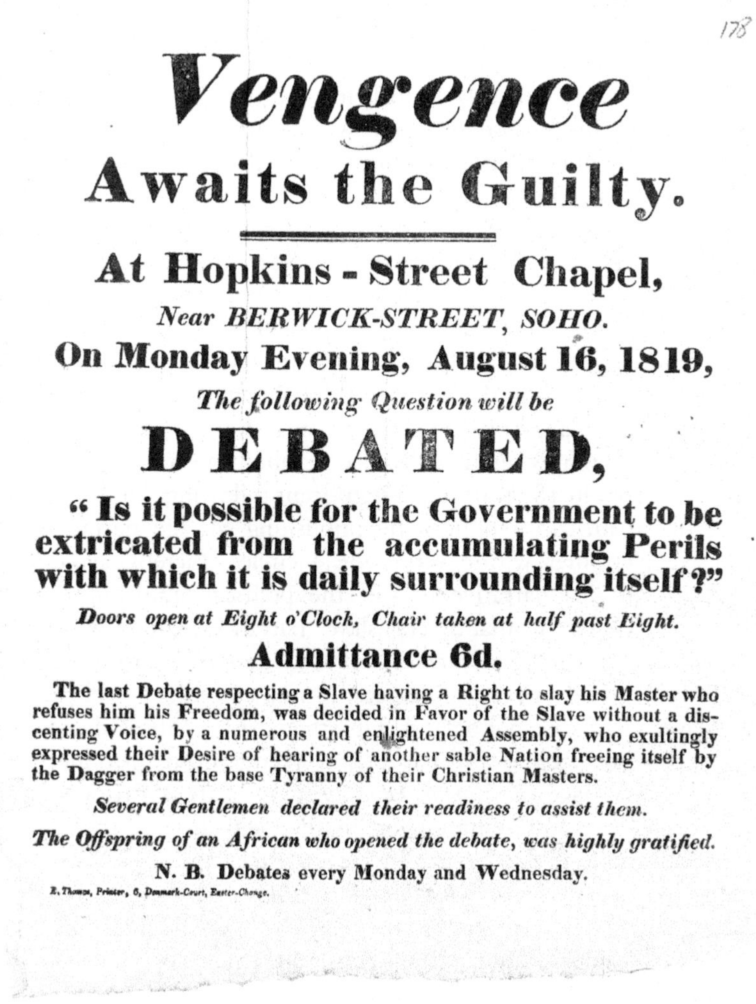

Vengence
Awaits the Guilty.

At Hopkins - Street Chapel,
Near BERWICK-STREET, SOHO.
On Monday Evening, August 16, 1819,
The following Question will be
DEBATED,

"Is it possible for the Government to be extricated from the accumulating Perils with which it is daily surrounding itself?"

Doors open at Eight o'Clock, Chair taken at half past Eight.

Admittance 6d.

The last Debate respecting a Slave having a Right to slay his Master who refuses him his Freedom, was decided in Favor of the Slave without a dis-centing Voice, by a numerous and enlightened Assembly, who exultingly expressed their Desire of hearing of another sable Nation freeing itself by the Dagger from the base Tyranny of their Christian Masters.

Several Gentlemen declared their readiness to assist them.

The Offspring of an African who opened the debate, was highly gratified.

N. B. Debates every Monday and Wednesday.

R. Thomas, Printer, 6, Denmark-Court, Exeter-Change.

Figure I.3 Handbill advertising a debate on August 16, 1819, "Vengeance Awaits the Guilty."
Courtesy of the National Archives of the UK.

colonies while proposing a different, distinctly African-Caribbean version of a more just society.[7] A government spy report written on August 10, 1819, recorded the debate and suggested Wedderburn was a threat to the British government: "After noticing the Insurrections of the Slaves in some of the West India Islands he said they fought in some instances for twenty years for 'Liberty' – and he then appealed to Britons who boasted such superior feeling and principles, whether they were ready to fight now for but a short time for their Liberties."[8] Inflammatory spy reports led to Wedderburn's arrest; he was jailed for sedition during the Peterloo Massacre. After his release on bail, Wedderburn "did not flinch," as McCalman aptly puts it, and he continued the debates.[9] However, within months, he was arrested again.

Although the jury recommended mercy, Wedderburn was given a two-year sentence for blasphemous libel in 1820. At his sentencing, the solicitor general declared, "the defendant is a most dangerous character, because he certainly possesses considerable talents, and those too of a popular nature, and calculated to do much mischief amongst the class of people to whom he was in the habit of addressing himself."[10] The idea that Wedderburn was dangerous precisely because he was too talented and popular indicates that when he published his abolitionist life narrative, *The Horrors of Slavery*, in 1824, he had a significant following. He continued to depart from mainstream politics by publishing his life narrative as an inexpensive pamphlet within ultra-radical circles, thereby avoiding the demand to edit his narrative to suit the political ambitions of white abolitionists. Other Romantic-era slave narratives, such as Olaudah Equiano's *The Interesting Narrative* (1789) and *The History of Mary Prince* (1831), were, to varying degrees, prompted, edited, and published by antislavery activists in England. Untethered by political demands for middle-class respectability and patriotism, Wedderburn introduced himself on the title page of *Horrors of Slavery* as "Late a Prisoner in His Majesty's Gaol": a representation of his life, reiterated in the narrative, that radically tracked the horrors of racialized slavery on a West Indian plantation to incarceration in an English prison. *Horrors of Slavery* also celebrated the rebellious practices of his enslaved mother, Rosanna, and his grandmother, Talkee Amy, as the sources of his emancipation from slavery rather than his residence on English soil.

While Romantic-era readers and government spies were alert to his presence, Wedderburn figures only marginally in contemporary Romanticist criticism. Wedderburn's work may have been neglected, in part, because of intractable questions about his authorship. In this book, Wedderburn's political theory will be discerned chiefly through his publications *Axe Laid to the Root* and *Horrors of Slavery*. However, there are other pamphlets and articles associated with his name. His first pamphlet, an antinomian political commentary, *Truth Self-Supported* (ca. 1802), was likely dictated to his publishers due to his illiteracy at the time.[11] Even if *Truth Self-Supported* was heavily edited and transcribed, Wedderburn returned to similar antinomian and anticlerical themes in the 1820s. Most scholars agree that he wrote the short satire "The Holy Liturgy," published in Richard Carlile's *The Lion* (1828). An anti-clerical satire published under his name, *Cast-Iron Parsons* (1820), however, was likely ghostwritten by the freethinker and pornographer George Cannon, alias Erasmus Perkins. Wedderburn's "radical patron" and collaborator, Cannon also wrote and then published Wedderburn's defense for his trial for blasphemy in 1820.[12] Unfortunately, Cannon's "defense" was so defiant as to ensure Wedderburn's imprisonment. Ryan Hanely notes, "historians have tended to represent the relationship between the two men as more mutually beneficial than was actually the case."[13] Moreover, questions about whether Cannon merely transcribed and polished or completely invented Wedderburn's defense remain. These questions are additionally complicated by the collaborative nature of ultra-radical print culture, which, Eric Pencek argues, emerged "in opposition to the underlying assumptions that go with individual authorship."[14] Wedderburn's embrace of collaborative authorship in opposition to private property challenges scholarship about his work.

Although uncertainty about the individual authorship of some texts within Wedderburn's oeuvre should be acknowledged, it should not be a barrier to analyzing the primary textual artifacts associated with him. As literary analysis instead of biography, this book does not detail every facet of Wedderburn's long, complicated, communal life and publications. *Robert Wedderburn, Abolition, and the Commons* limits its focus to Wedderburn's political contributions to Romantic print culture in the turbulent years before and after the Peterloo Massacre, *Axe Laid to the Root* (1817) and *Horrors of Slavery* (1824). Scholars agree that Wedderburn authored these texts because their content aligns with the Home Office's documentation of his speeches.[15] The government spy reports on his speeches verify the content and influence of Wedderburn's political activism, yet they are part of a repressive discourse intended to criminalize his politics. This book minimizes reliance on them. Another marker of Wedderburn's prominence during the years in which he wrote *Axe Laid to the Root* and *Horrors of Slavery* can be found in two caricatures by one of the Romantic period's "undisputed masters" of caricature, George Cruikshank.[16] *A Peep into the City of London Tavern* (1817) featured Wedderburn prominently alongside well-known radicals, and *The New Union Club* (1819) represented Wedderburn in alliance with abolitionists William Wilberforce and Zachary Macaulay. Both caricatures expressed

Figure I.4 George Cruikshank, *A Peep into the City of London Tavern by an Irish Amateur on the 21st of August 1817 – or a Sample of the Cooperation to Be Expected in One of Mr. Owen's Projected Paradises*, 1817.
Courtesy of the trustees of the British Museum.

anxiety about the extent and influence of Wedderburn's distinctively Black perspective on radicalism and abolition.

A Peep in the London Tavern (1817) was intended to mock the working-class movement toward "cooperation" by emphasizing significant differences in radical thought (Figure I.4). At the center of the caricature, the utopian proto-socialist Robert Owen stands on a table holding a copy of his *A New View of Society* (1813–16). A crowd has gathered to hear Owen speak, and several audience members, including the well-known radicals William Hone, Major John Cartwright, and Thomas Wooler, can be identified through their word bubbles. Wedderburn alone has risen above the other radicals by standing and stepping onto the table from which Owen speaks. Wedderburn contends, "I understand Slavery well! my mother was a slave. This would be but an improved system of Slavery – & without the solace of Revealed Religion & Faith."[17] Wedderburn must have been so well known that his biographical background would identify him to Cruikshank's audience even beyond London's radical circles.

Although Cruikshank would hardly have been sympathetic to Wedderburn's views, the word bubble correctly noted that Wedderburn's political thought emerged from his observation of enslaved Black women's strategic resistance to slavery. Wedderburn critiqued Owen's plan as "an improved system of Slavery," which astutely pointed out that Owen's moral concerns were limited to British workers in cotton mills while eliding the industry's dependence on American slavery for cotton. Cruikshank's summary of Wedderburn's critique uncannily anticipates Michael Morris's argument that Owen's improvements for textile workers were "a node in the global history of cotton" that illustrated British "improvement" at home depended on transatlantic slavery.[18] Wedderburn's publications demonstrate that he was indeed part of the political discussion about Owen's *New View*. His *Forlorn Hope*, a co-produced cheap weekly periodical published the same month as this caricature, accused Owen of being a "tool of the landholders" who hid the government's "inability to redress" the condition of the lower classes. Insisting that English workers must do more than cooperate to negotiate better pay, Wedderburn argued, "private property in land has been the cause of all the blood which has been shed in the last fifty years."[19] In other words, private property was the root of oppression, and liberation could be won only through land reparations that restored the commons and common rights throughout the British Empire, in Great Britain, Ireland, and, crucially, the West Indies.[20]

Like others in the crowd, Wedderburn can be further identified through the texts he carried with him, the Bible and William Wilberforce's anti-slavery writings. Wedderburn's status as a Black abolitionist was highlighted to distinguish him as a suspicious outsider to working-class politics whose ideas of transatlantic emancipation fit uneasily, if at all, with other working-class radicals. Although Cruikshank accurately depicted how

Wedderburn's political thought emerged, quite proudly, from his identity as the child of an enslaved woman and his lived experiences as a Black man in Jamaica, Wedderburn was an emancipationist who focused on land reparations instead of legal rights. He disagreed with Wilberforce's paternalist plan for a gradual transition from slavery to wage labor because it was designed to leave the colonial plantation economy intact. The idea that Wedderburn had Wilberforce "in his pocket" to back up his beliefs effectively denies Wedderburn's status as an original political theorist, and, moreover, reiterates a persistent misunderstanding of abolition that conflates the work of most antislavery activists with the position of William Wilberforce.[21] Cruikshank's racialized caricature of Wedderburn's physical features and behavior represent him as out of place and even menacing. Wedderburn waves his fist angrily while encroaching on Owen's space by stepping off his bench and placing his foot on the table. McCalman argues that his shoeless foot with bare toes sticking through the worn-out sock is meant to juxtapose Wedderburn's "ragged" appearance with Owen's neat dress.[22] Cruikshank minimizes Wedderburn's significant intellectual challenge to both English radicalism and abolition by depicting Wedderburn's disagreement with Owen as ill-mannered and physically aggressive. However, Wedderburn's foot on the table next to Owen demonstrates that his political ideas were a possible, even formidable, challenger to Owen's plans for reform.

Robert Wedderburn, Abolition, and the Commons endeavors to place Wedderburn's political thought at the center of that table instead of on the shoeless, tattered margins. By pulling Wilberforce "out of his pocket," Wedderburn's theories of abolition are revealed as a critique, not a celebration, of European concepts of freedom. For example, in *Axe Laid to the Root*, Wedderburn published a fictionalized open letter to Miss Campbell, a Jamaican Maroon, that argued, "yes, the English, in the days of Cromwell, while they were asserting the rights of man at home, were destroying your ancestors then fighting for their liberty" (4.54). Wedderburn challenged his white audience by asserting that the "rights of man" were accomplished while actively "destroying" the liberties of the Jamaican Maroons (and other colonized peoples, for he wrote about Cromwell's devastation of the Irish as well). Wedderburn confronts his readers with the dark underside of Romanticism's rights and radicalism, founded alongside and even because of Europe's imperialist land grabs and plantation slavery.

Moreover, by drawing on history as far back as the establishment of Jamaica as a British colony in 1655, Wedderburn emphasized that the expansion of the British empire also forced Black people in Jamaica to develop other forms of freedom in autonomous Maroon communities, where abolition and decolonization were already underway. Wedderburn centered Black histories and subjectivity while writing about British history and politics. Bakary Diaby recommends examining Black Romantic subjectivity because it would provide a model of revolution that "entail[s] having a revolutionary fragility forged by the oppressive weight of repressive power, a fragility in stark contrast to the reactive one that wields such power."[23] Many of the histories elaborated in Wedderburn's writing, such as the flight of the Jamaican Maroons or his enslaved mother's liberation tactics, drew upon and advocated for the efficacy of such "revolutionary fragility."

Robert Wedderburn, Abolition, and the Commons is indebted to the work of Manu Samriti Chander, who argues, "perhaps paradoxically, we need to cede Romanticism to its unacknowledged participants, those whose challenges to the field will also define it."[24] This book follows the political thought and activism of one unacknowledged participant, Robert Wedderburn, who proposed a model of freedom that profoundly reverses the white abolitionist belief that European models of liberty will eventually spread to the Caribbean. Wedderburn instead highlights Black Jamaican practices of freedom in collective slave revolt, Maroon villages, and traditional subsistence agriculture. Using Wedderburn's oeuvre as a "challenge to the field" of Romanticism, as Chander suggests, this book then rereads more familiar Romantic-era texts in light of the Black abolitionist geographies that Wedderburn introduced to his London audiences.[25] For example, Wedderburn's ideas about land-based freedom expose dramatic struggles over the provision grounds of enslaved laborers in Matthew Lewis's *Journal of a West India Proprietor*. Wedderburn's vindication of the freedom practices of his enslaved mother and grandmother in *Horrors of Slavery*, when read alongside *The History of Mary Prince,* prompts a reassessment of the influential tactics of Black women's activism in the abolition of slavery. Although Cruikshank represented Wedderburn's politics as a hostile outlier to even the most radical thought, this book invites Wedderburn's ideas into the political and textual histories of the Romantic period.

Wedderburn, Romanticism, and Black Studies

My reading of Wedderburn's life and writing is indebted to two distinct groups of scholars: scholars of Romantic-era working-class writers and scholars working in Black Atlantic studies. Malcolm Chase notes that Wedderburn participated in working-class agrarian movements toward a "People's Farm," which advocated for the restoration of the commons and a radical redistribution of land in England.[26] Iain McCalman's extensive archival research on Wedderburn's role in English radicalism is documented in *Radical Underworld* and his book-length collection of excerpts from Wedderburn's writing, *Horrors of Slavery and Other Writings, by Robert Wedderburn.* More than any other scholar, he laid the groundwork for understanding Wedderburn's influence in early nineteenth-century London. About *Axe Laid to the Root,* McCalman writes, "the periodical's most important contribution to popular radical ideology came from its sustained attempt to integrate the prospect of slave revolution from the West Indies with that of working-class revolution in England."[27] In addition to being a writer, Wedderburn was a famous orator who staged public debates. Michael Scrivener argues that Wedderburn's writing and oratory were both uniquely dialogic. Instead of using a singular voice, his thought was articulated through "a vivid performance of different roles."[28] David Worrall likewise emphasizes Wedderburn's oral debates. He asserts that "the forum in which Robert Wedderburn most vociferously developed his anticolonialist and revolutionary polemic was in a ruined loft in Soho's Hopkins Street."[29] This body of ground-breaking scholarship on Romantic-era working-class politics sought to include Wedderburn in the network of early nineteenth-century ultra-radicalism and print culture, so it tends to interpret Wedderburn's political writing as neatly aligning with or even derivative of white ultra-radical activists, such as his friend Thomas Spence.

The second group of scholars who have written about Wedderburn study Black British writers and Caribbean slave narratives. Often, this scholarship focuses on *Horrors of Slavery* (1824) and Wedderburn's sense of identity as a formerly enslaved, mixed-race person traversing London. Alan Rice attests to the cultural hybridity of Wedderburn's "unique and splendidly polyglot transatlantic dialect."[30] Helen Thomas suggests that by foregrounding his mixed-race identity, Wedderburn's "work exceeded and, in a sense, exacerbated, the parameters of spiritual discourse contained within earlier slave narratives."[31] Also noting his spiritual, prophetic style, Sue Thomas highlights Wedderburn's lively mixture "of both life writing and jeremiad," which sets a different tone from other West Indian slave narratives, particularly Olaudah Equiano's *Interesting Narrative.*[32] More recently, Michael Morris reads Wedderburn within the context of his Scottish father, James Wedderburn. The elder Wedderburn fled Great Britain to make new fortunes in Jamaica following the execution of his father after the Battle at Culloden in 1746.[33] Ryan Hanley situates Wedderburn within the publishing history of other Black British writers from the Romantic era, such as Equiano and Quobna Ottobah Cugoano, arguing that "unlike earlier black writers, Wedderburn never courted the approval of, or support from, 'respectable' authority figures, either within or peripheral to his own networks."[34]

While indebted to scholarship that situates Wedderburn either within working-class or Black Atlantic histories, this book is invested in bringing these strands of scholarship together to treat Wedderburn as a political theorist who brought distinctly African-Caribbean knowledge to his lower-class audiences in London. Wedderburn innovatively incorporated his life narrative into the realm of British working-class politics. Like me, Raphael Hoermann marvels that more work has not been done to take Wedderburn's political thought seriously. He conjectures that Wedderburn's "constant deliberate slippage between race and class and his call for violent transatlantic revolution might have contributed to his silencing."[35] For example, in Manisha Sinha's exhaustive transatlantic history of abolition, Wedderburn's work is discussed in only two paragraphs. Although Sinha laments that his work "has been ignored by historians of abolition," she only briefly acknowledges that his work provides "a blueprint for a postemancipation utopian black polity" without further explanation.[36] This book seeks to unravel and explain the troubling liminal dimensions of Wedderburn's utopian Black polity.

As a Black man who was formerly enslaved and as an impoverished working-class London radical who experienced persecution under British law, Wedderburn's writing appears to slip problematically between "wage slavery" and West Indian slavery. By celebrating the place-based freedom practices of enslaved people as worthy of emulation, Wedderburn, at first, appears to resonate with proslavery writers who sought to justify slavery as humane, or alternately, with working-class writers who claimed enslaved people in the West Indies had better living conditions than English workers. Elizabeth Bohls' argument that "the politics of slavery . . . played out to a significant degree as a politics of place" helps to explain why Wedderburn's politics did not resemble British abolitionist views.[37] Bohls notes that Romantic-era colonial histories and proslavery texts employed the landscape aesthetics of the picturesque to obfuscate the brutal reality of slavery in the West Indies. On the other hand, British abolitionists acknowledged slavery's brutality, but they also carefully contained that brutality within the geographic boundaries of the West Indies to reassure readers that freedom and opportunity reigned for all in England. In other words, antislavery activists imagined freedom as a transplant: British liberal freedoms, which resided in England, would be planted in the West Indies and extended to enslaved people. Wedderburn jettisoned the geographic paradigms of both antislavery and proslavery writers by insisting that Black place-based freedom practices in the West Indies were superior to British individualist freedoms.

Deciphering Wedderburn's celebration of Black geographies, in which land-based West Indian insurrection was an essential touchstone, requires a turn toward scholarship in Caribbean and Black studies. Wedderburn's lived experiences with enslaved people in Jamaica taught him about resistance to the emergent plantation economy. C. L. R. James argues,

> wherever the sugar plantation and slavery existed, they imposed a pattern. It is an original pattern, not European, not African, not a part of the American main, not native in any conceivable sense of that word, but West Indian, *sui generis*, with no parallel anywhere else.[38]

On his father's sugar plantations and then on the docks of Kingston, Wedderburn negotiated and observed the frontiers of the Caribbean plantation economy. To be economically viable, sugar production required large monoculture farms. Eric Williams notes that the rise of sugar plantations was responsible for "changing flourishing commonwealths of small farmers into vast sugar factories owned by a camarilla of absentee capitalist magnates and worked by a mass of alien proletarians."[39] While the movement to large-scale agriculture was taking place across the British empire, West Indian plantations were distinctive because, Sidney Mintz explains, "so much of the industrial processing of the cane was also carried out on the plantations."[40] In addition to his experiences on sugar plantations, Wedderburn explains that in his early work as a jobbing millwright, he was able to travel through many parts of Jamaica:

> Though only a lad, I was yet capable of making observations on passing occurrences; being reared in Kingston, and having also lived eighteen months in Spanish town, and the like period in Port Royal; possessing an inclination to rove, gave me a still better opportunity to observe the manners and customs of that country.[41]

From Jamaica's port cities to rural plantations, Wedderburn's experiences with agro-industrialist plantation slavery provided highly sophisticated insights into the workings of Great Britain's economy that were unavailable to most London radicals. If the large commodity plantation is a land-based form of control that reorganized environmental and social relationships, the African-Jamaican place-based freedoms championed by Wedderburn, on the provision grounds of enslaved people and in Maroon villages, offered a radically different, decolonial foundation for radical politics.

Wedderburn insisted that abolition must be grounded in land and food sovereignty, and not just the law. His view resonates with Sylvia Wynter's distinction between narratives of the plantation versus those of the provision grounds. Provision grounds were plots of land given to enslaved people in the Caribbean to grow their own food. Outside of the plantation's gaze and near mountains unsuitable for growing commodity crops, the provision grounds were located outside of the view and control of plantation overseers. As enslaved and formerly enslaved people cultivated common culture and traditional knowledge on the provision grounds, they developed distinct Black geographies that countered the dehumanizing experiences of plantation slavery. Wynter explains:

> For African peasants transplanted to the plot all the structure of values that had been created by traditional societies of Africa, the land remained the Earth – and the Earth was a goddess; man used the land to feed himself; and to offer first fruits to the Earth; his funeral was the mystical reunion with the earth. Because of this traditional concept the social order remained primary. Around the growing of yam, of food for survival, he created on the plot a folk culture – the basis of a social order – in three hundred years.[42]

In Wynter's view, the provision grounds were sites of hybrid creole culture that remained tied to West Indian land and African traditions. Rarely pictured on planters' maps, these Black geographies became, Wynter argues, "a source of cultural guerilla resistance to the plantation system."[43] Drawing on Wynter, scholars of Black geographies explore how liberation from slavery was "as much about the struggles over physical geographies as it is about consciousness, cultural refusals, and discourse."[44] Fundamentally opposed to the abolition imagined by Wilberforce, in which freedom was a gift that required continued obedience to Britain's colonial rule, Black geographies were and are, as Katherine McKittrick notes, a "poetics that envisions a decolonial future."[45]

The Black geographies championed by Wedderburn, such as those of the provision grounds and Maroon settlements, contested private property by building reparative commons. Alex A. Moulton notes, "these communities and farming plots enabled the (re)constitution of a commons and were sites of repair; spaces where African identities were reformed into New World Black identities."[46] Like Moulton, Wedderburn represented Black geographies in Jamaica as "sites of repair" that inspired his transatlantic political theory: He argued, "the state of society, truly desirable by the enlightened philanthropists, in which the monopoly of the common benefits of nature would be unknown, and every man able to procure his subsistence with a healthy exertion of labour, could have the leisure to cultivate his intellect, and liberty to expand his virtue" (*Axe* 3.46). In his view, freedom required access to communally held land, which enabled equity in accessing "the common benefits of nature," healthy homes, food, and leisure. When Wedderburn argued that justice must include "an equal share of the profit of the land and its appurtenances," he outlined and championed African-Jamaican Black geographies as both literal places and as stories that advocated for restoring land to dispossessed people. The radical nature of "staying put" on the land continues in Jamaica, where, Rachel Goffe argues, the "squatter" is "an ancestor of Black radical traditions that have long run counter to plantation logics of property, surveillance, and disposability."[47]

Arguing that freedom was found in actively reclaiming or "squatting" on colonial land rather than appealing to the law, Wedderburn told stories of liberatory Black geographies to his working-class London audience. Like the contemporary abolitionist Ruth Wilson Gilmore, Wedderburn argued that "freedom is a place."[48] Colonizer maps rarely included Black geographies, but the project of reimagining colonial land was often noted in writing. Judith Madera, for example, proposes that African American literature can be understood as a project of remapping. She claims, "to gain representation in the symbolic structures of white territorialization, black authors had to write over white principles of containment. They had to dismantle dominant organizational codes of place."[49] Robert Wedderburn wrote against the dominant discourse of colonial land grabs and plantation monoculture to suggest that African Caribbean people were already cultivating abolitionist, decolonial futures through communally held land.

Rereading Romanticism's Planter Picturesque

Awareness of the Black abolitionist geographies championed by Wedderburn uncovers new critical readings of Romantic-era natural histories of Jamaica. John Barrell surmises that most Romantic-era representations of landscape were "expressions of an attempt to occupy, so to speak, the place to which they were applied; to appropriate it and to destroy in it what was unknown."[50] Colonial natural histories were additionally compelled to assuage the conscience of the British public by erasing the toil and suffering of enslaved people. The planter picturesque, according to Elizabeth Bohls, "used landscape aesthetics to reimagine the traces of trauma in the form of aesthetic appeal."[51] A notable example of the planter picturesque can be found in James Hakewill's *Picturesque Tour of the Island of Jamaica* (1825), a book of "seductively beautiful" illustrations of peaceful, pastoral plantations where human figures are "mere

Figure I.5 James Hakewill, "Spring Garden Estate, St. Georges," from *A Picturesque Tour of the Island of Jamaica.* London: Hurst and Robinson, 1825. Courtesy of the Yale Center for British Art.

staffage – that is, human decoration – in the best picturesque tradition."[52] Hakewill's illustration of the Spring Garden Estate in St. George's parish presents the plantation as a lush environment strictly controlled by orderly straight lines and buildings (Figure I.5). All visible human figures are walking on a straight, narrow paved road that facilitates the export of plantation commodities while maintaining order. The ripe sugar cane to the left side of the engraving wave as if in motion, which, like other images that deploy the planter picturesque, as Evelyn O'Callaghan observes, seeks to "naturalize colonial transplantation, masking the materialist matrix of the plantation economy by imposing an aesthetic screen of picturesque composition."[53] Mountains rise in a blurred distance, the sites of the Black geographies of the provision grounds and Maroon communities that functioned outside of the gaze and logic of the plantation. Nathan K. Hensley argues, "traces of such halfway freedoms exist in the white supremacist archive only as minor notes, blank spaces–in Hakewill's work, arguably not at all."[54] However, by reading Hakewill alongside Wedderburn, the contours of the minor notes of freedom and resistance become more visible.

The written description accompanying the illustration includes the places and practices of New World Black communities:

> This estate contains nearly three thousand acres of land, of which five hundred and eighty are in cane cultivation of plants and ratoons. On it are six hundred negroes; many of them settled on it from father to son, and who regard their houses and provision grounds (of which they have between three and four hundred acres) as an inheritance, the possession of which they enjoy with uninterrupted security. With their surplus produce, and their pigs and poultry, they supply even to the distance of Anotto Bay, and from this traffic derive a very considerable profit.[55]

Not illustrated because they do not fit into the planter picturesque, Hakewill wrote of aspects of the provision grounds that Wedderburn championed. First, they established kinship, evolving into "family grounds" that were communally possessed and utilized. Material representations of kinship undermined slavery because, as Orlando Patterson proposes, slavery's "natal alienation" severed "all formal, legally enforceable ties of 'blood,' and from any attachment to groups or localities other than those chosen for him by the master."[56] Second, these grounds were so productive that an internal market thrived in accommodating the surplus. Elizabeth DeLoughrey argues that the provision grounds "supported a vibrant internal market economy in which slaves provided the majority of the region's subsistence and gained significant amounts of currency, autonomy, and even freedom."[57] Due to the abundant success of the Black ecological project of the provision grounds, Caribbean internal markets became a viable alternative to the capitalist economy. Third, enslaved people accumulated profit from this practice. The idea that enslaved people could rightfully earn property through the provision grounds and internal markets but still be property themselves becomes a repeating, troubling, and glaring contradiction in British writing about slavery in the West Indies.

Undoubtedly, Hakewill and other proslavery writers documented the provision grounds and internal markets as part of a larger argument that West Indian slavery was humane and desirable. Yet simultaneously, the narrative reveals Black geographies that challenge slavery. Planters rarely visited provision grounds, which tended to be located one to ten miles away from the plantation on land unsuitable for commodity crops. In a liminal space outside the plantation and next to the mountains, enslaved people had a margin of freedom. In his introduction to the book, Hakewill expressed anxiety about mountain grounds that had not been fully colonized: He noted that the colony of Jamaica spanned over 2,724,265 acres, yet over 1,914,809 of these acres remained "mountains" that were uncultivated.[58] He urged for more enclosure and colonization because, in Great Britain as well as the Caribbean, as Barrell notes, "the enclosure of uncultivated land, with the object of cultivating it, was a way of bringing it into that part of the landscape which because it was cultivated was known, and no longer hostile."[59] Indeed, the potential hostility of the unenclosed Jamaican mountains was used to justify Hakewill's argument that slavery must continue.

Concerning this geography, Hakewill asked a probing question that would become a crisis after emancipation: "Suppose the negro emancipated, what motive would he have for working?" He directly expressed concern that the geography and climate of Jamaica might facilitate freedom from wage labor for capitalist agriculture:

> Unlike the peasant of Europe, who if he do not work must starve, he [the Jamaican laborer] has only to betake himself to the woods, where, if no law gives the power of dislodging him, he will immediately find himself at ease, and look at perfect indifference on all beyond his hut and his plantain ground.[60]

The provision grounds were a threat not only to plantation slavery but wage-labor plantation futures. In Wedderburn's oppositional political history, "perfect indifference" to the colonial plantation economy required access to land. Hakewill implied it was merely the tropical climate of Jamaica that allowed Black people to subsist outside of the global food system because the survival of African-Caribbean land-based commons and markets challenged one of European enslavers' primary assumptions, that Africans were "bereft of farming skills and knowledge, and were given these skills and knowledge by white planters."[61] Both ecologically and culturally, the mountains provided an alternative to the monoculture of the sugar cane plantation. Hakewill's fears demonstrate why Wedderburn was a champion of the African-Jamaican provision grounds and Maroon communities.

Countering the Romantic picturesque, Wedderburn's political writing often represented freedom through an abolitionist grotesque, moments in which the produce generated by Black agricultural and ecological knowledge invaded the boundaries of plantations. By putting Wedderburn in dialogue with other Romantic-era texts, this book explores numerous instances where plantations were terrorized, not by scarcity or ineptitude, but by the *success* of Black geographies. For example, Matthew Lewis documented that the people he enslaved kept innumerable pigs that, when loosed, destroyed his sugar cane as quickly as a fire, and Queen Nanny of the Maroons grew pumpkins almost overnight, reterritorializing British land and nourishing an army of Jamaican Maroons. Jamaica's prolific pumpkins continued to trouble the British imagination even after abolition, as Thomas Carlyle vividly portrayed in his racist depiction of "Quashee" surrounded by pumpkins, food that provided freedom from the compulsion to work for a wage on British sugar plantations.[62] The following chapters explore these and other Romantic-era Black geographies in detail.

Chapter 1 discusses the political ideas outlined in Wedderburn's *Axe Laid to the Root* (1817), an inexpensive weekly periodical for working-class readers that Wedderburn wrote and published as he rose to leadership of the Spencean Philanthropists in 1817. *Axe Laid to the Root* instructed its white, lower-class readers about the radical potential of African-Jamaican land and food-based liberation. The provision grounds, plots set apart from the plantation for enslaved people to grow their own food, were a source of resistance to plantation capitalism, providing food sovereignty and communal identity. The ecological knowledge of the Jamaican Maroons was another source of resistance to plantation economies. Finally, Wedderburn's writing in "cheap" periodicals aspired to cultivate a transatlantic alliance between the English lower classes, the colonized Irish, and free and enslaved people in Jamaica. The chapter concludes by discussing George Cruikshank's *The New Union Club*, which features Wedderburn as a central figure within abolitionist circles. Despite Cruikshank's intention to dismiss him as a crude entertainer, Wedderburn remained a prominent figure in the caricature, a reminder that Wedderburn's *Axe Laid to the Root* supplemented his influential preaching and public debates in London. Wedderburn attempted to persuade his white lower-class audience that Black resistance was a viable political strategy, destabilizing the white abolitionist view that liberation would arise from transporting English freedoms to the colonies and extending them to enslaved people.

Chapter 2 explores how Wedderburn's view of Black-led abolition was further outlined in his life narrative, *The Horrors of Slavery* (1824). The narrative initially emerged as a series of letters that Wedderburn wrote to a working-class periodical, *Bell's Life in London*, after the editor had questioned whether plantation owners would ever enslave their own mixed-race children. The question prompted Wedderburn to share his life story, in which he represented himself as a "product" of plantation slavery and testified to his father's sexual and moral depravity as a "slave-dealer." Although the letters prompted threatening replies from his white half-brother, Andrew Colvile, Wedderburn defiantly republished the *Bell's Life* letters as a pamphlet sold by the ultra-radical booksellers Richard Carlile and Thomas Davison. *Horrors of Slavery* radically tracked his life from the horrors of slavery on a West Indian plantation to his harsh sentence of solitary confinement in an English prison for blasphemous libel. *Horrors* argued that freedom from slavery was haunted by an unrepaired traumatic past and ongoing prosecution by the British government, making it an essential supplement to more commonly studied Romantic-era slave narratives, such as Equiano's *Interesting Narrative.*

Horrors of Slavery also announced an antislavery politics largely unacknowledged by Romantic-era abolitionists: place-based, self-liberation led by Black women. Chapter 3 proposes that Wedderburn significantly reworked the Romantic, abolitionist figure of the sorrowful, enslaved Black mother by celebrating his African-Jamaican mother and grandmother's communal, place-based resistance to slavery. Wedderburn's mother, Rosanna, demanded that his enslaver father manumit him. His grandmother, Talkee Amy, was a skilled higgler and obeah woman who, in Wedderburn's terms, "trafficked on her own account." Similar freedom practices are then traced throughout *The History of Mary Prince* (1831). Mary Prince's repeated petit marronage demanded enslavers' acknowledgment of her kinship with her parents and husband. As a West Indian higgler, like Talkee Amy, Prince used the produce from the provision grounds of the enslaved to assert freedom in fugitive markets. Instead of representing an individual's journey from enslavement to British liberal freedom, Wedderburn and Prince's life narratives do the reverse; they were both Black and British, lived in London, and brought stories of Black women's place-based freedom practices to a white audience.

Guided by Wedderburn's argument that land-based freedom must be guarded "above all" for Black self-emancipation, Chapter 4 asserts that tensions over provision grounds permeated Matthew Lewis's encounters with enslaved people in his *Journal of a West India Proprietor* (1818, published in 1834). When Matthew Lewis arrived at his Cornwall plantation in Westmoreland, Jamaica, the people on his estate celebrated for two days. Lewis was flattered by the fawning and praise, but the celebration quickly shifted to negotiations for more time at the provision grounds. After granting an additional day per week on the provision grounds as "a matter of right," Lewis documented that enslaved people were growing poisons, unleashing fires, harboring crowds of destructive livestock, and providing sustenance for self-liberated Black people. Despite noting these dangers, Lewis wrote to William Wilberforce detailing his plan for emancipation by giving enslaved people his plantation as reparations, a proposal he feared to be "dangerous to the island." Lewis's *Journal* recorded that his plantations were undermined, not by overt rebellion, but rather by the success of the Black ecological project: The botanical and animal ecologies of the provision grounds were anticipatory abolitionist commons that would be drawn upon in the coming emancipation.

Black abolitionist geographies were cultivated to their fullest extent in Maroon villages. Chapter 5 moves backward in time to trace the Maroons' decolonial relationship with the environment, starting with Queen Nanny, a leader in the First Maroon War and a present-day National Hero of Jamaica. Narratives of Nanny's warfare against the British noted that her fight included growing pumpkins in the rugged Blue Mountains. The chapter then turns to a critically neglected Romantic-era text, R. C. Dallas's *History of the Maroons* (1803). Although primarily a military history, Dallas repeatedly admired the Maroons' communal "superabundance." Similarly, J. G. Stedman's *Narrative of a Five Years' Expedition* (1796), accompanied by William Blake's illustrations, described Maroon settlements as viable, sustainable societies that were notable alternatives to plantation capitalism. The Maroons' agricultural and culinary "superabundance," documented by Dallas, Stedman, and Blake alike, suggests a Romantic-era ecological critique rooted in communal decolonial practices, which supplements the Romantic figure of the solitary walker who critiques society by communing with nature.

Chapter 6 proposes that the provision grounds continued to trouble the Victorian imagination because, as Malcom Ferdinand observes, it was "*an abolition of slavery on the condition that the colonial plantation continues.*"[63] The radical nature of Black-led agriculture emerged vividly after the abolition of slavery in 1834 when newly freed Black people challenged the plantocracy by staying put on their communal provision grounds. For example, letters from the overseer on Lord Holland's Jamaica estate documented that formerly enslaved people viewed their homes and provision grounds as a commons, so "they cannot think of paying any rent." Both antislavery and proslavery writers developed strategies for displacing Black Jamaicans from their land. Abolitionist Joseph Sturge, for example, recommended importing provisions from Haiti to weaken Jamaica's internal markets and make workers dependent on wages. Thomas Carlyle's notorious "Discourse" (1849) seethed with racist rage focused on "Quashee" surrounded by pumpkins, a synecdoche for independent, agriculturally successful Black people. In Carlyle's essay, the planter picturesque becomes an abolitionist grotesque of "waste fertility," an environment of seemingly out-of-control plants and animals swarming around free Black people unwilling to participate in Britain's wage labor economy. Carlyle's coinage of "waste fertility" inadvertently illustrated the Black geographies championed by Wedderburn.

The Conclusion reads Wedderburn's final pamphlet, *An Address to the Lord Brougham and Vaux* (1831), as a contribution to the early nineteenth-century political "war of representation" about whether Black people in the West Indies would be willing to work for wages after emancipation. Although seeming to reiterate the proslavery claim that enslaved people in the West Indies had better living conditions than European wage laborers, Wedderburn's vision of dwelling on the land outlined a nuanced, speculative decolonial future. The conclusion finally argues that narratives of the Romantic revolutionary age should include Black abolitionist geographies, a revolution cultivated on common land with pigs, pumpkins, and yams.

Wedderburn's Black geographies were not spectacular, nor did they have the overt insurrectionist telos of stories that dominate histories of Black self-emancipation, such as Tacky's War or the Haitian Revolution. David Scott observes that Wedderburn was a "conscript of modernity," working within limitations that may chafe against scholarly and political desires for revolutionary clarity and heroic action toward the abolition of slavery. Attention to Wedderburn's place-based, communal freedoms responds to Scott's call for "a story more attuned to the productive ways in which power has shaped the conditions of possible action, more specifically, shaped the cognitive and institutional conditions in which the New World slave acted."[64] The provision grounds functioned precisely this way: They were shaped by the conditions of power, as the planters allotted them, and then enslaved people created freedom practices within them. Malcom Ferdinand provocatively argues that emancipation erased such Black geographies. He claims, "*the vitality present in the breaking of chains and in mad dashes took precedence over the patience of planted yams and paced-out forests.*"[65] Wedderburn's writing invites us to reconsider the political importance of the insurgent multispecies communities of planted yams and forest paths forged by Black people in the West Indies under the dehumanizing system of slavery. At the same time, it is paramount to avoid creating an idealized version of these difficult-to-carve-out spaces. Jenny Sharpe warns, "an uncritical celebration of slave resistance and resilience risks overlooking the conditions of subjugation and dehumanization that in many instances prevented an opposition to slavery, overt or otherwise."[66] To avoid overlooking the painful, circumscribed conditions of plantation slavery, this book attempts, as Saidiya Hartman suggests, to "represent the various modes of practice without reducing them to conditions of domination or romanticizing them as pure forms of resistance."[67]

With those caveats in mind, this book attempts to recover Wedderburn's place in politics, challenging redemptive histories of abolition that focus on Wilberforce and other white antislavery activists as heroic figures.[68] Wedderburn's abolitionist geographies found a place in the Romantic era so prominent that he was depicted in caricatures with other well-known radicals, spied upon by the British government, and even jailed for his influence. While his treatment was in keeping with the paranoid repression of the post-Waterloo era, the response to his activism still suggests that scholars should take his work more seriously. Wedderburn's writing provides a rare glimpse into what Vincent Brown describes as "an oppositional political history taught and learned on Jamaican plantations – a radical pedagogy of the enslaved – shaped the slaves' goals, strategies, and tactics as they rehearsed bygone battles and considered future possibilities."[69] By centering that oppositional pedagogy, *Robert Wedderburn, Abolition, and the Commons* attends to stories of Black Caribbean practices of freedom that can productively challenge and stretch Romantic-era narratives about the landscape, the abolition of slavery, and radical politics.

CHAPTER 1

Against Private Property
Wedderburn's *The Axe Laid to the Root*

As he rose to leadership of the Spencean Philanthropists in London, Robert Wedderburn wrote and published six issues of *The Axe Laid to the Root, or a Fatal Blow to Oppressors* (1817) (Figure 1.1). A three-halfpence, "cheap" periodical, *Axe Laid to the Root* emerged in dialogue with other radical broadsheets and pamphlets that flourished after William Cobbett published "To the Journeymen and Labourers" in November 1816. Cobbett's cheap *Register* provided a blueprint for avoiding the Stamp Act and getting radical political writing into the hands and minds of working-class readers.[1] Wedderburn's political message differed sharply from Cobbett's *Register* and other radical publications of the period: Wedderburn argued for a transatlantic alliance between the radicals of England's lower classes and enslaved people in the West Indies. As the title suggests, Wedderburn's journalism aspired to be an axe to the root of private property in land. Without the abolition of private property, reform in England and abolition in the West Indies were "only an attempt to heal, without extracting the core" of the transatlantic plantation system (*Axe* 1.9). Scholars have emphasized the influence of Thomas Spence's advocacy for land nationalization on Wedderburn's thought. For example, Helen Thomas argues that *Axe* "advanced claims for land reformation on the plantocratic islands of the West Indies according to Spence's directive and denounced concepts of English liberty as *myths* propounded by priests, kings and lords."[2] Although he indeed denounced English concepts of liberty, Wedderburn's ideas did not derive from a Spencean "directive." Instead, Wedderburn traded in Spencean rhetoric to instruct his white, lower-class readers in London about the radical potential within African-Jamaican practices of insurrectionary land and food reclamation.

The difficulty of interpreting Wedderburn's work can be located in the title, *Axe Laid to the Root*, which nodded simultaneously to Christ's radical teaching, "the axe is laid unto the root of the trees: therefore every tree which bringeth not forth good fruit is hewn down, and cast into the fire";

No. 1. Price Threehalf-Pence.

THE

AXE LAID TO THE ROOT,

OR A

Fatal Blow to Oppressors,

BEING AN ADDRESS TO

THE PLANTERS AND NEGROES

OF THE

ISLAND OF JAMAICA.

Printed by A. Seale, 160, Tottenham Court Road; and Published by Robert Wedderburn, 8, Church Court, St. Martin's Lane, London.

To the Editor.

Sir,

In your sketch which you style 'a review of Sir Robert Wilson's late publication,' you say, you open this volume with mingled feelings of sorrow and disgust. Sir, this is no proof of impartiality; and you seem to approve of his services in the late war, and ascribe to him well earned laurels; you consider he is now about to barter these laurels for the blood stained violets of Napoleon. Is the violet more stained than the eagle, or the British lion? You charge Sir Robert with raising insiduous means to embroil this country in war with Russia. There is no danger of your governors daring to venture a contest with that gigantic power. But not to follow you in your incoherent remarks, as the work is before the public, they will judge its merits without your feeble assistance. I have not neglected to watch the progressive power of Russia to its present height, (from the reign of Catherine the great, who in defiance to all Europe, disposed of Poland agreeable to her sovereign will,) down to the present moment, when Alexander is directing his army, navy, and his counsel, by the most able men of civilized Europe. England also, has contributed to her power, by improving her ships of war. Have not the citizens of London, by spreading a princely table before the Emperor on his late visit, convinced him that such feasts may be had in Russia, by means of his exertion? Is he not giving premiums to English artists and others, to accomplish his great designs? You say in your comment, that Russia is without the sinues of war; I say, that power will supply itself at the expense of humanity and justice. The feudal system there established, is the strength of the Russian empire; the barons holding the land and its inhabitants as private property; at the will of their Emperor are always subservient to his views, which must of necessity be ambitious. I remain, your obedient.

A Critic 1 Observer.

Figure 1.1 Title page, Robert Wedderburn's *Axe Laid to the Root,* 1817. Courtesy of the National Archives of the UK.

to Tom Paine's call for secular revolution, "lay then the axe to the root, and teach governments humanity"; and to the African proverb, "if you are a big tree, we are a small axe."[3] At the end of the first issue, Wedderburn announced that his goal was to bring Black freedom practices to his London audience: "I am a West-Indian, a lover of liberty, and would dishonour human nature if I did not shew myself a friend to the liberty of others" (*Axe* 1.7–8). Wedderburn's love of liberty emerged from his experiences as a marginalized and oppressed person in several parts of the British Empire: In Jamaica, he was raised by his enslaved mother and grandmother; aboard a British Navy ship, he was subject to harsh discipline, and finally, in London, he emerged as an artisan tailor only to be put out of work by the rise of the factory system. These combined experiences led him to theorize a transatlantic revolution against empire. Peter Linebaugh and Marcus Rediker argue, "Wedderburn was in fact a strategically central actor in the formation and dissemination of revolutionary traditions, an intellectual organic to the Atlantic proletariat."[4] Scholarship about Wedderburn's transatlantic radicalism, however, has not explored Wedderburn's central heuristic for thinking about revolution and freedom: the provision grounds, plots set apart from the plantation for enslaved people to grow their own food.

In the first issue of the *Axe*, he declared, "Above all, mind and keep possession of the land you now possess as slaves; for without that, freedom is not worth possessing; for if you once give up the possession of your lands, your oppressors will have power to starve you to death" (*Axe* 1.4). Enslavers distributed provision grounds, yet they were creatively appropriated by African Caribbean people and turned into a commons, where shared property, time, and resources resisted the practices and subjectivities inculcated by the violent exploitation of the plantation system. Sylvia Wynter explains, "the planters gave the slaves plots of land on which to grow food to feed themselves in order to maximize profits. We suggest that this plot system was . . . the focus of resistance to the market system and market values."[5] Wedderburn's political writing argued that African-Jamaican provision grounds were an emergent commons that arose during and after the disasters of dispossession and enslavement. Enslaved people cultivated intergenerational polycultures (against plantation monoculture) by growing sweet potatoes, cassava, maize, taro, plantains, pigeon peas, and other vegetables.[6] When Wedderburn insisted that the provision grounds were a model for transatlantic abolitionist futures, his ideas resonated with what Katherine McKittrick calls Black geographies, "innovative black diaspora practices that, in fact, spatialize acts of survival" and provide models of "how the land and nourishment can sustain alternative worldviews and challenge practices of dehumanization."[7]

Axe Laid to the Root outlined and advocated for Black abolitionist geographies within early nineteenth-century Romantic print culture. The chapter first explores Wedderburn's advocacy for land-based resistance, which was modeled on provision grounds that allowed enslaved people to cultivate commons in creative relationships with land, plants, and animals. Provision grounds resisted the extractive logic of the plantation. A second source of guerilla resistance to the plantation, the Jamaican Maroons, is explored in the following section. Wedderburn's representation of Jamaican Maroon culture did not emphasize flight from slavery as much as the Maroons' development of local ecological knowledge and food sovereignty as sources of continuing independence. The third section explores Wedderburn's cultivation of a transatlantic alliance between the English lower classes, the colonized Irish, and free and enslaved people in Jamaica. The chapter concludes with a discussion of George Cruikshank's *The New Union Club* (1819), which features Wedderburn as a central figure within abolitionist circles. Despite Cruikshank's intention to dismiss him as a crude entertainer, Wedderburn remained a prominent figure in the caricature, which recorded anxiety about the potential influence of Wedderburn's ideas in nineteenth-century London.

Provision Grounds as Commons

The six issues of Wedderburn's *Axe Laid to the Root* outlined plans to abolish West Indian slavery and foment transatlantic worker liberation. Strategies ranged from a universal worker's strike to violent revolt, and all were revolutions initiated from below. White plantocracy must be overthrown, and further freedom from enslavement, according to Wedderburn, would occur as formerly enslaved people demand continued use of the provision grounds as commons: "When you are exorted [*sic*] to hold the land, and never give it up to your oppressors, you are not told to hold it as private property, but as tenants at will to the sovereignty of the people" *(Axe* 1.6). Wedderburn's vision of Black liberation took place not only by throwing off the institution of slavery but also by refusing to base any post-slavery society on property ownership. Keeping hold of the provision grounds after emancipation served as reparations for slavery and as the grounded, material basis for a new society. Culturing diverse crops on the provision grounds transformed work from oppressive slave labor on plantations to creative community building through working the land as "tenants to the people," not as property owners. Instead of conceiving freedom as access to the liberal right to own private property, Wedderburn insisted that freedom should be established by creating commons that abolish private property altogether.

As a leader of the Spencean Philanthropists in London, Wedderburn championed English lower-class demands for the "people's farm." The people's farm was a concept at the center of Thomas Spence's radical agrarian scheme for land nationalization, which was initially developed during the radical years of the 1790s.[8] In his *Restorer of Society to Its Natural State*, Spence argued, "the land shall no longer be suffered to be the property of individuals, but of the Parishes."[9] Spence doggedly advocated for the people's farm in pamphlets, ballads, and songs until his death in 1814. In the 1810s, when Spence knew Wedderburn, he was making similar arguments for the abolition of private property. Spence took great care to distinguish his agrarian radicalism from mainstream English radicalism. For example, in his final publication, written just before his death, Spence wrote, "What a Grand Mistake to class Jacobins and Levellers together; can they be called Levellers who wish individually only to enrich themselves, and to accumulate all they can of both Lands and Effects, without regard to the Public welfare?"[10] Other scholars have emphasized Spence's influence on Wedderburn. Iain McCalman argues, for example, "Wedderburn's fiery extempore speeches contain little in the way of original political theory."[11] Ryan Hanley suggests Wedderburn "accommodated Spencean land reform within his own distinctive brand of antislavery rhetoric."[12] Instead accommodating Thomas Spence's "people's farm," however, Wedderburn's advocacy introduced London radicals to distinctive practices of Black land reclamation and food sovereignty on Jamaican plantations. Raphael Hoermann surmises that "Wedderburn's position marks a theoretical advance as he points towards a Black Atlantic relocation of the axis of transatlantic liberation."[13] Wedderburn's theoretical contribution lies in relocating the geography of liberation: Wedderburn looked to African-Jamaican provision grounds as viable models for regrounding people in shared communal land after the disaster of plantation slavery.

Wedderburn's commitment to and development of this African-Caribbean model can be found in *Axe*'s initial open letter, which was addressed to enslaved Jamaicans. Wedderburn admonished:

> Above all, mind and keep possession of the land you now possess as slaves; for without that, freedom is not worth possessing; for if you once give up the possession of your lands, your oppressors will have power to starve you

> to death ... which will force you to commit crimes in order to obtain subsistence [*sic*]; as the landholders in Europe are serving those that are dispossessed of lands; for it is a fact, that thousands of families are now in a starving state; the prisons are full: humanity impells [*sic*] the executive power to withdraw the sentence of death on criminals, whilst the landholders, in fact, are surrounded with every necessary of life. Take warning by the sufferings of the European poor, and never give up the lands you now possess, for it is your right by God and nature, for the "earth was given to the children of men." (*Axe* 1.4–5)

In this passage, Wedderburn used Spencean phrasing, the "earth was given to the children of men," to persuade readers that keeping land as a commons, instead of individual property, was a Christian philosophy.[14] Thomas Evans, the former leader of the Spencean Philanthropists, for example, used similar language in his pamphlet, *Christian Policy, or the Salvation of Empire* (1816): "I propose, that all feudality be abolished, and the territory of those realms be declared to be the people's farm; that there be no other tenure, but leasehold."[15] Wedderburn's language about keeping "possession" of the provision grounds as "tenants" further corresponds with J. M. Neeson's definition of the English commons, which allowed for "possession without ownership" of land and food production. By 1817, however, the English commons were largely enclosed, which meant, in most instances, "the extinction of common right."[16] Wedderburn's *Axe* was written in the form of open letters, much like Cobbett's *Register* and other early nineteenth-century working-class periodicals. Although the letters were addressed to enslaved people in Jamaica, the periodical was primarily distributed to lower-class readers in London.[17] Therefore, when Wedderburn admonished enslaved people to "keep possession of the land," it was a performance informing his white, laboring-class audience that African Caribbean people were already enacting a "people's farm" on their provision grounds. Wedderburn not only integrated Black resistance to slavery with working-class radicalism but also championed Black thought and practices as *models* for the English lower classes.

By telling enslaved people to "take warning" from the sufferings of the European poor, Wedderburn may appear to have asserted, like white proslavery writers, that the British lower classes were in worse condition than enslaved people in the Caribbean. Although working-class radicals used the term "wage-slavery" to suggest that wage earners in Great Britain were no better off than enslaved people in the West Indies, Wedderburn did not intend to equate wage labor with chattel slavery.[18] Instead, as

Worrall argues, by making this connection, "Wedderburn is mirroring and mocking his original disbelief at English passivity," thereby goading his audience into action.[19] Aligning the interests of the British lower classes with enslaved people in Jamaica, Wedderburn argued that the transition from subsistence economies to monoculture plantations in Europe and the West Indies dangerously dispossessed people from land, food, and power. The urgency of sugar production ushered in several features of factory discipline that only later spread to England, such as labor force organization and time consciousness.[20] Wedderburn's experience with the sugar plantation factory and its place in the global commodity food system led him to view emancipation from slavery, like emancipation from serfdom, as primitive accumulation; as Karl Marx notes, "these freedmen became sellers of themselves only after they had been robbed of all their own means of production."[21] By drawing the connection between plantations in the West Indies and large consolidated farms in England after enclosure, Wedderburn was not equating wage labor with slavery but instead called attention to the continuity between West Indian plantations and the factory system emerging in England. Wedderburn's politics held up land-based forms of resistance to the plantation economy in the Caribbean as more effective, progressive, and inclusive than white working-class radicalism.

Although they were initially intended to force enslaved people to grow their own food, Wedderburn noted that the provision grounds also grew practices of freedom through Black culture and creativity. Jamaica's mountainous terrain resisted sugar production, thus allowing room for extensive provision grounds on land unsuitable for large-scale commodity production. Located several miles outside the plantation and next to mountain wilderness, provision grounds facilitated the "evasion of the overseer's lines of sight."[22] B. W. Higman's study of plantation survey maps reveals that on these grounds, enslaved people "were sometimes able to pattern small areas according to their own conceptions of spatial order."[23] Mintz calls provision grounds "proto-peasant" because although they were "created at the insistence of the masters to reduce the costs of feeding slaves, the plots and then markets were to become training grounds for freedom, a basis for the eventual rise of a free peasantry."[24] The tension between the demands of the European colonizers' plantations and the freedoms associated with the peasant economies of the provision grounds exploded, as discussed in the final chapters, after Emancipation in 1838.

The movement toward large-scale agricultural projects was also taking place in England. In a vivid coinage, Cobbett called it a movement of

"Bull-Frog Farmers," who "like the *Bull-Frogs* of the American swamps, have swallowed up the small-farmers, as the Bull-Frogs do the little chirping frogs."[25] Cobbett viewed these consolidations as violence against the poor, as did Wedderburn, who argued, "it is inconsistent with justice, that a few should have the power to till or not to till the earth, thereby holding the existence of a whole population in their hands. They can cause a famine, or create abundance" (*Axe* 1.9). Wedderburn not only viewed plantation land grabs as violent, but he also prophetically anticipated that landowners would artificially create scarcity and famine to discipline the landless poor, a strategy that was actively proposed by Thomas Carlyle in his 1849 essay, "Occasional Discourse on the Negro Question." Although English laborers were not enslaved, Wedderburn suggested that the food sovereignty of the African-Jamaican provision grounds remained a model of resistance to the transatlantic plantation ecologies of the British Empire. For example, in his letter to "A Superabundant" in the second issue of *Axe*, Wedderburn asserted, "the land is engrossed by land-holders, who have made laws to deprive us of the privilege of planting a potatoe [*sic*]" (*Axe* 2.20). Defying Malthusian biopolitical theories of nature's scarcity, which naturalized society's failure to feed a "superabundant" poor population, Wedderburn evoked the potato, thus connecting the food of impoverished people in England and Ireland with the yam, the food of enslaved people in the West Indies. Ground provisions became a figure for transatlantic food sovereignty and land-based freedom.[26] Mary Louise Pratt points out that, in Romantic-era natural histories and agricultural treatises, "the system of nature overwrote local and peasant ways of knowing within Europe just as it did indigenous ones abroad."[27] Alert to this erasure, Wedderburn argued for the urgency of retaining local subsistence cultures throughout the British Empire. When Wedderburn championed the provision grounds, he offered a new theory of freedom, outside of abolitionist and proslavery English political views, that emerged directly from distinctly African-Caribbean communal food and land practices.

For Wedderburn, the superabundant poor can strategically wield their numbers against those in power. In an open letter to enslaved Jamaicans, Wedderburn advised, "the equality of your present station in slavery, is your strength. You all feel the injury – you are all capable of making resistance" (*Axe* 1.14). The equal and complete dispossession of enslavement facilitated collaborative practices of resistance, in which "union among you, will strike tremendous terror to the receivers of stolen persons" (*Axe* 1.4).[28] For the London readers of *Axe Laid to the Root*, this advice to enslaved people in Jamaica was a performance that suggested the lower classes have been deceived by the idea that if they work hard within the cash nexus, somehow they will be able to provide for their families. In this way, Wedderburn warned about believing Great Britain's national narrative, which, Catherine Gallagher explains, arose from the "relatively new ability of a society to misrepresent the resources available to laborers – that is, to promise prosperity through high money wages and then betray that promise by a scarcity of provisions."[29] The unequal dispossession among the lower classes facilitated that narrative, motivating an allegiance to work that created a barrier to finding common interests in overthrowing private property. Wedderburn discerned the need to create solidarity among laboring classes of people who were disposable under agricultural capitalism, because, as Linebaugh argues, "human solidarity is the foundation of commoning."[30] Yet Wedderburn's commons were the African Caribbean provision grounds and, as discussed in the next section, the settlements of the Jamaican Maroons. These commons were designated spaces and cultural practices that produced local food sovereignty, which was designed to compel those in power into cooperative negotiations.

Provisions of the Jamaican Maroons

Wedderburn's insistence on the connection between land use and freedom continued with a second example of Black resistance to colonial plantations, the Jamaican Maroons. In the first issue of *Axe Laid to the Root*, after describing the provision grounds as the foundation for workers' liberation, Wedderburn's writing shifted into a prophetic mode: He predicted that within twenty years, Jamaica would be in the hands of Black people. At this point, the Jamaican Maroons become a second, related model of freedom:

> The island of Jamaica will be in the hands of blacks within twenty years. Prepare for flights, ye planters, for the fate of St. Domingo awaits you. Get ready your blood hounds, the allies which you employed against the Maroons. Recollect the fermentation will be universal. Their weapons are their bill-hooks; their store of provision is every were [*sic*] in abundance; you know they can live upon sugar canes, and a vast variety of herbs and fruits,—yea, even upon the buds of trees. You cannot cut off their supplies. (*Axe* 1.12)

Instead of representing the Maroons' resistance as a flight from the plantation, Wedderburn suggested that their infamous guerilla warfare required guerilla gardening, or at least guerilla foraging. Although Maroon culture was not as directly agricultural as the provision grounds, the Maroons' freedom relied on their "store of provision" cultivated through local and traditional ecological knowledge of the "vast variety" of forageable foods in the Jamaican landscape. Even sugar cane shifted from a plantation commodity to a form of subsistence that fueled resistance. Wedderburn further reversed imagery associated with the biblical millennium: Swords are not turned into plowshares and pruning hooks, but pruning hooks, the tools of the enslaved on commodity plantations, are weaponized against their enslavers.[31] Morris argues that in the aforementioned passage Wedderburn "recalls that the Haitian slaves used their billhooks to combat their masters, and the Maroons could survive periods of hardship by sucking on the meagre rations of sugarcane during their wars against the British."[32] Yet Wedderburn also strategically conflated weaponry with food: The representation of pruning hooks as weapons also metaphorically reinforced the idea that food sovereignty was a form of combat against the British Empire. Wedderburn's representation of the Jamaican Maroons then resonates with Alex A. Moulton's depiction of the Maroons as communal landholders: as "a runaway peasantry" who "provided an example of the power of Black land holding, which became increasingly mirrored by the free Black peasantry."[33]

The food sovereignty cultivated in Maroon villages and provision grounds strategically fought against what Rachel B. Herrmann calls "victual imperialism": British and American colonizers strategically controlled the food of indigenous and enslaved people to gain power. Herrmann contends that "scholars must reexamine how enslaved and formerly enslaved people traded, produced, stole, transported, and regulated foodstuffs" as forms of resistance.[34] Wedderburn's insights about the Maroons, noted in depth in the forthcoming chapter on Maroon ecologies of warfare, can be confirmed by reading British military narratives, which inadvertently recorded the Maroons' extensive agricultural societies. Military campaigns against them were waged chiefly by destroying their fields and food. Wedderburn alluded to such campaigns when he argued, "the Maroons were human beings, and ought not to be hunted down by Britons acting the blood-hound's part" (*Axe* 4.55).[35] By depicting the Maroons as rational community-builders, while the British colonizers are animalized and conflated with the dogs they used to pursue Maroons during the Second Maroon War, Wedderburn suggested – *to his London audience* – a reversal of European accounts of civilization.

His vision provided inspiration for establishing counter-modernities that were at once in step with Romanticism but also radically outside of it. The Maroons' cultivation of a creolized food commons must have resonated with Wedderburn's lower-class audiences, since food debates in England, as Gallagher and Greenblatt have established, encompassed multiple laboring class issues, such as "the proper level of wages, the effect on population growth, the danger of setting wages according to the cheapest possible staple food, and the social consequences of having two standard foods, wheat bread for the middle classes and potatoes for the poor."[36] William Cobbett spoke to this host of labor issues when he advocated for subsistence through cultivating a cottage economy as resistance to the insecurity of wage labor. Wedderburn situated the food freedoms of the Maroons and the provision grounds of the enslaved next to English movements for a cottage economy.

To demonstrate, for his London audience, the transatlantic political potential of the counter-modernities developed by the Maroons, Wedderburn contrasted the Maroons' successful freedom struggles to those of the "silly Irish rebels," who used armies and military maneuvers that imitated the British Empire's strategies (*Axe* 1.12). An anonymous eighteenth-century manuscript described the Maroons' place-based strategies in similar terms: "Their knowledge of the woods & Mountains and their Robust Hardinness and activity, screened them continually from the pursuits of our parties."[37] Wedderburn's opposition to symmetrical warfare, Ajmal Waqif argues, was due to how he favored the Maroons' "guerrilla strategy that exploited their knowledge of mountain and jungle."[38] The Maroons lured British troops into fighting by traversing treacherous mountain paths, where their knowledge of the landscape gave them an advantage. Wedderburn prophesied that tactics of marronage would migrate from Jamaica to England in the second issue of *Axe Laid to the Root*. After discussing numerous legalized abuses of the English poor, he prophesied: "Be not mistaken, the rising generation, for want of industrious habits, will not starve quietly. They will be fed at the hazard of their lives and liberty. Hunger will compel them to rush into your houses, more murder than ever, will be committed by not exposing your goods" (*Axe* 2.21). Using performative, prophetic speech just after describing the food sovereignty cultivated by Jamaican Maroon communities, marronage became a model of freedom that might easily migrate to England and begin to agitate for change, like Wedderburn himself.

Wedderburn further instructed his white audience in the political possibilities inherent in Maroon culture in the last two issues of *Axe Laid to the Root*, where he published a series of letters between himself and a fictional interlocutor, "Miss Campbell," a half-sister of part Maroon ancestry who became a plantation owner and enslaver in Jamaica.[39] In the first letter, Wedderburn admonished Miss Campbell, "you have fallen from the purity of the Maroons, your original," because she followed the European practice of plantation slavery (*Axe* 4.54). Although Wedderburn stated that Miss Campbell had fallen, she still had the potential to perform Afrocentric women's leadership. The purity Wedderburn mentions, however, should not be misconstrued as a racial identity but rather as a superior model of political allyship worthy of emulation by his white readers in London. Shelby Johnson insightfully argues: "Although Wedderburn begins the passage by having Elizabeth utter a demand for vengeance on behalf of the 'blood of [her Maroon] ancestors,' Elizabeth troubles any reading of history that would understand revolution as solely or always the result of enslaved resistance."[40] By representing Miss Campbell as a Maroon and mixed-race enslaver, Wedderburn suggested to his London audience that white people complicit in slavery can be transformed and join the struggle for abolition based on the example of African-Jamaican marronage.

In holding out Miss Campbell as an example of potential liberation from slavery through marronage, Wedderburn radically challenged dominant European representations of the Maroons. Frances R. Botkin outlines the history of Anglo-cultural depictions of the Maroons through figures like Three-Fingered Jack, whose menacing African masculinity "compromised production on the plantation and threatened the lives of Anglo-Jamaicans."[41] Throughout his writing, Wedderburn insisted that women also can engage in combat and marronage. In his recommendations for a new society at the end of his second issue of *The Axe Laid to the Root*, Wedderburn wrote, "let every individual learn the art of war, yea, even the females, for they are capable of displaying courage" (*Axe* 2.26). The letters to Miss Campbell in the last issues of *Axe Laid to the Root* reveal Wedderburn's ideal of Black women's leadership. Wedderburn also noted that he was initially inspired to write to her because she purchased his brother's freedom, and "the greatness of the deed has inspired me with a zeal to extend freedom beyond present conception" (*Axe* 4.53). Miss Campbell's leadership inspired Wedderburn to develop a new, more expansive concept of freedom. He went on to fully develop his vision of Black women as liberators in his life narrative, *The Horrors of Slavery*.

Other letters to and from Miss Campbell in *Axe Laid to the Root* detailed her decision to manumit the people she had enslaved. The manumission included land-based reparations; she transformed her estate into a common for their shared possession and use. At this point, the letter switched to past tense, declaring prophetically that she had already released her slaves: "Miss Campbell then cried, the land is yours, not because

Wedderburn, the Spencean says so, for I have read the word of God, and it says, the Lord gave the earth to the children of men. You are the children of men as well as others" (*Axe* 4.59). Freedom here was represented as a lively synthesis of Maroon culture, the provision grounds, and the practices of early Christians who shared everything. This model of abolition was far removed from the white savior narratives of British abolitionists because it required Black leadership and land reparations for enslaved people. Wedderburn's abolitionist vision crucially restored territory to dispossessed Black people.

When Miss Campbell liberated the people that she enslaved and gave them her land for communal use, her actions resonated with Queen Nanny, a Maroon hero who fought against the British in the First Maroon War (1728–39). Nanny was a formidable military leader because she was also a gardener who reterritorialized land and saved her people by growing pumpkins. Although Nanny was not mentioned in Wedderburn's letters with Miss Campbell, in his vision of abolition, a rebellious Maroon woman similarly established a territory for dispossessed New World Africans.[42] Miss Campbell declared the abolition of her private property – both in land and people – to the local magistrate to have it recorded. The magistrates replied with concern for Miss Campbell's sanity, and they warned her to "keep your slaves upon your own estate, for fear they should corrupt others, and turn their brains to think that liberty and possession of the soil is better than slavery and the whip" (*Axe* 6.85–6). Miss Campbell replied, "I will obey you, and keep them on our estate, but they have been talking about it this month past to the country negroes on the market days. I told them not to speak of it, but they talked of it the more" (*Axe* 6.86). Defying the need for abolition initiated by the British government, Miss Campbell declared that abolition had already materialized when she transformed her plantation into a reparative commons. Her response to the magistrate warned that "talk" about her mode of abolition had already been exchanged at the internal markets alongside the surplus food from the provision grounds. "Talk" about freedom pushed abolition forward, according to Miles Ogborn, and such talk should be understood as "anticipatory speech acts which attempted to shape the future through making new collectives."[43] Therefore, Miss Campbell's response was nothing short of a threat that word of land reparations was out and circulating among Black Jamaicans.

Wedderburn's letters with Miss Campbell evoked a convergence of land-based Black abolitionist ecologies: freedom materially and ideologically spread by the communal possession of land and the internal markets.

J. T. Roane theorizes that Black commons in America functioned as an "insurgent cartography" that rejects settler futurity and landscapes of domination.[44] Miss Campbell rejected settler futurity by transforming her plantation into commons: "I can show no title deeds that are just. Those who sold it to me murdered them who lived on it before" (*Axe* 4.59). In this statement, Wedderburn anticipated the insights of Édouard Glissant, who argued that due to the plantation machine's extermination of indigenous peoples, it was necessary to create "a new relationship with the land: not the absolute ontological possession regarded as sacred but the complicity of relation."[45] As a mixed-race enslaver and descendent of Maroons, Miss Campbell embodied that complicity of relation, and as she acknowledged the genocide of indigenous people as part of the plantation system, Wedderburn pointed out that freedom within the British system of propertied ownership unjustly continued the original theft of land in the Caribbean. The only way forward was for abolition to include a land-based transition from plantation ecologies to Black commons.

Wedderburn within Romantic-Era Political Culture

Wedderburn believed ardently in the power and potential of the English cheap periodical. In his first, co-produced journal, *The Forlorn Hope* (1817), Wedderburn argued, "the press has opened a fair field to combat in, where the few stand on equal ground with the many."[46] The six issues of *Axe Laid to the Root* were published in London by Arthur Seale, a former London Corresponding Society member who published many radical nineteenth-century texts, including the political pamphlets and broadsides of Thomas Spence and millenarian texts of Richard Brothers and Joanna Southcott.[47] Wedderburn's "cheap" periodical published for working-class readers redeployed the established dialogic form of the radical weekly periodical using the voices of "the many" to speak through various genres – open letters, political commentary, and poetry. Although others penned the abolitionist poems, Wedderburn likely wrote most of the prose, including the letters to himself and his responses, as already noted about his correspondence with Miss Campbell. Eric Pencek argues that Wedderburn's many voices rejected the "author-function" because private property is one of "the underlying assumptions that go with individual authorship." More pragmatically, Wedderburn's many voices secured his anonymity: "However memorable the individual Wedderburn may be, in polemical action, his voice becomes the voice, not of a revolutionary, but of the revolution."[48] Hanley describes this style as "authorial schizophrenia," yet this chapter argues that its polyvocality tended and grew what Sonya Posmentier calls a "plot" that "emerges from the dialectic between freedom and constraint."[49] Posmentier, using Wynter, uses the provision grounds as a verb to theorize that "provisioning" in writing is the "action of material and spiritual sustenance which is always underway in poetics."[50] Just as provision grounds and Maroon villages cultivated polycultures of yams, pumpkins, and pigs on the margins of monoculture sugar plantations, the many voices in *Axe Laid to the Root* were deployed to "call in" many readers to receive spiritual sustenance that offered alternatives to the logics of plantation capitalism and liberal individualism.

England's weekly radical periodicals of the early nineteenth century, Jon Klancher notes, "confront their readers as collectives and representatives of collectives ... The radical text was not meant to form a singular bond between reader and writer, but to bind one reader to another *as* audience."[51] By alternately addressing enslaved people in Jamaica and the lower classes in England, Wedderburn suggested both groups have a united interest in resisting British governance. Just before Wedderburn's publication of *Axe Laid to the Root*, William Cobbett published his highly influential cheap *Political Register*, "To the Journeymen and Labourers of England, Wales, Scotland, and Ireland" (1816), which brought together both skilled and unskilled laborers, as well as men, women, and children into a communal, politicized reading audience.[52] Cobbett, however, was a virulent racist who sought to include the white working-classes in politics while scapegoating enslaved people in the West Indies.[53] At the same time, as James Chandler observes, Cobbett had a "deeply ingrained transatlantic orientation" through his exchange of periodicals and ideas across the Atlantic.[54] Wedderburn shared this transatlantic orientation, and perhaps that is why, despite Cobbett's well-known racism, Wedderburn championed his work.

Wedderburn specifically praised William Cobbett's mass distribution of the *Political Register* as a fight for the "liberty of the press," and in this matter he appears to agree with E. P. Thompson, who argued, in the "groundswell of Radical propaganda" of that period, the most influential journalistic voice was that of William Cobbett.[55] In the fifth issue of *Axe Laid to the Root*, Wedderburn published a prophetic essay supporting Cobbett's forthcoming *A Grammar of the English Language* (1818). Wedderburn's "A Hodge Podge Effusion Produced by Reading Cobbett's *Register*" explained that Cobbett's pioneering of cheap publications provided prophetic inspiration from which Wedderburn could launch his own political theories: "With the breath of truth blow into a flame the fire kindled by Cobbett, never to the extinguished" (*Axe* 5.76).[56]

Wedderburn viewed his periodical as inspired by and even a continuation of the work of Cobbett, which demonstrated his intellectual flexibility and determination to create what Kevin Gilmartin calls "rhetorical bricolage," a text that accommodates contradiction by combining "elements from across discourse boundaries such that the antecedent discourses are fundamentally altered in the resultant structures."[57]

Wedderburn and Cobbett believed that universal literacy was the foundation of a just society, and both championed using plain language over learned. Olivia Smith suggests that Cobbett's *Grammar*, the publication Wedderburn praises, depicted "the act of learning grammar by one of his readers as an act of class warfare."[58] Wedderburn's friend Thomas Spence articulated similar goals for literacy in his *The Grand Repository of the English Language* (1775). Spence's grammar book, Saree Makdisi argues, "had in mind not only British plebians but also 'Negro slaves' and the inhabitants of India when developing his phonetic spelling system for English."[59] Wedderburn had a similarly global vision for universal literacy. In his address to enslaved people in Jamaica, Wedderburn outlined several political policies for a post-emancipation society, including the establishment of a common language and literacy: "Let the alphabet be engraven [*sic*] on your trees, and on every public wall, for knowledge is god-like strength, which will regulate your physical force" (*Axe* 2.29).[60] Moreover, he argued that all children should be freely educated, and the children should wear various colored caps that symbolized their degrees of literacy so that their development would be marked and applauded publicly.

E. P. Thompson famously proposed, "class happens when some men, as a result of common experiences (inherited or shared), feel and articulate the identity of their interests between themselves, and as against other men whose interests are different from (and usually opposed to) theirs."[61] Wedderburn attempted to extend this sense of class beyond the "English" by addressing many distinct classes of oppressed people in Jamaica: free mixed-race people living in Kingston reading radical publications, enslaved Black people tending provision grounds, and Maroons honing guerilla foraging and gleaning practices. Moreover, instead of returning to nostalgic European models of "old England," like William Cobbett, Wedderburn ridiculed the idealization of England's medieval institutions. Just after his documentation of England's excessive use of capital punishment for petty theft, Wedderburn quoted the phrase "Oh the Roast of Beef of Old England?" in quotation marks with a question mark at the end to suggest that the medieval English "tradition" of hospitality was not an inclusive or realistic model for transnational liberation

(*Axe* 2.21). Throughout the periodical, Wedderburn directly addresses English inhospitality toward the Irish: "Oh! Ye poor of Ireland, your death, through starvation, will be a perpetual, yea, an eternal monument of disgrace to the landholders, it will be an immortal book, wherein will be read the wicked system of private property in land" (*Axe* 5.70). Addressing the impact of empire in Jamaica and Ireland, *Axe Laid to the Root* sought to create transatlantic solidarity among colonized peoples.

At the same time, Wedderburn also directly addressed the lower classes in London. In the second issue of *Axe Laid to the Root*, for example, he protested the Metropolitan Paving Acts (1817), which allowed the city to seize land for widening roads and to prosecute people who held signs, shops, or gardens near the streets. The Metropolitan Paving Act "facilitated the prosecution of hawkers blocking the pavement, flying dustmen, coach drivers committing traffic offences, and much else besides."[62] Wedderburn declared the Act was "a war against garden pots and sign boards" (*Axe* 2.19) that targeted the lower classes who created subsistence gardens and small businesses on these urban commons. Wedderburn's discernment of an urban commons in London, something entirely unnoticed by Cobbett and other radicals, was perhaps inspired by being raised by his grandmother, Talkee Amy, a higgler who expertly navigated the markets of Kingston, Jamaica. The control of urban spaces was part of a Romantic-era project that Saree Makdisi identifies as "Occidentalism," which racialized common people to justify the enclosure of urban commons like sidewalk markets. By outlawing street hawkers, the British government stopped urban markets that redistributed food and bookseller stalls that sold cheap subversive ballads and pamphlets.[63] Wedderburn compared English system of property to a "Bandditi [sic] of Robbers" that strategically starved the lower classes: "If you resist, it is death; if you tamely submit, you perish for want of subsistence" (*Axe* 2.21). By highlighting how incarceration and capital punishment were used to punish the English poor for attempting to procure food, Wedderburn illustrated how liberal forms of freedom based on the free market and private property laid the groundwork for criminalizing independent subsistence in both England and the West Indies.

Axe Laid to the Root addressed many different and opposing groups of people – mainstream English radicals, the English poor, Irish Catholics, free mixed-race people, enslaved people, and Jamaican Maroons – to cultivate radical transatlantic solidarity. There are only six issues of *Axe Laid to the Root*, and why the publication ceased production is unknown. However, it was part of the "ultra-radical press of bewildering vigour and ephemerality" that flourished just before the Peterloo Massacre.[64] The periodical's unpredictable circulation amongst the poor throughout London allowed Wedderburn to champion models of creative Black resistance that white abolitionists did not acknowledge. Wedderburn was skeptical of the Evangelical "respectability" endorsed by British abolitionists such as William Wilberforce and Hannah More. Moreover, Wedderburn does not call upon dominant British abolitionist tropes that, as Elizabeth Bohls argues, "implicitly distance British bodies from African persons and practices by invoking a visceral disgust" through depicting bloody or sweating bodies that put enslaved people in a "passive posture."[65] Instead *Axe Laid to the Root* repeatedly held out empowered examples of Black liberation.

In most studies of the intensification of radical activity leading up to the Peterloo Massacre, Wedderburn is referred to, if at all, as a minor player in Romantic-era radicalism. However, in 1819, a year Ian Haywood asserts "marked the apotheosis of single-print graphic caricature's intervention into the political public sphere," George Cruikshank's *The New Union Club* (1819) depicted Wedderburn as dangerously influential (Figure 1.2).[66] This caricature along with numerous government spy reports on his political speeches demonstrated that Wedderburn's political

Figure 1.2 George Cruikshank, *The New Union Club, Being a Representation of What Took Place at a Celebrated Dinner, Given by a Celebrated ____Society*, 1819. Courtesy of the trustees of the British Museum.

advocacy for African Jamaican land and food-based insurrection were circulating and significant enough to be feared by the establishment. *The New Union Club* represents a meeting at the philanthropic African Institution as a degenerate sexual orgy, where abolitionists, including William Wilberforce, Zachary Macaulay, and William Smith (MP for Norwich), are "presented as victims of unbridled black hedonism," according to Marcus Wood.[67] In an incisive seven-page analysis of the caricature, Wood does not mention Wedderburn's name, even though he stands on a table at the center of the print. Such critical silence, unfortunately, echoes Cruikshank's silencing of Wedderburn: As the main speaker at the meeting, Wedderburn was poised as though mid-sentence, with a dramatic gesture and open mouth, yet he lacked a word bubble, unlike the white participants in the meeting. Moreover, he is crowded by other distracting images designed to pull the viewer's attention away from him. The print enunciated how Wedderburn's enemies and allies alike acknowledged his influence while dismissing him as a mere entertainer, a dismissal that this book attempts to remedy.

Recent readings of Wedderburn's influence acknowledge his place in the caricature. Jenna M. Gibbs suggests that Wedderburn's "table-top oratory incites the lawless anarchy Cruikshank believed would erupt after emancipation and universal suffrage."[68] Johnson argues that the image "visually registers (with a degree of sardonic horror) the collective energy Wedderburn's speeches frequently invite."[69] These readings attempt to recover Wedderburn's influence but do not attend to his voicelessness. Compared to *A Peep in the London Tavern*, another Cruikshank caricature that features Wedderburn, discussed in the Introduction, this Wedderburn is more appropriately dressed. Yet his behavior is racially caricatured as even more inappropriate: He clutches his genitals in a masturbatory pose while speaking dramatically and voicelessly to what appears to be an unheeding crowd. Depicted on the same horizontal level as a Black musician, Wedderburn is further diminished as a mere performer rather than a serious political activist. Only one young man listens, and his attentiveness to Wedderburn makes him unaware that his hair and coat have been lit on fire by the child behind him. The caricature warns of Wedderburn's dangerously charismatic hold over his listeners while dismissing the substance of his politics.

The paintings on the wall behind Wedderburn also offer suggestions about Wedderburn's influence. A painting to the right of Wedderburn depicts "the King of Hayti and his Black guards," and Johnson points out that the painting "conjoins Wedderburn's presence as a radical agitator to

Haiti's post-revolutionary state and to the unholy specter of a Black sovereignty both at home and abroad."[70] The painting just above his head depicts St. Paul in a speaking posture identical to Wedderburn's. St. Paul speaks 1 Timothy 5:8: "But if any provide not for his own, and especially for those of his own house, he hath denied the faith, and is worse than an infidel," a verse that, in this context, conveyed the stereotypical working-class message that antislavery advocates should care for the poor of England instead of worrying about enslaved people in the West Indies. Further suggesting that the presence of Black people would diminish the prospects of the white working class, in the right corner, a white, disabled sailor is being forcibly removed by an able-bodied Black sailor. Caring for one's own "house" or race contradicted Wedderburn's message of a transatlantic alliance against plantations. Wedderburn would have at least appreciated that Cruikshank modeled this print on James Gillray's *The Union Club* (1801), which ridiculed the Irish and their supporters, because Wedderburn sought to create solidarity between the starving people of Ireland and enslaved people in the West Indies.

Cruikshank's caricature reminds us that Wedderburn's *Axe Laid to the Root* was a supplement to extensive preaching and public debates that he held in London. His publications are artifacts that provide a limited window into Wedderburn's vision for a transatlantic alliance against private property. However, he also clearly valued writing as a vehicle for activism, and he noted: "I must give vent, I have commenced my carear [*sic*], the press is the engine of my destruction" (*Axe* 4.53). Black intellectuals like Wedderburn, Paul Gilroy argues, outlined traditions and ideas that "supported countercultures of modernity that touched the workers' movement but are not reducible to it. They supplied important foundations on which it could build."[71] Wedderburn imagined this foundation as a Black commons that arose after dispossession. Throughout his career, Wedderburn envisioned a transatlantic abolitionist future based on a foundation of African Jamaican countercultures that refused individual property ownership. *Axe Laid to the Root* asserted that Black practices of the provision grounds might be transplanted from the periphery of the West Indian colonies to the metropole of London, strategically destabilizing the white abolitionist view that liberation arises from transporting English freedoms to the colonies and extending them to enslaved people.

CHAPTER 2

From Plantation to Prison
Wedderburn's *The Horrors of Slavery* and London's Radical Press

Robert Wedderburn's most well-known work, *The Horrors of Slavery* (1824), boasts a unique publication history within early nineteenth-century London's radical press. Published seven years after *Axe Laid to the Root*, Wedderburn continued cultivating the intersection of working-class and antislavery interests by initially revealing his life narrative through a series of letters to the working-class periodical *Bell's Life in London*. Wedderburn then republished the *Bell's Life* letters as a pamphlet with ten additional pages of personal narrative. By choosing to publish his life narrative as a series of unsolicited letters to a popular working-class Sunday paper and then as a self-published "cheap" pamphlet within ultra-radical circles, Wedderburn avoided the demand to edit his life narrative to suit the political ambitions of white, middle-class abolitionists. Other Romantic-era slave narratives, such as Olaudah Equiano's *The Interesting Narrative* (1789) and *The History of Mary Prince* (1831), were edited and published by abolitionists in England. This chapter analyzes the publication history of Wedderburn's *Horrors of Slavery*, thereby addressing, in part, the problem that Manu Samriti Chander and Patricia A. Matthew outline: "Olaudah Equiano and his *Interesting Narrative* have served too long as the single abolitionist/antislavery text in Romanticism."[1] Untethered by mainstream abolitionist political constraints, Wedderburn's life narrative illustrated how an unrepaired traumatic past haunted his "freedom" from West Indian slavery. By introducing himself as "Late a Prisoner in His Majesty's Gaol," his life narrative radically tracked the horrors of racialized slavery from the West Indian plantation to incarceration in an English prison (Figure 2.1).

Scholars who have assessed the entirety of Wedderburn's writing career argue that *Horrors of Slavery* was less politically radical than his earlier *Axe Laid to the Root* because it amounted to a "personal vindication" of the lives of his enslaved mother and grandmother.[2] In Wedderburn's case, however, the personal was political. Anthony Bogues proposes that slave narratives should be read as political treatises that "probed alternative meanings of

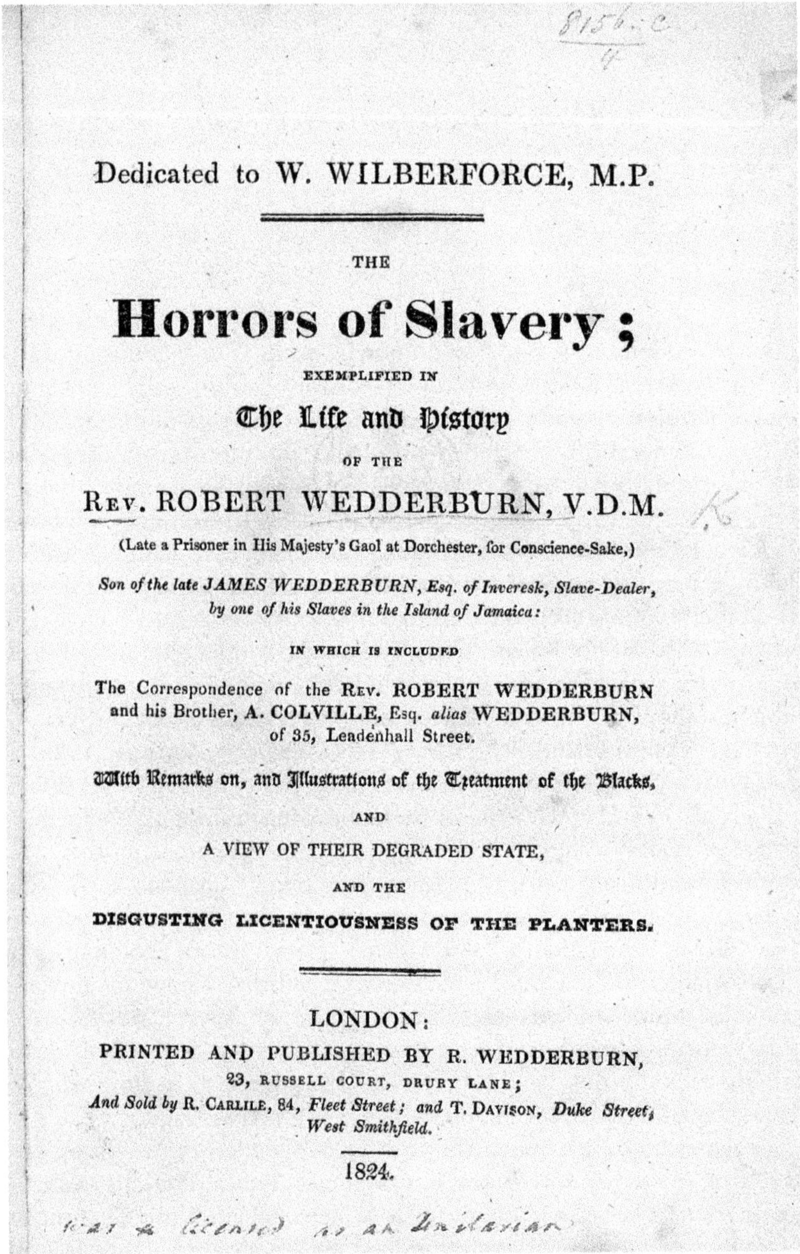

Dedicated to W. WILBERFORCE, M.P.

THE

Horrors of Slavery;

EXEMPLIFIED IN

The Life and History

OF THE

REV. ROBERT WEDDERBURN, V.D.M.

(Late a Prisoner in His Majesty's Gaol at Dorchester, for Conscience-Sake,)

Son of the late JAMES WEDDERBURN, Esq. of Inveresk, Slave-Dealer, by one of his Slaves in the Island of Jamaica:

IN WHICH IS INCLUDED

The Correspondence of the REV. ROBERT WEDDERBURN and his Brother, A. COLVILLE, Esq. *alias* WEDDERBURN, of 35, Leadenhall Street.

With Remarks on, and Illustrations of the Treatment of the Blacks,

AND

A VIEW OF THEIR DEGRADED STATE,

AND THE

DISGUSTING LICENTIOUSNESS OF THE PLANTERS.

LONDON:

PRINTED AND PUBLISHED BY R. WEDDERBURN,

23, RUSSELL COURT, DRURY LANE;

And Sold by R. CARLILE, 84, *Fleet Street;* and T. DAVISON, *Duke Street, West Smithfield.*

1824.

Figure 2.1 Title page from *Horrors of Slavery*. London, 1824.

racial slavery, natural liberty, and natural rights."[3] Wedderburn's life narrative, like his former publication, *Axe Laid to the Root*, strategically destabilized the British antislavery view that liberation would take place by transporting essentially English freedoms to the colonies and extending them to enslaved people. *Horrors* not only vindicated the freedom practices of his enslaved Jamaican mother and grandmother, as discussed in Chapter 3, but it also courageously illustrated how the violence of plantation slavery followed free Black British citizens into England.

The first part of this chapter explores the origins of Wedderburn's life narrative in his letters to *Bell's Life*, which were prompted by the editor's questions about whether enslavers in the West Indies would sell their own children. After Wedderburn's initial public letter describing his father's depravity, subsequent issues of *Bell's Life* revealed an argumentative exchange between Wedderburn and his white half-brother, Andrew Colvile, who wrote to *Bell's Life* to defend his father's reputation. Colvile's letters failed to recover the elder Wedderburn's reputation and further served to illustrate the starkly inequitable futures of the white and Black "children of a Slave-Dealer." The second part of this chapter discusses Wedderburn's republication of those letters in the pamphlet *Horrors of Slavery*, which explicitly traced his life journey from being enslaved on a plantation in Jamaica to being a prisoner of conscience in Dorchester Gaol. By outlining a British Black man's life trajectory from a West Indian plantation to poverty and prison in England, *Horrors of Slavery* foreshadows Catherine Hall's warning: "This 'romance' of Abolition disguises more than it explains, and produces its mechanisms of amnesia – as it still forcefully does in public life in Britain, with the invocation of 'Wilberforce' as the archangel of liberty."[4] As a self-publishing "unrespectable" radical, Wedderburn was not pressured to replicate the antislavery convention of celebrating British liberal freedoms; therefore, *Horrors of Slavery* is an essential supplement to more commonly studied Romantic-era slave narratives.[5]

"Brother or No Brother—That Is the Question": Wedderburn's Letters to *Bell's Life in London*

Horrors of Slavery originated in a series of letters that Wedderburn wrote to the editor of *Bell's Life in London* between February 15 and March 28, 1824. A popular weekly paper with a circulation of 10,000, *Bell's Life* advertised itself as "combining, with the News of the Week, a rich Repository of Fashion, Wit and Humour, and the interesting incidents of Real Life." Among radical newspapers, *Bell's Life* was unique in its content, "with its unabashedly broad coverage of sporting subjects, its lurid crime stories, and its advertisements for louche songbooks."[6] Unlike most other "cheap" publications, *Bell's Life* appealed to a diverse audience, from the lower classes to middle-class writers, such as Charles Dickens, Thomas Hood, and Robert Southey, who all read it "in spite of its cheap format and its sometimes racy tone."[7] By publishing his life narrative in a working-class journal in the 1820s, moreover, Wedderburn further challenged "the emergence and consolidation of a specifically working-class racism in radical print culture."[8] Like *Axe Laid to the Root*, Wedderburn's letters to *Bell's Life* sought to cultivate a relationship between working-class interests and abolition.

Wedderburn's first letter responded to a February 15, 1824, article, "The Blessings of Slavery," which summarized a London Tavern meeting of persons with monetary interests in West Indian Colonies. After publishing the names of the people who attended the meeting, the editor reported that the attendees complained of "the injustice of deteriorating their property (their fellow men) and of emancipating their Slaves, without remuneration to their masters, who had *bought* them."[9] The editor's critical commentary was evident in his emphasis that the "property" discussed in the meeting is "their fellow men." A sharper critique was directed toward the intergenerational nature of chattel slavery, described as "*Chains* and *Whips* for a RACE yet UNBORN." Orlando Patterson calls this cruelty "natal alienation"; slavery severs the "ties of birth in both ascending and descending generations."[10] The *Bell's Life* editor documented evidence of natal alienation by citing a report of a man in Liverpool who "had boasted of the profit he had made by a Negro-girl who had borne him three children, *all of whom he* SOLD, *with their heart-broken mother, on his quitting Jamaica!*" After citing this anecdote, the editor asked, "how many of the Slave-Dealers present at the London Tavern, on Tuesday last, have enhanced their profit by similar disposals?"[11] The question of planters' habitual "disposal" of their Black kin prompted Wedderburn to reply with his own story of his father's sexual violence toward his enslaved mother, Rosanna, and of the elder Wedderburn's financial and emotional abandonment of his mixed-race children.

When *Bell's Life* issued the following week's "The Blessings of Slavery" column, the editor introduced Wedderburn's letter with a disclaimer: "He has given his name and address, or we could not have published an account so monstrous."[12] By naming himself and his father, Wedderburn's initial letter about his life experience provided more evidence to support *Bell's Life*'s claim that enslavers improved their income by having children with the women they enslaved:

> Your observations on the Meeting of the Receivers of Stolen Men, call for my sincere thanks, I being the descendant of a Slave by a base Slave-Holder, the late JAMES WEDDERBURN, Esq. of Inveresk, who sold my mother when she was with child of me, HER THIRD SON BY HIM!!![13]

Wedderburn's letter transformed the *Bell's Life* conversation about slavery, previously between white writers, by consciously inserting his Black Caribbean perspective into the conversation. Instead of presenting himself as a passive object of study that merely illustrated the consequences of slavery, as his story might be told in the pages of an antislavery periodical, Wedderburn emerged as a lively interlocutor whose agency in telling his own story prompted his half-brother's contentious, threatening replies.

Within the institution of slavery, Hortense Spillers contends, "the denied genetic link becomes a chief strategy of an undenied ownership, as if the interrogation into the father's identity—the blank space where his proper name would fit—were answered by the fact, de jure, of a material possession."[14] Wedderburn's first letter filled that blank space with James Wedderburn's name in bold capital letters. After publicly claiming his genetic relationship with his father, he detailed his father's repeated assaults on his enslaved mother, Rosanna, who "was FORCED to submit to him, being *his Slave*, THOUGH HE KNEW SHE DISLIKED HIM!"[15] Wedderburn emphasized his enslaver father's sexually predatory behavior by using what Marcy J. Dinius identifies as "radical typography" through which "voice and the emotion in the text are visible and thereby audible in its typography."[16] By using the typography of capital letters for emphasis, Wedderburn asserted, controversially at that time, that even a long-established relationship between an enslaver and a woman he enslaved could not be consensual. If, as Mary Louise Pratt argues, British colonization and slavery were promoted as mutually beneficial by replicating stories of "transracial love plots" that were "imaginings in which European supremacy is guaranteed by affective and social bonding," Wedderburn's assertion that his mother was continually raped throughout a years-long "relationship" with her enslaver undermined that fantasy.[17]

To further undermine the fantasy of affective bonding, Wedderburn explained that his experience as a mixed-race child of an enslaver was, in fact, commonplace rather than unique. Giving an account of two mixed-race relatives who were sold into slavery in America by their uncle, Wedderburn insisted that their enslaver "*had a little shame*, for the law in Jamaica allowed him to sell them, or even had they been his children – *so much for humanity and Christian goodness*."[18] Again using typography to emphasize the monstrosity of the denied genetic link that Spiller notes,

Wedderburn also highlighted how continuing kinship among whites – in this case, white brothers having access to each other's property in people – required the erasure of any kinship with their mixed-race children. Wedderburn concluded the letter, "oh, what barbarism!" His emphasis on European barbarism reflected the discourse that Stefan M. Wheelock identifies as the "rhetoric of black prophetic denunciation [that] belongs to this antislavery culture of hope and expectation."[19] The hope and expectation of acknowledging kinship between poor mixed-race Britons and their white relatives underlaid Wedderburn's initial letter, which prompted an unexpected, enraged reply from his half brother.

The March 21, 1824, edition of *Bell's Life* dramatically introduced "A LETTER FROM *ANOTHER* SON OF THE LATE SLAVE-DEALER, JAMES WEDDERBURN, Esq."[20] By reiterating the name of the father and then putting correspondence under the heading, "Brother or No Brother – 'That Is the Question?,'" the editor of *Bell's Life* alluded to the well-known antislavery medal and slogan, "Am I Not a Man and a Brother?" In this way, the editor concurred that acknowledging kinship and therefore sharing property fueled the conflicted exchange. The posture of Wedderburn in relation to his brother, however, was far from the abolitionist trope of the individualized "grateful slave" begging for release. George Boulukos argues, the grateful slave trope depicted "African slaves as capable of becoming devoted to their masters and even embracing their condition."[21] The figure of the grateful, compliant, formerly enslaved person not only attempted to eliminate traumatic memory but also elided Black knowledge of and capacity for self-emancipation. By emphasizing justified rebelliousness on the part of enslaved and formerly enslaved people, including himself, Wedderburn refused the diffused racism of British antislavery sentimentalism. Brycchan Carey contends that "abolitionist ethics rooted in sentimental philosophy came at considerable risk of perpetuating racial ideologies that saw Africans and other non-Europeans merely as feeling rather than as rational individuals."[22] Wedderburn refused abolitionism's performative sentimentalism by demanding acknowledgment of his kinship with his Scots family. When Wedderburn's half brother, Andrew Colvile, wrote the letter to *Bell's Life*, he was living in London as chairman of the West India Dock Company and Member of the Committee of the Hudson's Bay Company.[23] Given his prominent position in London society, the editor's description of Colvile as merely "another brother" must have angered him as much as it illustrated the stark contrast in the futures of white and mixed-race brothers.

Colvile's letter sought to restore his father's reputation after Wedderburn's "foul slander upon the character of the respected dead." First declaring that his father "never had any child by, or any connection of *that kind*, with the mother of this man," Colvile then undermined his own statement by demonstrating his own private knowledge of Rosanna's character, although in his lifetime his father had enslaved hundreds of people. He claimed Rosanna was sold to another enslaver because she had "so violent a temper" and was often "occasioning a disturbance in the house." Continuing to reveal his family's familiarity with Rosanna's life story, Colvile asserted, "several years afterwards, this woman was delivered of a mulatto child, and as *she could not tell who was the father*, her master, in a foolish joke, named the child Wedderburn." Based on established stereotypes about Black women as angry and promiscuous, Colvile's demeaning description of Wedderburn's mother was followed by the accusation that Wedderburn had asked for money in the past "upon the *strength of his name*." Colvile thereby revealed that his motivation for defending his father's reputation was to maintain his claim on inherited property.

It is unclear why Colvile publicly defended his father at this time, because James Wedderburn had already been named as Robert Wedderburn's father in his trial for blasphemous libel four years earlier in 1820. At the trial, Wedderburn declared that "he was the offspring of a female slave, by a rich European planter." The word "planter" has an asterisk that names the father as James Wedderburn in a footnote at the bottom of the page.[24] Even before the trial, in the first issue of *Axe Laid to the Root*, Wedderburn clearly outlined his heritage: "Be it known to the world, that, I Robert Wedderburn, son of James Wedderburn, esq. of Inveresk, near Musselborough, by Rosannah his slave, whom he sold to James Charles Shalto Douglas, esq. in the parish of St. Mary, in the island of Jamaica, while pregnant with the said Wedderburn, who was not held as a slave, (a provision being made in the agreement, that the child when born should be free.)" (1.3). Thus, Wedderburn had claimed James Wedderburn as his father throughout his life. The wide circulation of *Bell's Life* in more respectable audiences must have prompted Colvile's sudden decision to defend his father. The state of mixed-race children from the West Indies was precarious. As Michael Morris explains, "white parentage provided potential access to a source of financial as well as cultural capital that was unavailable to their enslaved and free black compatriots (although Wedderburn remained debarred from this inheritance, a feature that fueled much of his anger)."[25] Colvile's denial of his mixed-race brother was rhetorically ineffective. The *Bell's Life* editor declared that Colvile's letters provided even more evidence that Wedderburn's account of his parentage was "literally true." Making a distinction between "slave-dealers' logic" and the working-class mission of *Bell's Life in London*, the editor argued that "our columns are as open to one part of the father's family as another." The editor further suggested that since Colvile and Wedderburn now both resided in London, Colvile should not allow the "dearest ties to consanguinity" to be "trampled upon by a sordid thirst of interest" produced by the institution of West Indian slavery.[26]

After the editor advocated a more equitable distribution of Colvile's private wealth, Wedderburn continued his assertion of kinship in his reply to his brother in the March 28, 1824, edition of *Bell's Life*. Expressing surprise "that any person would have had the temerity, not to say audacity, to have contradicted my assertions, and thereby occasion me to PROVE the deep depravity of the man to whom I owe my existence," Wedderburn's response asserted two points: first that his mother was a virtuous woman caught in an impossibly violent situation, and second, that the European men in his family perpetuated trauma in their thirst for plantation profits.[27] Wedderburn defended his mother, Rosanna, as "a woman, virtuous in principle, but a Slave, and a sacrifice to the unprincipled lust of my father." He denied Colvile's assertion that his mother was promiscuous, defying the idea that an enslaved woman can consent to a sexual relationship with her enslaver. While denying his mother's promiscuity, Wedderburn surprisingly celebrated Colvile's description of Rosanna as an angry and unmanageable housekeeper: "Yes, and I glory in her *rebellious* disposition, and which I have inherited from her." As discussed in Chapter 3, Rosanna angrily fought for freedom for her mixed-race children by forcing the elder Wedderburn to acknowledge his kinship with them. The pamphlet version of *Horrors of Slavery* celebrated the tactics of his mother and grandmother as the origin of Wedderburn's freedom.

Asserting kinship was inseparable from the demand for a redistribution of Colvile's wealth, a product, like Wedderburn himself, of plantation slavery. Wedderburn unashamedly admitted that he asked his father for money, claiming it was based on a biblical "ground of *right*."[28] Citing Deuteronomy 21:10, 17, which states that if a man has two wives, the children of his favorite wife should not get the entire inheritance, but the firstborn of the hated wife should have a "double portion" of the estate, Wedderburn claimed this right based on the Bible. He also unashamedly asserted his own need: At the time, bread prices were high, and his wife was pregnant. By documenting his repeated bids for paternal care,

Wedderburn's life narrative demonstrated a "willful familiarity" with the Scots side of his family, which, according to Elahe Haschemi Yekani, "no longer follows eighteenth-century conventionalised accounts of slavery that humbly (and sentimentally) petition on behalf of the 'poor Africans.' It demonstrates a more outrageous familiarity with his father and brother, identified by name and address."[29] Wedderburn performed this willful familiarity by insisting that Colvile remembered when "I visited my father, who had the inhumanity to threaten to send me to gaol if I troubled him." He reminded Colvile that his father did not then deny his parentage, but rather asserted that his mixed-race son was a "lazy fellow" who should not be given financial assistance. Wedderburn's unwavering insistence on his kinship with both the white and Black sides of his family rebelled against the way chattel slavery rendered people into "genealogical isolates," who, according to Orlando Patterson, were "denied all claims on, and obligations to, his parents and living blood relations."[30] His life narrative can be understood as a performance that testified to various strategies of reclamation of those severed genealogical lines.

Wedderburn's attempts to connect with his white kin in England ended with legal threats, which gestured toward the way British law was wielded unfairly against free Black Britons. James Wedderburn threatened to send his son to jail if he continued to ask for money, and Colvile ended his letter by threatening to sue. Wedderburn, however, was undeterred by these threats: "I mean to publish my whole history in a cheap pamphlet, and to give the public a specimen of the inhumanity, cruelty, avarice, and diabolical lust of the West India Slave-Holders; and in the Courts of Justice I will defend and prove my assertions." Nicole N. Aljoe argues that West Indian slave narratives, unlike their American counterparts, were often viewed as legal records that anticipate "going to law" and "frequently announce themselves as substitutes for – and even anticipations of – courtroom and Parliamentary testimony."[31] Wedderburn's pamphlet even more radically attempted to "go to law" and challenge the foundations of property and plantation slavery by asserting his right to be acknowledged as a member of the Wedderburn family, even if his mother was enslaved by his father.

Analyzing *Horrors of Slavery* within the context of its initial, partial publication in a radical weekly newspaper reveals that Wedderburn asserted Black self-liberation instead of appealing to abolitionists for assistance. He also continued to assert, even demand, that members of London's lower classes dialogue with him about the cause of abolition and the status of Black people in Britain. In seeking this dialogue, Wedderburn was out of step with other radicals of the 1820s. As Ryan

Hanley documents, "as demands for an extended franchise became more urgent, the black slave was increasingly represented to emergent working-class readerships as being different from, and inferior to, them.[32] However, Wedderburn continued to cultivate solidarity between the English working classes and enslaved people in the Caribbean by choosing to retain the entirety of the text from *Bell's Life* – his own, the editor's, and Colvile's – when he published *Horrors of Slavery* as a pamphlet later that year.

"A Prisoner for Conscience-Sake": Life Narrative from Plantation to Prison

The pamphlet version of *Horrors of Slavery* began with an additional thirteen-page life narrative and ended with a new summary of the public conflict with his half brother. It also reframed Wedderburn's initial letters in terms of the two-year sentence (1820–22) that he served for blasphemous libel. The pamphlet's title page emphasized Wedderburn's identity as "Late a Prisoner in His Majesty's Gaol at Dorchester, for Conscience-Sake," and the additional life narrative drew connections between plantations in the West Indies and prosecution and prison in England. On the one hand, emphasizing his recent prison sentence in the pamphlet may have been designed to establish credibility with other English ultra-radicals, who had also been prosecuted under the Six Acts after the Peterloo Massacre. Richard D. Altick observes that under the Six Acts, "prosecution of offending printers, booksellers, and hawkers was swift, and the sentences handed down upon conviction were severe."[33] By reframing his life narrative in light of his recent prison sentence, Wedderburn evoked the fame and support he received during his initial arrest for sedition in September 1819 (Figure 2.2). At the same time, this reframing of his life narrative, through the title page and preface to William Wilberforce, who visited him in prison, outlined the trajectory of a mixed-race child born in Jamaica from plantation slavery to incarceration in England.

After the initial charges for sedition failed, Wedderburn was released, rearrested, and finally convicted of blasphemous libel on February 25, 1820. He subsequently spent two years in Dorchester Gaol at the same time as the radical publisher, Richard Carlile, another political prisoner under the Six Acts. Carlile was convicted of blasphemous and seditious libel after publishing a critique of the Peterloo Massacre in *The Republican* and republishing Thomas Paine's *Common Sense*, *Rights of Man*, and *Age of Reason*. Wedderburn was not allowed to visit Carlile in prison. Still, they were acquainted, and Wedderburn even collaborated with him to publish

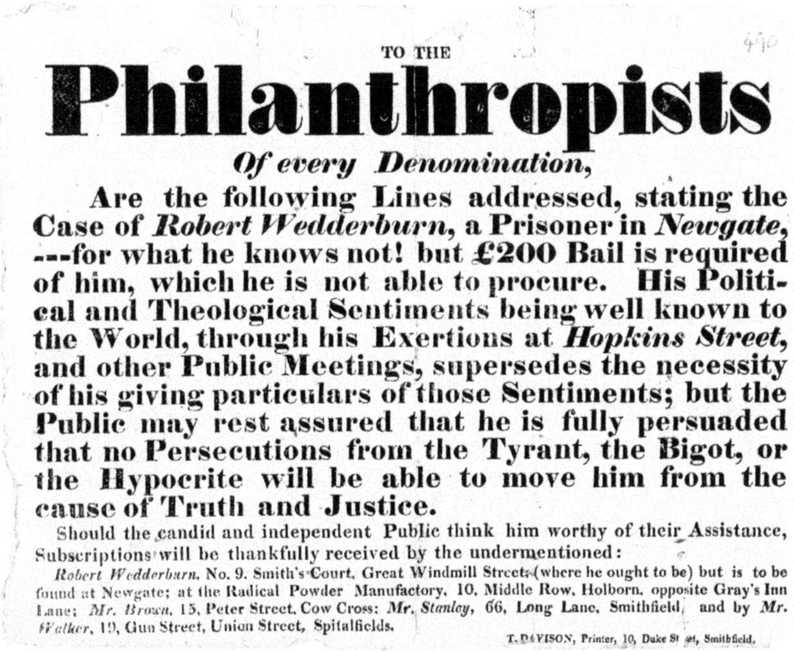
TO THE

Philanthropists

Of every Denomination,

Are the following Lines addressed, stating the Case of *Robert Wedderburn*, a Prisoner in *Newgate*, ---for what he knows not! but £200 Bail is required of him, which he is not able to procure. His Political and Theological Sentiments being well known to the World, through his Exertions at *Hopkins Street*, and other Public Meetings, supersedes the necessity of his giving particulars of those Sentiments; but the Public may rest assured that he is fully persuaded that no Persecutions from the Tyrant, the Bigot, or the Hypocrite will be able to move him from the cause of Truth and Justice.

Should the candid and independent Public think him worthy of their Assistance, Subscriptions will be thankfully received by the undermentioned:

Robert Wedderburn, No. 9. Smith's Court, Great Windmill Street, (where he ought to be) but is to be found at Newgate; at the Radical Powder Manufactory, 10, Middle Row, Holborn, opposite Gray's Inn Lane; *Mr. Brown*, 15, Peter Street, Cow Cross; *Mr. Stanley*, 66, Long Lane, Smithfield, and by *Mr. Walker*, 19, Gun Street, Union Street, Spitalfields.

T. DAVISON, Printer, 10, Duke Street, Smithfield.

Figure 2.2 Handbill printed by T. Davison raising bail money for Wedderburn after his arrest in 1819.
Courtesy of the National Archives of the UK.

his satire, "Diabolical Liturgy," in the *Lion* in 1828. While Wedderburn and Carlile were in Dorchester Gaol, William Wilberforce visited both. Wedderburn recounted this prison visit in his dedication to *Horrors of Slavery*, which further framed the correspondence in *Bell's Life* as an outgrowth of his time in prison. It is impossible to know precisely what transpired between the two men. The preface mentioned that Wilberforce encouraged Wedderburn to write an autobiographical narrative to assist his campaign to end slavery in the West Indies. Wilberforce must have been aware of Wedderburn's talent and influence; after all, at his sentencing, the solicitor general testified that Wedderburn was dangerous because "he certainly possesses considerable talents, and those too of a popular nature."[34] Wilberforce likely wanted to guide Wedderburn's talent away from publishing cheap ultra-radical periodicals, such as *Axe Laid to the Root*, into a more conventional, politically useful slave narrative.

Slave narratives were often prefaced by endorsements from white abolitionists who vouched for the authenticity of the narrative. Wedderburn's dedication to Wilberforce cited this convention while refusing to ask for any endorsement. The preface to *Horrors* addressed Wilberforce satirically by ventriloquizing the antislavery trope of the "grateful slave": "an oppressed, insulted, and degraded African – to whom but you can I dedicate the following pages, illustrative of the treatment of my poor countrymen?"[35] This submissive position contrasted sharply with Wedderburn's defiant tone, celebrating his status as a former prisoner of conscience. As a member of Parliament, Wilberforce created and enforced the laws that landed Carlile and Wedderburn in prison. Although remembered as an abolitionist and animal rights activist, Wilberforce was also a notorious enemy of working-class interests. He advocated for laws that enforced moral codes among the poor and voted for the Combination Acts, which prohibited labor organizing, and labor organizing, as Joseph Albernaz argues, was at the heart of much of Wedderburn's work.[36] While the preface began by calling Wilberforce a "glorious benefactor" and "tower of strength," it also recorded his moral and literal abandonment, leaving Wedderburn in a solitary prison cell with "your advice, for which I am still your debtor" and two "books beautifully bound in calf." While some scholars accept that *Horrors* complied with Wilberforce's request for a reformed narrative, Raphael Hoermann reasons that by thanking Wilberforce for the advice and books that left him in "debt," Wedderburn was "employing money-lending imagery that emphasizes their socioeconomic disparity."[37] By highlighting Wilberforce's advice and expensive books, moreover, Wedderburn insinuated that he experienced the visit as performative, "ghostly consolation" rather than authentic material help.

Wedderburn's audience would have known about Wilberforce's visit because Carlile wrote extensively about Wedderburn's trial and jail sentence in *The Republican*. Upon Wedderburn's release, Carlile summarized the racialized mistreatment of Wedderburn in both the courts and prison: Although the jury had recommended mercy, Judge Abbott was a "persecuting bigot" who sentenced Wedderburn to two years. The severity of the sentence was followed by racialized mistreatment within the prison, where Wedderburn was subject to solitary confinement in which "no prisoner was allowed to go near him to converse."[38] Carlile declared, "the case of Wedderburn has been abominable, comparing his treatment with the common treatment of other prisoners. Instead of being treated with leniency suitable to his alleged misdemeanor, he has been treated with marked severity." Carlile's rant against racially motivated punishment was explicitly directed toward the "Canting Wilberforce," who visited the jail and afterward "pronounced him [Wedderburn] an honest, conscientious man." Calling out the purely performative nature of Wilberforce's prison visit, Carlile asked rhetorically, "did he think Wedderburn had fair play I should like to know?" Carlile implied that Wilberforce's publicized prison visits served him more than the prisoners, which resonates with Wedderburn's representation of Wilberforce's "ghostly consolation" in the preface. Convicted of blasphemous libel, Wedderburn merely interpreted the Bible for himself, as Carlile concluded his open letter, "the conduct of Wedderburn was strictly moral, your conduct in persecuting him was immoral in the extreme, the punishment to which you have subjected him is inhuman on your part, and the part of those who have participated in it." Despite Wilberforce's humanitarian prison visit and his campaigns to abolish slavery, he participated in Wedderburn's racialized prosecution and imprisonment in England. Therefore, by dedicating *Horrors of Slavery* to Wilberforce, Wedderburn simultaneously evoked the horrors of plantation slavery, which Wilberforce tried to abolish, and the horrors of the English prison, where Wilberforce visited him as a "free" person.

Although Carlile was Wedderburn's ally, his willingness to call out racism on English soil was limited.[39] As a Black writer, Wedderburn was unduly criticized by enemies and allies alike. His writing and political advocacy evinced a similar structure to the writing persona of the "Brown Romantic," who, according to Manu Samriti Chander, was forced to negotiate "a subject position of 'exclusive inclusion,' which systemically relegates the colonial writer to outsider status no matter which option he chooses."[40] Wedderburn was compelled to negotiate a place within the Romantic forms of the radical periodical and the slave narrative. Yet, his content chafed against the messages of both working-class and abolitionist writers. Wedderburn's *Horrors* stands apart from other Romantic-era slave narratives as a self-published work unconcerned with garnering the approval of the middle-class antislavery audience. Published by the pornographer and ultra-radical William Dugdale and sold by the radical booksellers Richard Carlile and Thomas Davison, *Horrors of Slavery* was allied with the same ultra-radical working-class print cultures as his earlier periodical, *Axe Laid to the Root*.

Wedderburn enunciated his complex identity and political views on the title page, where he described himself as a political prisoner and spiritual authority, the "Rev. ROBERT WEDDERBURN, V.D.M." The acronym V. D. M. indicated a minister without a university degree, and, as Sue Thomas points out, political activists often obtained this license to avoid prosecution.[41] Wedderburn's exploitation of this loophole was made clear at his trial, where it was documented that with his license, "he made use of it for the purpose of undermining and reviling the Religion of the Country."[42] By signaling that he was a minister, Wedderburn also claimed authority as an interpreter of the Bible, aligning himself with his first publication, *Truth Self-Supported; or a Refutation of Certain Doctrinal Errors* (c. 1802). Michael Morris asserts that *Truth Self-Supported* "developed a powerful antinomian position of 'Gospel Liberty' free from the confines of the church and state law."[43] Thirty-four years later, Wedderburn continued to call upon his credentials as an antinomian radical who used the Bible to critique not only slavery but also European forms of Christianity. Wedderburn asserted an authority not acknowledged in the *Bell's Life* letters by self-claiming his identity as a minister and committed ultra-radical.

If, as David Scott contends, Black autobiographical narratives "offered the unique possibility of dramatically staging the black self in a way that vindicated both its essential humanity and its potential for worthy achievement," then Wedderburn's emphasis on his complex professional and racial identity was significant.[44] On the title page and in the new material added to his pamphlet, Wedderburn declared himself to be "son of the late JAMES WEDDERBURN, Esq. of Inveresk, Slave-Dealer, by one of his Slaves in the Island of Jamaica." James Olney points out that an established convention of slave narratives was to adopt a new last name suggested by a white abolitionist "to accord with new social identity as a free man."[45] Wedderburn cited and spurned this convention by proclaiming his mixed-race identity as a product of the plantation system of Jamaica. If the implications of having an enslaver for a father were not enough, in bold upper-case letters, Wedderburn advertised that his pamphlet would indeed detail the "**DISGUSTING LICENTIOUSNESS OF THE PLANTERS**." Whereas other slave narratives often downplayed the sexual violence of specific plantation owners in fear of alienating the sensitivities of their white, English audience, Wedderburn highlighted sexual violence as the reason for his existence.

As advertised, the pamphlet's additional life narrative provided even more details about the painful inheritance of being the son of a "slave-dealer." The first sentence declared, "the events of my life have been few and uninteresting. To my unfortunate origin I must attribute all my miseries and misfortunes." Alluding directly to Olaudah Equiano's *The Interesting Narrative* (1789), which recorded incidents that are "interesting" because they "have not happened to many," Wedderburn emphasized that his life began and has remained both "uninteresting" and "unfortunate" due to racial oppression, which was the *common* experience of Black people, both free and enslaved, in the British empire.[46] Lisa Lowe argues that Black autobiography "served as a particularly powerful genre for the individual achievement of liberty through ethical education and civilization." Moreover, the British "canonization of Equiano's autobiography as the quintessential narrative of progress" reassured readers that "the slavery of the past is overcome and replaced by modern freedom."[47] By alluding to and contradicting Equiano's individualist narrative, Wedderburn's autobiography remained firmly connected to ongoing, collective Black experiences of oppression in the West Indies and Europe.

Equiano and Wedderburn were both what Scott calls "conscripts of modernity," and perhaps that was why Equiano narrated his journey out of enslavement with a tone of "extravagant deference," according to Elizabeth Bohls, that "takes pains to separate the crimes of slavery from the glories of the British nation."[48] Wedderburn instead portrayed himself as an angry but resilient victim of the British empire. Seeking justice both in the West Indies and in England, Wedderburn rhetorically combined, Sue Thomas notes, the genres of "life writing and jeremiad."[49] Wedderburn further claimed that he published *Horrors* to enact intergenerational justice: "I deem it an act of justice to myself, to my children, and to the memory of my mother, to say what I am, and who were the authors of my existence; and to shew [*sic*] the world, that, not to my own misconduct is to be attributed my misfortunes, but to the inhumanity of a MAN, whom I am compelled to call by the name of FATHER" (*HoS* 4). Wedderburn recorded his unapologetically traumatic life history to memorialize his mixed-race heritage. At the same time, by insisting that his life story was common enough to be "uninteresting," his experiences illustrated collective racialized oppression that put the "freedoms" of Great Britain into question.

Wedderburn further complicated the geographic imagination of British antislavery activists by locating the origin of his existence in the English suppression of the Scots. His grandfather "exerted himself strenuously in the cause of the Pretender" and was executed for his role in the Battle of Culloden (*HoS* 5). An evocative memory from after his arrival in London in the late 1770s recalled viewing the rebel's skull over the Temple Bar and wondering whether it was his grandfather's. Morris argues that Wedderburn's discussion of his grandfather amounts to "Scottish-Creole discourse" by "invoking both the rebellion and the degrading traitor's death, Wedderburn is able at once to legitimate his own insurrectionary politics and undermine the respectability of his adversary Colvile, who denies his family claims."[50] Ryan Hanley considers this to be only radical moment in *Horrors of Slavery*: "In terms of radical sentiment [it] contained only a passing mention of Wedderburn's paternal grandfather's role in the

Jacobite rising of 1745."[51] Including the history of his grandfather's execution for revolt against the British expressed anticolonial sentiments as it uncannily evoked the common treatment of enemies of the British Empire.

From a Caribbean perspective, the public executions of Scottish rebels in London would resonate with ongoing, publicized spectacles of the brutal executions of enslaved people in the British West Indies, where, after drawn-out executions, the bodies were left in public view to continue the intimidation. Simon Gikandi notes that writers about the West Indies "made them central to their narratives irrespective of their political positions."[52] Vincent Brown contends, "executed slaves became important symbols, entering history in a way that masters could not control and making history in ways that have often escaped notice."[53] Wedderburn's explicit narration of his Scottish grandfather's execution by hanging, beheading, and quartering emphasized that one of his first experiences on English soil was not deliriously breathing in the air of freedom but rather observing the bones of his white kin, who had been brutally executed for revolting against the empire. However, the persecution of Scottish rebels, as Wedderburn's existence made clear, perpetuated the growth of slavery and Jamaican plantations.

Wedderburn followed his description of British colonialism at home with an explanation of why his Scots father and uncle went to Jamaica: "Our family estates were confiscated to the King, and my dear father found himself destitute in the world, or with no resource but his own industry" (*HoS* 6). Two colonial injustices were recorded simultaneously: The Scots' estates were confiscated after the rebellion, and Wedderburn was not included in "our family estates" because he was the child of an enslaved woman. The suppression after the Battle of Culloden, as scholars note, only further fueled the British empire because many Scotsmen, including Wedderburn's father, went to the West Indies to replenish fortunes plundered by the British crown.[54] Wedderburn emphasized that his father was corrupted by his desire for wealth and not by the climate of Jamaica: "While my dear and honoured father was poor, he was chaste as any Scotchman, whose poverty made him virtuous; but the moment he became rich, he gave loose to his carnal appetites, and indulged himself without moderation, but as parsimonious as ever" (*HoS* 6). Thus, Wedderburn described his father's transformation from a traumatized child of a Scottish rebel to a dissolute enslaver violently oppressing hundreds of people in Jamaica.

Helen Thomas argues that Wedderburn's writing "interweaves within the dominant network a fabric articulating the proud and rebellious nature of his mixed ancestral and cultural identity, inherited from his African mother and grandmother, and his white grandfather."[55] This mixed ancestral heritage resonated with his advocacy for ending slavery and for supporting working-class rights in England, as the first paragraph of his narrative announced:

> I am the offspring of a slave, it is true; but I am a man of free thought and opinion; and though I was immured for two years in his Majesty's gaol at Dorchester, for daring to express my sentiments as a free man, I am still the same in mind as I was before, and imprisonment has but confirmed to me that I was right. (*HoS* 4)

Combining his racialized childhood experience in Jamaica with his current oppression by the British government, Wedderburn emphasized the short journey from plantation slavery to an English prison, anticipating what McKittrick calls "plantation logics," in which incarceration and segregation perpetuate the structures of slavery after legal emancipation.[56] In Wedderburn's imagination of a post-emancipation future, he admonished, "have no prisons" (*Axe* 2.29), foreshadowing Ruth Wilson Gilmore's assertion that abolition must tackle the question of how to "diminish and remedy harm" instead of putting people in cages.[57] By emphasizing that he was recently a prisoner of conscience and a product of plantation slavery, Wedderburn radically combined the slave narrative of the West Indies with the prison narrative of Europe, refusing to make sharp distinctions between the two. At the end of *Horrors of Slavery*, Wedderburn expressed a longing to return to the West Indies: "I should have gone back to Jamaica, had I not been fearful of the planters; for such is their hatred of anyone having black blood in his veins, and who dares to think and act as a free man, that they would most certainly trumped up some charge against me, and hung me" (*HoS* 24). While the penal system in Jamaica was far more violent, in either England or Jamaica "daring to express his sentiments as a free man" would lead him to prosecution by the state.

Horrors of Slavery is an essential supplement to understanding slave narratives in the Romantic period due to its publication history within an ultra-radical working-class print culture instead of middle-class abolitionist networks. By continuing to assert that working-class radicalism and abolition were linked, Wedderburn's life narrative resonates with Lowe's assertion that "the liberal arguments to end slavery contributed to the ideology of free wage labor that was necessary to buttress industrialization at home."[58] This allowed Wedderburn to use his experiences to critique not just slavery but also "freedom" in England. Wedderburn published his life narrative, remarkably, after being jailed for blasphemous libel and threatened with a lawsuit by his half brother. Raymond Williams argues, "of all periods in British history, that between 1815 and the 1830s is outstanding for its struggle for freedom of the press." He notes with admiration that radical writers and publishers continued to publish and preach when "it was a struggle to speak and to live, against a State power which was prepared to use any method to oppose and to repress democratic activity."[59] Wedderburn played a part in this struggle for an independent working-class print culture. Yet, he participated as a Black man at constant risk of incarceration. He insisted that he inherited the courage to speak out from his enslaved mother, Rosanna, noting, "I glory in her *rebellious* disposition, and which I have inherited from her."[60] Chapter 3 analyzes how *Horrors of Slavery* represents Black women as the sources of his courage and freedom.

CHAPTER 3

Black Women's Abolitionist Geographies in The Horrors of Slavery *and* The History of Mary Prince

Slave narratives that have shaped Romanticists' understanding of the Black British presence within the period, notably Olaudah Equiano's *The Interesting Narrative* and *The History of Mary Prince*, were published by British abolitionists whose antislavery politics imagined freedom as a gift that would be generously bestowed on grateful, enslaved people in the West Indies. Robert Wedderburn self-published *Horrors of Slavery* (1824) within ultra-radical networks in London, so his life narrative was not shaped by the political ambitions of white, middle-class antislavery activists. Eschewing any demand for middle-class "respectability," Wedderburn defiantly announced on the title page that he was "Late a Prisoner in His Majesty's Gaol," and his narrative radically tracked his racialized life experiences from plantation slavery in the West Indies to prosecution and prison in England. In an even more radical departure from antislavery politics, Wedderburn championed Black women, not his residence on English soil, as the source of his liberation from slavery. Wedderburn documented that his mother, Rosanna, tactically rebelled against his enslaver father and then offered to be sold to another enslaver: "One of the conditions of the sale was, that her offspring, your humble servant, was to be free, from its birth, and I thank my God, that through a long life of hardship and adversity, I have ever been free in both mind and body: and have always raised my voice in behalf of my enslaved countrymen!"[1] Rosanna negotiated his manumission in Jamaica, and Wedderburn insisted that his radical activism in London emerged directly from her liberation tactics. *Horrors of Slavery* then recorded Black West Indian women's influence on radical politics in London.

Saidiya Hartman laments that in the archive of slavery, "the stories that exist are not about them [enslaved Black women], but rather about the violence, excess, mendacity, and reason that seized hold of their lives."[2] *Horrors of Slavery* provides a notable exception to lurid representations of violence against Black women. The violence and horrors of slavery indeed seized Wedderburn's mother and grandmother, as the pamphlet's title contends. Yet the narrative also asserted that their communal, place-based resistance to slavery led to Wedderburn's freedom, thereby reworking the Romantic, abolitionist trope of sorrowful, enslaved Black mothers, who were represented, as "Debbie Lee points out, as "utterly sentimentalized and in need of pity and salvation."[3] Although scholars who assess the entirety of Wedderburn's career suggest that *Horrors of Slavery* abandoned radical politics to write a "personal vindication," his vindication of his mother and grandmother was radically political as it attended to the trauma of their continuing enslavement while championing their place-based freedom practices.[4]

Unlike Wedderburn's self-published *Horrors of Slavery*, *History of Mary Prince* is a highly mediated text transcribed and edited by antislavery activists, so there is no clear answer to the question asked by Jenny Sharpe: "How can we read the slave narrative as a record of what the slave could not speak into being or was obliged to forget?"[5] Potential and partial answers to that question can be found intertextually. If, as Edlie L. Wong argues, Wedderburn "proffer[s] an understanding of black female agency that was often erased from the petitions, pamphlets, and addresses published and circulated by organized British antislavery," then reading *History of Mary Prince* next to *Horrors of Slavery* reveals similar abolitionist geographies cultivated by Black women in the West Indies.[6] One strategy for abolition was petit marronage, a practice that Neil Roberts describes as "fugitive acts of truancy away from the zone of enslavement."[7] Wedderburn mentioned that Rosanna resisted her mistreatment by fleeing from his father's plantation and seeking "asylum" from Wedderburn's uncle. She then demanded that his enslaver father acknowledge his parental obligations by manumitting his mixed-race children. In this light, Mary Prince's repeated episodes of petit marronage demanded enslavers acknowledge kinship with her parents and, later, her husband. In both narratives, Black women assert place-based liberation strategies – by quarreling in the enslaver's home, fleeing and hiding from their enslavers, and finding community in spiritual practices – that map abolitionist geographies of kinship. The demand for an enslaver to acknowledge Black kinship was radically self-emancipatory because, as Hortense Spillers argues, the "property/kinless constellation" was central to slavery: "If kinship were possible, the property relations would be undermined, since the offspring would then 'belong' *to* a mother and father."[8] Rosanna and Prince undermined plantation-based property relations by demanding that enslavers acknowledge Black parentage and kinship, which performed place-based resistances to slavery that British antislavery writers failed to recognize.

Wedderburn outlined a second example of enslaved Black women's freedom practices in stories of his grandmother, Talkee Amy, a skilled higgler and obeah woman who, in Wedderburn's terms, "trafficked on her own account" (*HoS* 10).[9] Shauna J. Sweeney recommends reading West Indian higglers as "fugitive market women" who "invite us to disentangle marronage from formal sovereignty and to conceptualize it as a set of antislavery practices with multiple iterations."[10] The *History*'s editor, Thomas Pringle, may have highlighted Prince's higglering to emphasize her work ethic. Yet as fugitive market women, Talkee Amy and Mary Prince both navigated and cultivated Black geographies and economies within the system of slavery. By higglering in the internal markets, they also participated in what Julius S. Scott called "the common wind": Black networks of information, both rumors and facts, which sought to raise expectations for freedom and create possibilities for insurrection against the plantation system.[11] The depictions of higglering in these life stories recorded strategic resistance to plantation spaces and surveillance.

Patricia A. Matthew contends that new scholarly work in Romanticism should "challenge the idea of the benevolent abolitionist and bring Black women's lives in the eighteenth and nineteenth century into sharper focus."[12] This chapter aspires to address, albeit partially, the gap in scholarship that Matthew notes. Bakary Diaby likewise emphasizes that scholars should not forget Black women when evaluating whom we cite and uphold "as producers of theoretical knowledge."[13] While Rosanna and Talkee Amy were not "theorists," Wedderburn described them as producers of abolitionist knowledge and practices that were developed communally on the margins of West Indian slavery. At a time when white women's voices were directing abolitionist discourse, *Horrors of Slavery* announced a politics largely unacknowledged by Romantic-era antislavery: place-based, self-liberation led by Black women.[14] These stories of Black women's freedom practices may seem unfamiliar, because, as Katherine McKittrick argues, "the dispossessed black female body is often equated with the ungeographic." During slavery, Black women were constrained by plantation geographies, yet they also cultivated fugitive place-based knowledge and deployed environmental strategies to resist enslavement. As McKittrick explains, "the real and imaginary geographic processes important to black women are not just about limitations, captivities, and erasures; they are also about everyday contestations, philosophical demands, and the possibilities the production of space can engender for subaltern subjects."[15] Wedderburn's stories of Rosanna and Talkee Amy illustrated just such everyday contestations, which makes *Horrors of Slavery* an illuminating intertext for reading *History of Mary Prince*. The following section discusses Wedderburn's celebration of his mother and grandmother and argues that their stories mapped self-emancipatory places and practices in Jamaica. The second half of the chapter then locates similar abolitionist geographies in the *History of Mary Prince*. Black women's geographies in these life narratives countered the plantation system's exploitation of land and people in favor of communal, material, and place-based forms of liberation that supplement histories of Romantic-era abolition and women's activism.

"I Have Inherited the Same Disposition": Wedderburn's Rebellious Matriarchs

As explored in Chapter 2, *Horrors of Slavery* began as a series of letters published between February 15 and March 28, 1824, in the working-class weekly paper *Bell's Life in London*. The paper ran a series of antislavery articles, and Wedderburn was prompted to write and share his life story after the *Bell's Life* editor questioned whether plantation owners would ever attempt to enslave their own mixed-race children. In his letters to *Bell's Life*, Wedderburn represented himself as a "product" of plantation slavery and testified to his father's sexual and moral depravity as a "slave-dealer." After Wedderburn's initial letter was published, subsequent issues of *Bell's Life* highlighted an argumentative exchange between Wedderburn and his white half-brother, Andrew Colvile, who wrote to *Bell's Life* to defend his father's reputation. Colvile asserted that Wedderburn's mother, Rosanna, was resold to another enslaver because she had "so violent a temper" that she continually created "a disturbance in the house." Colvile also claimed that Rosanna was promiscuous: Wedderburn received his last name as a "foolish joke" because Rosanna "could not tell who was the father" of her children (*HoS* 15). Wedderburn reframed his mother's violent temper as a determination to avenge the wrongs against her, which, according to Raphael Hoermann, "undermines the abolitionist rhetoric of sympathy, which turns the shackled passive slave into an object of white pity."[16] In fact, Wedderburn's championing of Black women's resistance to slavery enunciated a history that, as Hartman points out, "remains marginal or neglected in the narratives of black insurgency, resistance, and refusal."[17] While histories of slave rebellion still fail to acknowledge the everyday resistances of Black women, in *Horrors of Slavery*, Wedderburn translated Rosanna's angry and unmanageable behavior into a heroic disposition toward justice.

Spurred by his half-brother's "insolence to revile her memory in the most abusive language, and to stigmatize her for that which was owing to the deep and dark iniquity of my father" (*HoS* 5), Wedderburn republished the *Bell's Life* correspondence as a pamphlet, *Horrors of Slavery* (1824), which included ten pages of additional narrative that detailed the experiences of his mother and grandmother. In the additional narrative, Wedderburn further illustrated the justness of his mother's anger and rebellion by describing his father's cruel treatment of her, as he announced, "I will not leave the world without some testimony to the injustice and inhumanity of my father" (*HoS* 8). Rosanna was trained as a lady's maid, and she was purchased by his father so that he could add her to a house "full of female slaves, all objects of his lusts" (*HoS* 8). Beyond satisfying his sexual appetite, the father created additional income because he then enslaved and sold his own children:

> My father ranged through the whole of his household for his own lewd purposes; for they being his personal property, cost nothing extra; and if any one proved with child – why, it was an acquisition which might one day fetch something in the market, like a horse or pig in Smithfield. (*HoS* 7)

This description of Wedderburn's father referred back to the original question, posed by the editor of *Bell's Life in London*: "How many of the Slave-Dealers present at the London Tavern, on Tuesday last, have enhanced their profit by similar disposals?"[18] The question of enslavers selling their own children was initially depicted as a father treating the women and children he enslaved like animals, a common trope in abolitionist literature. Brycchan Carey notes that stories about enslaved people being treated like animals were "deliberately deployed to invoke sympathy for enslaved people and to shock the British and American public into opposing slavery."[19] However, Wedderburn also cannily reversed this abolitionist trope by zoomorphizing his father as livestock. At one point, the elder Wedderburn was described as a "perfect parish bull" and at another, "a bantam cock upon his own dunghill" (*HoS* 7, 8). By animalizing his father's depraved behavior through violent, patriarchal animals, Wedderburn emphasized the uncivilized, predatory nature of the European plantation system while downplaying representations of enslaved people as passive animals to be pitied.

Rosanna's strategic resistance to the sexual violence of her enslaver also significantly revised another common trope in Romantic-era antislavery literature, the figure of the despairing Black mother. Debbie Lee argues, "anti-slavery verse stresses the black mother's singleness, and along with it her despair and destruction, with the underlying implication that she is an example of failed domesticity."[20] Wedderburn's depiction of Rosanna's agency and maternal care countered sentimental depictions of Black single mothers who failed to care for their children and instead blamed his father for any despair. He asked, "was it likely that my poor mother could practise the Christian virtue of humility, when her Christian master provoked her to wrath?" (*HoS* 9). His tone echoed William Blake's early antinomian writings in *The Marriage of Heaven and Hell*, in which the prophet Isaiah stated, "I was then persuaded, & remain confirm'd; that the voice of honest indignation is the voice of God, I cared not for consequences but wrote."[21] Rosanna expressed her righteous indignation by speaking and fighting against the elder Wedderburn's mistreatment. Finally, she fled from his home, as Wedderburn noted, "my uncle, Sir JOHN WEDDERBURN, my father's elder brother, had given my mother an asylum in his house, against the brutal treatment of my father" (*HoS* 9).[22] During her "asylum" in another enslaver's home, Rosanna negotiated her resale to another enslaver, in which "one of the stipulations of the bargain was, that the child which she then bore should be FREE from the moment of its birth. I was that child" (*HoS* 9). Rosanna's petit marronage forced the elder Wedderburn to admit his parentage by manumitting his children with her, and her demands amounted to a radical refusal to comply with, in Hartman's words, "the mother's only claim – to transfer her dispossession to the child."[23] Reframed as righteous, even prophetic, "honest indignation," Rosanna's petit marronage led directly to Wedderburn's manumission from slavery.

Wedderburn's story of his mother's marronage provided a model of Black women's self-liberation practices instead of advocating for British freedoms to be bestowed on grateful enslaved people.[24] He even claimed to have inherited his mother's anger as his political model: "I have not the least doubt but that from her rebellious and violent temper during that period, that I have inherited the same disposition – the same desire to see justice overtake the oppressors of my countrymen – and the same determination to lose [sic] no stone unturned" (*HoS* 9). Wedderburn's proud declaration that he inherited his mother's angry "disposition" signaled that her rebellious affect was part of an assemblage of practices of resistance, and further hinted that Black women's freedom practices could be productive not only in the West Indies but also in Great Britain. However, Rosanna's agency was also limited. Hartman contends, "those of us who have been 'touched by the mother' need acknowledge that her ability to provide care, food, and refuge often has placed her in great jeopardy and, above all, required her to give with no expectation of reciprocity or return."[25] Although she managed to negotiate her mixed-race children's freedom, Rosanna was never freed from slavery. Her influence, however, lived on in Wedderburn's depictions of Black women as emancipators, which recur in his writing. In his earlier publication *Axe Laid to the Root* (1817), Wedderburn described a mixed-race Maroon figure, Miss Campbell, who liberated the people that she enslaved, and thereby, as Shelby Johnson observes, centered "on a Black woman's presence in his anticolonial and antipatriarchal politics."[26] Miss Campbell's anticolonial politics also established Black geographies through making reparations for enslaved people by giving them her plantation. Wedderburn's *Horrors of Slavery* suggested that Black abolitionist spaces could be established even within the home of an enslaver, where Rosanna negotiated his freedom.

Repeatedly countering antislavery writers' representations of Black women as despairing victims, Wedderburn portrayed his enslaved grandmother, Talkee Amy, as another influential advocate for his freedom. Wedderburn recorded that he was raised from age four by Talkee Amy, "who earned her livelihood by retailing all sorts of goods, hard or soft, smuggled or not, for the merchants of Kingston" (*HoS* 10). While Talkee Amy sold her enslaver's goods, she navigated the ports of Kingston and developed her own business smuggling merchandise. As Wedderburn relates, "she trafficked on her own account with the goods of other merchants, having an agency of half-a-crown in the pound allowed her for her trouble" (*HoS* 10). Here the word "trafficked" activated both meanings of the word: first, to buy and sell goods, and second, to communicate revolutionary ideas. Talkee Amy's name further signaled the significance of market conversations. Wedderburn explained that her name signified a "chattering old woman." Yet in Jamaica, the pass given to enslaved people to leave a plantation was called a "talkee talkee." The name "talkee talkee" indicated, Miles Ogborn notes, that enslaved people recognized the insurrectionist "relationship between speech and mobility across boundaries."[27] By calling his grandmother "Talkee," Wedderburn evoked the freedom of "passes" that allowed enslaved people to leave their plantations and cultivate insurrectionary relationships. Talkee Amy's name gestured toward the anticipatory abolitionist geographies outside of plantations.

Along with her name and economic savvy, Talkee Amy was depicted as an agent within what Scott has called "the masterless Caribbean": Talkee Amy lived in Kingston, where she would have been able to procure uncommon forms of freedom.[28] Olaudah Equiano's *Interesting Narrative* paid tribute to the distinctive cultural atmosphere of the Black Kingston markets, a depiction with which Wedderburn's readers would have been familiar:

> When I came to Kingston, I was surprised to see the number of Africans who were assembled together on Sundays; particularly at a large commodious place, called Spring Path. Here each different nation of Africa meet and dance after the manner of their own country. They still retain most of their native customs: they bury their dead, and put victuals, pipes and tobacco, and other things, in the grave with the corps [*sic*], in the same manner as in Africa.[29]

Talkee Amy's work as both a market higgler and an obeah practitioner who performed burials resonates uncannily with Equiano's description of Kingston.[30] A central part of the Jamaican internal marketing system, higglers allowed enslaved people to sell excess produce and other crafts from their provision grounds. Alex A. Moulton notes, "what was meant to be a system of added exploitation became one of Black economic agency, especially for Black women, an unintended effect."[31] Sweeney defines this economic agency as "market marronage," which "constituted a distinct form of enslaved resistance bound up with black women's unique ability to carve out a modicum of economic independence within the heart of slavery."[32] Wedderburn's story of Talkee Amy illustrated the connection between petit marronage and market marronage because they both involved taking leave from the controlling scrutiny of European enslavers. Selling legal and illegal goods, Talkee Amy was as independent as an enslaved woman could be at that time, and "such was confidence the merchants of Kingston had in her honesty, that she could be trusted to any amount" (*HoS* 10). It is possible, moreover, that this description of Talkee Amy resonated positively with Wedderburn's lower-class readers in London, particularly those who were dispossessed by enclosure and the curtailment of women's quasi-independent cottage production.[33]

Talkee Amy's skills for negotiating market marronage extended beyond her own interests and were deployed on behalf of her grandson. Wedderburn recalled, "I never saw my dear father but once in the island of Jamaica, when I went with my grandmother to know if he meant to do any thing for me, his son" (*HoS* 10). The journey from Kingston to Wedderburn's estate in Westmoreland parish, a round-trip of approximately 240 miles by car today, would have been arduous and complicated. The trip demonstrated that higglers had "unique opportunities to move from town to country and back again under the auspices of conducting legitimate business."[34] The unofficial pathways of higglers, like those of the Maroons, which I discuss in Chapter 5, were abolitionist geographies at work in and between plantations. Moreover, the story of an enslaved

Black woman traveling across the island to demand that a white plantation owner acknowledge his mixed-race son reiterated Rosanna's model of resistance to slavery through claiming kinship and inheritance. Wedderburn's father replied with "abusive language" and declared he would not support his mixed-race children.[35] In response, Talkee Amy "called him a mean Scotch rascal, thus to desert his own flesh and blood; and declared, that as she had kept me hitherto, so she would yet, without his paltry assistance" (*HoS* 10). This declaration of kinship and independence – although enslaved, she worked to make enough money to feed, clothe, and care for her free grandson – alluded to the abolitionist economies and ecologies within and alongside official colonizer geographies.

Talkee Amy's liberation practices emerged from a liminal space between slavery and freedom, local and global markets, and legal and illegal economies. Although she was trusted, esteemed, and apparently "masterless," Talkee Amy lived precariously as an enslaved person, and the following paragraph of *Horrors of Slavery* transitioned abruptly to a more familiar scene in antislavery literature.[36] Talkee Amy's enslaver, Joseph Payne, was captured along with his ship and crew by the Spanish, and Payne was condemned to death. Following this turn of events, Talkee Amy was accused of being an obeah woman who "bewitched the vessel," and as punishment, she was flogged for witchcraft while the eleven-year-old Wedderburn watched.[37] Wedderburn's description of Talkee Amy's punishment disclosed how charges of obeah were deployed against powerful Black women. Moreover, it offers a Black perspective on Romantic-era obeah, a practice that had captured the British Romantic imagination.

Obeah, Diana Paton outlines, was a set of "healing and solidarity-building practices" that were not fully understood by white colonizers; it emerges in colonial discourse as a "conceptual framework for making sense of Africans' and African Caribbeans' relationship to the spiritual world."[38] British narratives were at cross purposes to minimize the importance of obeah as a collective power while at the same time stoking fear of it as an excuse to control the enslaved population. Janelle Rodriques argues, "in fictional narratives of this period, slave rebellions go hand-in-hand with Obeah, even as they are portrayed as isolated grievances between particular slaves and particularly malicious owners."[39] Jeffrey Cottrell notes that Romantic-era "obeah fictions" were directed primarily at categorizing Black women and pointed toward "a key moment in the development of dominant cultural strategies for subjectifying and controlling its citizens."[40] Wedderburn's recollections of his grandmother directly countered

Romantic "obeah fictions" as the story moved on, defiantly, to emphasize Talkee Amy's continuing leadership within Kingston's Black community.

Soon after the punishment, the only child of the woman who accused Talkee Amy died. The bereaved mother then was forced to beg Talkee Amy, an obeah practitioner and "transmitter of preslavery epistemologies," to arrange the funeral.[41] For his London audience, Wedderburn translated the significance of Talkee Amy's spiritual role in the burials of enslaved people by comparing it to Irish wakes: "The good old woman instantly set about assisting her in her child's funeral, it being as great an object to have a decent burial with the blacks in Jamaica, as with the lower classes in Ireland" (*HoS* 12). By putting Talkee Amy's role as an obeah woman in solidarity with the colonized people of Ireland, Wedderburn emphasized that obeah was a community-building religious practice in which Black women created value for dispossessed human lives. Talkee Amy's spiritual practices then countered Romantic-era representations of obeah as "the knowledge of poisons, spells, and other subtle weapons to be used against the white population," which, as Lizabeth Paravisini-Gebert argues, made it "an ever-present element in Gothic texts produced in and about the West Indies."[42] Wedderburn's *Horrors of Slavery* provided a significant alternative to Romantic-era depictions of obeah through gothic tropes.

By officiating the child's funeral, Talkee Amy was further employed in what Thomas W. Laqueur has called "necrogeography," the spatial practices of burial that cultivated the "unbreakable bond between the materiality of the corpse and the consciousness—individual and collective—of those who live with the dead."[43] Laqueur explores the large working-class funerals encouraged by trade unions in England, a phenomenon with which Wedderburn's lower-class audience would have been familiar, particularly after the Peterloo Massacre. Burials of enslaved people in Jamaica also had notable political implications. Vincent Brown documents the importance of Black burial grounds: "Last rites in Jamaica articulated the first principles of slave society—the meaningful codes of conduct that organized public life and its categories of belonging."[44] Talkee Amy's funeral for the child cultivated her own, the child's, and the community's dignity while, at the same time, reclaiming colonized land by creating an abolitionist necrogeography in Jamaica. Moreover, funerals for enslaved people were recognized as potentially insurrectionist gatherings. For example, Matthew Lewis recorded a story of a rebellion being organized at a child's funeral in his *Journal of a West India Proprietor*.[45] Far more than personal vindication then, Wedderburn's stories of his grandmother and mother in *Horrors of Slavery* mapped Black abolitionist geographies within enslavers' homes, in the markets, along higglers' pathways, and on cemetery plots.

Horrors of Slavery was written at a significant point in time after the end of the slave trade and as emancipation was on the horizon. Lisa Lowe proposes that slave narratives were important cultural documents in this period because "liberal emancipation required a literary narrative of the self-authoring autonomous individual to be distilled out of the heteronomous collective subjectivity of colonial slavery."[46] Thwarting established convention, Wedderburn signed off on his pamphlet with an ominous note alluding to collective revolt: "In a future part of my history I shall give some particulars of the treatment of blacks in the West Indies, and the prospect of general massacre and rebellion there, from my own experience. In the meantime, I bid my readers farewell" (*HoS* 24).[47] From his opening insistence that his life was "uninteresting" because it was part of common racialized mistreatment experienced by Black people, until his conclusion about collective revolt, Wedderburn's ostensibly individual life narrative constantly gestured toward the collective subjectivity of colonial slavery. Moreover, his celebration of his enslaved mother and grandmother's freedom tactics as the source of his own liberation allows readers to locate similar instances of Black women's abolitionist geographies, collectively networked through kinship and markets, in *The History of Mary Prince*.

Abolitionist Geographies in *The History of Mary Prince*

The preface to *The History of Mary Prince* stated that her life story was "taken down from Mary's own lips" and then "pruned into its present shape" by Susanna Strickland. The editor, Thomas Pringle, assured readers that he endeavored to retain "Mary's exact expressions and peculiar phraseology," but his added notes and preface indicated that the *History* was shaped to advocate for the political goals of white abolitionists.[48] Kerry Sinanan cautions: "It is difficult to access the resistance of the historical subject, Mary Prince, when what we know of her is the product of a cultural artifact produced within the hierarchical dynamics of the Anti-Slavery Society driven by the political demands of British abolitionism."[49] Although *The History* was transcribed and edited by antislavery activists, when read alongside Wedderburn's self-published *Horrors of Slavery*, similar communal, place-based resistances to slavery emerge. Katherine

McKittrick's nuanced portrayal of Black women's geographies supports this reading. She explains,

> rather than attempting to complete black women's geographies by "finding" them or "discovering" them, I am emphasizing that geography and black women have *always* functioned together and that this interrelated process is a new way to "enter" into space (conceptually and materially), one that uncovers a geographic story predicated on an ongoing struggle (to assert humanness and more humanly workable geographies).[50]

Like Wedderburn's mother and grandmother, Prince entered and navigated spaces in a way that asserted her humanness by rebelliously claiming kinship and participating in unofficial local economies. These Black abolitionist geographies were not explicitly mapped, but instead, Prince's struggle against slavery and her relationship to place materialized as interrelated processes. Since Black geographies were not officially mapped, Judith Madera argues, they are often found "at the intersection of both place and text," and such texts described "places as limit situations and places as possibility."[51] Mary Prince's narrative mapped the "limit situations" of trauma alongside areas sown with abolitionist possibility through narrating Black women's self-emancipatory navigation of place.[52]

While Wedderburn described Black women's spatial practices within the context of Jamaica, Mary Prince's resistances were spatialized throughout various locations in the West Indies. Mary Prince was born enslaved in Bermuda. When she was almost twelve, her enslaver, Mrs. Williams, forced her to work for another woman, Mrs. Pruden, who lived several miles away. Prince described this experience as traumatic because it separated her from her family: "When I kissed my mother and brothers and sisters, I thought my young heart would break, it pained me so" (*HMP* 8). While the narrative appears to serve British antislavery tropes by suggesting that Prince's flights back to the home of Mrs. Williams demonstrated loyalty to her enslaver, Prince's petit marronage also stubbornly performed a self-emancipatory attachment to her family, like Wedderburn's mother, Rosanna.[53] Her first petit marronage occurred after Prince asked for permission to visit Mrs. Williams when she was sick, and she stayed "longer than she had given me leave to do" (*HMP* 8). Narrated immediately after documenting her heartbreak over being separated from her mother and siblings, who remained with Mrs. Williams, the flight performed attachment to her family of origin. She was then violently struck by Mrs. Pruden for stealing her time.

A second flight from Mrs. Pruden occurred at Mrs. Williams's death, as Prince recalled, "my grief was so great that, forgetting I had the baby in my arms, I ran away directly to my poor mistress's house; but reached it only in time to see the corpse carried out" (*HMP* 9). In this gothic scene, Prince arrived with Mrs. Pruden's baby in tow as her enslaver's corpse was removed from the premises. By "forgetting" she was holding the baby but nonetheless running with the child for five miles, Prince's petit marronage separated Mrs. Pruden from her child as she reunited with her family. Neil Roberts explains that "during marronage, agents struggle psychologically, socially, metaphysically, and politically to exit slavery, maintain freedom, and assert a lived social space while existing in a liminal position." Understanding freedom from slavery through marronage, Roberts reasons, allows for attention to "degrees of agency" that challenge the "mistaken rigid division between potentiality and actuality."[54] Even though running to her enslaver's home elicited the antislavery trope of the faithful slave who is attached to her enslaver, when read as petit marronage, Prince's flight to Mrs. Williams's home appears as an act of rebellion that reestablished her connection with her family.[55]

Prince's episodes of petit marronage escalated as she reached maturity. After being sold to Captain I–, she was beaten several times severely and habitually pinched, slapped, and emotionally abused. After one beating, Prince responded by running away to her mother. Her mother could not help her legally, so "she hid me up in a hole in the rocks near" (*HMP* 18). Knowledge about and access to this cave required navigating Caribbean geographies, and it turned out to be a place of marginal freedom that allowed a brief respite from slavery through reconnection with kin and community. Such abolitionist geographies, J. T. Roane argues, "disrupted mastery and efficacy in terms of labor discipline, control, and domination and required the articulation of a unique set of paths, hiding spots, and techniques of anti-surveillance and weaponization."[56] Although she must return to her enslaver, Prince's father escorted his daughter to confront her enslaver about his mistreatment. By running to her mother and then having her father intervene with Captain I– Prince challenged the foundation of slavery, in which "kinship loses its meaning," according to Spillers, "*since it can be invaded at any given and arbitrary moment by the property relations.*"[57] Prince's reclamation of one of the meanings and functions of kinship – parental care – gave her temporary reprieve from her abuse, and her enslaver "did not flog me that day" (*HMP* 18). If, as Spillers asserts, the "denied genetic link becomes a chief strategy of an undenied ownership," then Prince's flight to her family challenged that ownership.[58] Prince enacted this challenge through her careful navigation of unofficial pathways and caves on the margins of West Indian slavery.

Prince's tactical navigation of place can also be detected in her description of Turk's Island, where enslaved laborers in the salt industry suffered painful blisters on their legs that "eat down in some cases to the very bone" (*HMP* 19). Even in this most panoptic and cruel place, Prince reestablished kinship connections by monitoring the island's port and incoming ships. Searching incoming boats for family members, one day Prince found her mother on a sloop loaded with enslaved people. Although her mother had "lost her senses" and does not recognize her, Prince also discovered:

> She had a sweet child with her – a little sister I had never seen, about four years of age, called Rebecca. I took her on shore with me, for I felt I should love her directly; and I kept her with me a week. Poor little thing! her's [*sic*] has been a sad life, and continues so to this day. (*HMP* 23)

Thus, on Turk's Island, Prince continued to abandon her work tactically in order to navigate places where she might reconnect with her kin. Matthew Rowney notes, "Prince's various ways of repurposing and withholding her labour takes part in a figurative smuggling as well."[59] Such figurative smuggling, in this case, included caring for her sister for a week to "love her directly." This story resonated with her elopement with Mrs. Pruden's baby, where caretaking skills combined with the navigation of plantation geographies allowed Prince to resist dehumanization by forging emotional connections with her family. Like Wedderburn, Prince emphasized kinship as the source of freedom instead of individual work and merit. The note attached to this passage, written by Pringle, added that Prince had very little information about her seven brothers and three sisters; the exception was the same sister that she "loved directly," Rebecca, who remained enslaved in Bermuda. Although this was hardly a celebratory outcome of Prince's petit marronage, the note provided evidence that Prince's determination to cultivate kinship and humanity through her strategic navigation of Caribbean places enabled ongoing intelligence about her sister.

The brutalizing economic and ecological practices on Turk's Island contrasted with Prince's later work as a higgler in Antigua's internal markets, where her petit marronage transformed into market marronage:

> I had a good deal of time to myself, and made the most of it. I took in washing, and sold coffee and yams and other provisions to the captains of ships. I did not sit still idling during the absence of my owners; for I wanted, by all honest means, to earn money and buy my freedom. Sometimes I bought a hog cheap on board ship, and sold it for double the money on shore; and I also earned a good deal by selling coffee. By this means by degrees I acquired a little cash. (*HMP* 27)

Prince's knowledge of agriculture, gardens, ports, and markets allowed her to earn money toward buying her freedom. Sharpe maintains that the editor shaped Prince's discussion of higglering so that it "is cast in the more favorable light of honest work and good economic sense."[60] Yet at the same time, when reading Prince's narrative through Wedderburn's accounts of Talkee Amy, another enslaved Black woman who "trafficked on her own account," Prince's higglering can be understood as a strategic development of freedom within communal Black counter-plantation practices. As Sweeney suggests, higglers "blazed their own trails through plantations, pens, and town centers, carving out distinct cartographies of freedom and family during slavery."[61] Indeed, the rebellious potential of Prince's higglering was revealed when she asked to buy her freedom after making a substantial amount of money. In response, Mrs. Woods "called me a black devil, and asked me who had put freedom in my head" (*HMP* 31).

The subversive potential of the Caribbean internal markets can also be located in their time, on Sunday afternoons, the only time of rest given to enslaved people. However, many enslaved people sold the abundance from their provision grounds in the thriving local markets instead of resting. Prince noted,

> after that [feeding animals on Sunday mornings], those that have yams or potatoes, or fire-wood to sell, hasten to market to buy a dog's worth of salt fish, or pork, which is a great treat for them. Some of them buy a little pickle out of the shad barrels, which they call sauce, to season their yams and Indian corn. It is very wrong, I know, to work on a Sunday or go to market; but will not God call the Buckra men to answer for this on the great day of judgment—since they will give the slave no other day? (*HMP* 28)

This description was framed as an apology for the Sunday markets, a well-known practice among enslaved people that missionaries and abolitionists lamented because it interfered with church attendance. However, by asserting that enslavers created the need for Sunday markets "since they will give the slaves no other day," the narrative also gestured toward unremitting demands by enslaved people for more days to tend their provision grounds and markets.[62] Chapter 4 proposes that Matthew Lewis's *Journal of a West India Proprietor* documented tense negotiations with the people he enslaved over allowing more days to access their provision grounds.

While networking within internal markets, Prince's resistance to slavery grew with her proficiency as a higgler. Constantly in conflict with her enslavers, Prince was asked to find another enslaver to buy her. Through her networks, twice Prince found new enslavers, and both times the

Woods refused to sell her (*HMP* 27). Like Talkee Amy, Prince "trafficked on her own account." Prince goes so far as to market herself, and in this way, as Sharpe argues succinctly, "Prince undermined her master's right of ownership by asserting her status as property."[63] Although the threatened abandonment by the Woods was calculated to create insecurity in Prince so she would become more compliant, their threats instead had the opposite effect of creating more independence, which coincided with her growing determination to forge autonomy through spiritual practice.

On the surface, Prince's conversion to the Moravian faith was much more acceptably Christian than Talkee Amy's subversive role as an obeah woman. Nevertheless, Prince's conversion and religious practice were directly tied to rebellion against the plantation system, because her initial conversion occurred on Christmas. Plantation slavery was continually thwarted by underground resistance. Yet, as Robert Dirks notes, "once each year, the Christmas revelers brought these normally invisible efforts out into the open, celebrating them by means of eye-catching spectacles and dramatic enactments."[64] In the British West Indies, any meeting held at Christmas tied it to the potential for slave rebellion or at least a self-directed "taking time" away from the plantation. While the implications of Prince's Christmas conversion were not drawn out in her narrative, they were revealed in the trial of Wood v. Pringle. The cross-examiner stated, "she knows Christmas time. The natives then have a 'stir up;' they dress in white, and dance, but if the ministers know of their dancing they prevent it."[65] Whatever Prince may have known about Christmas "stir-ups" does not appear in the narrative. Yet, her Christmas conversion clearly led to increased petit marronage: "This meeting had a great impression on my mind, and led my spirit to the Moravian church . . . I did not then tell my mistress about it; for I knew that she would not give me leave to go. But I felt I *must* go" (*HMP* 29). Spiritual conversion then became a Christmas rebellion since Prince's selection of a church without permission from her enslaver further rebelled against her status as property.

The Moravians allowed marriages of enslaved people, and Prince's marriage enacted another reclamation of herself from her enslavers, which was confirmed by their violent response. Prince was flogged when the Woods' found out about her marriage, and Mrs. Wood declared that she did not want a Black man near her home or for a Black man's clothes to be washed with hers. Prince noted, "she was fearful, I think, that I should lose her time, in order to wash and do things for my husband" (*HMP* 30). Prince's conversion and marriage withdrew labor and reclaimed kinship, just as she had done since her initial flights from Mrs. Pruden. The

Moravian church, in both Antigua and London, facilitated Prince's abolitionist geographies because that network of affiliation provided the courage for Prince to finally take her legal freedom when, for the fourth time in London, the Woods' "opened the door and bade me get out" (*HMP* 32).[66]

Mary Prince's journey from a Bermuda plantation to Thomas Pringle's servants' quarters in London demonstrates further, as Alan Bewell suggests, that "her story should also be read as the story of immigration, of a Black West Indian woman's struggle to put down roots in London," even though Pringle never imagined "what kind of new relationship the British needed to build with people whose presence in Britain stemmed from its colonial past."[67] *History of Mary Prince* revealed that Caribbean Black geographies contested the liberal, individualist forms of freedom advocated by British antislavery activists. Even more importantly, her narrative resisted framing slavery through an "abolitionist geography," which, as Elizabeth Bohls proposes, was a pervasive narrative strategy that "took great pains to distinguish colonies from the metropole, the sugar islands from the British Isles – strategically absolving metropolitan readers' guilt while urging them to take action for change."[68] Instead of celebrating her freedom on English soil, Prince openly lamented living in England: "I was sorry I had come from Antigua, since mistress would work me so hard" (*HMP* 32). Even after leaving the Woods, Prince wanted to return to the West Indies: "I still live in the hope that God will find a way to give me my liberty, and give me back to my husband" (*HMP* 37). For Prince, legal freedom in England failed to provide her the liberty to live within the community and kinship she had already cultivated in Antigua.

Wedderburn's *Horrors of Slavery* also emphasized the difficulties of being a Black immigrant in London. As argued in Chapter 2, Wedderburn's life story tracked directly from his birth in West Indian slavery to legal "freedom" in an English prison. If legal freedom led to starving in city streets or to languishing in prison, then Black freedom in these texts was inscribed in their anticipatory abolitionist geographies – in hiding places, provision grounds, Black churches, and internal markets – that, countering antislavery geographies that located freedom in Great Britain, remained in the West Indies. Instead of representing an individual's journey from enslavement to British liberal freedom, Wedderburn and Prince's life narratives do the reverse; they were both Black and British, lived in London, and brought stories of Black women's place-based freedom practices to a white audience. Vincent Brown contends that during Tacky's Revolt (1760) in Jamaica, the insurgent rebellion created "countermappings [that] reveal a geography of hope and possibility, fugitive territories carved out through political struggle that were difficult to maintain, paradoxical in their alliances, and, in most cases, yet to be past."[69] Although Brown does not include the everyday practices of Black Caribbean women in this geography of hope, *Horrors of Slavery* and the *History of Mary Prince* recorded that Rosanna, Talkee Amy, and Mary Prince were cultivators of insurgent abolitionist geographies within and around the plantation system.

CHAPTER 4

Provisions and Pigs
Black Geographies in Matthew Lewis's *Journal of a West India Proprietor*

When Matthew Lewis arrived at his newly inherited Cornwall plantation in Westmoreland, Jamaica, on January 2, 1816, the enslaved people on his estate celebrated all night. He promised them a festival day the following Saturday, which lasted until Sunday evening. Lewis was flattered by the fawning and praise during this first encounter with the people he enslaved.[1] Nevertheless, as soon as these celebrations ceased, the negotiations began. He recorded: "But first they requested to have tomorrow to themselves, in order that they might go to the mountains for provisions" (*Journal* 81).[2] Lewis was interested in ameliorating the conditions of enslaved people, so he immediately agreed that the Monday after his arrival would be set aside to cultivate and harvest the provision grounds. If, as Mary Louise Pratt argues, in colonial travel writing, arrival scenes were "potent sites for framing relations of contact and setting the terms of its representation," then negotiations over the provision grounds set the terms for Lewis's relationships with the people he enslaved.[3] Distributed by enslavers, provision grounds were plots set apart from the plantation for enslaved people to grow their own food. Compelling enslaved people to travel several miles from the plantation to less-productive mountain land to grow and harvest food during their limited time for "rest" benefited plantation owners. At the same time, due to their distance from the gaze of plantation overseers, provision grounds were creatively cultivated as communal sites of food and culture that resisted the brutalizing subjectivities inculcated by the violent plantation system. Chapter 1 argued that Robert Wedderburn championed provision grounds as a central heuristic for theorizing Black self-emancipation in the West Indies and, more surprisingly, workers' rights in England. In the first issue of his *Axe Laid to the Root*, for example, Wedderburn declared, "above all, mind and keep possession of the land you now possess as slaves; for without that, freedom is not worth possessing; for if you once give up the possession of your lands, your oppressors will have power to starve you to death" (*Axe* 1.4).

Guided by Wedderburn's argument that access to provision grounds must be guarded "above all" for Black self-emancipation in the West Indies, this chapter argues for reading Lewis's *Journal of a West India Proprietor* (1818, published in 1834) as a record of negotiations over access to the provision grounds. A primary concern upon his arrival and before his final departure, tensions over provision grounds framed Lewis's records of his encounters with enslaved people.

Within the field of Romanticism, Matthew Lewis is most well-known as the author of the enormously popular and influential gothic novel *The Monk* (1796). Written when he was only nineteen years old, *The Monk* contributed significantly to the development and explosion of this Romantic genre. Lewis had not visited Jamaica before writing *The Monk*. Still, he was keenly aware of slavery in the West Indies because his father, with whom he had a vexed relationship, owned plantations in Jamaica. Thus, *The Monk*, like other gothic novels, as Lizabeth Paravesini-Gebert argues, "mirrors a growing fear in British society around 1800 of the consequences of the nation's exposure to colonial societies, nonwhite races, non-Christian belief systems, and the moral evils of slavery."[4] In 1812, Lewis was unavoidably confronted with his own complicity in the moral evils of slavery when he inherited two Jamaican sugar plantations, which included approximately 600 enslaved people. Upon his inheritance, Lewis promptly "gave up literature for sugar" and threw his energy into actively managing the plantations.[5] However, his writing did not entirely cease, and throughout two trips to Jamaica between 1815 and 1818, he kept detailed travel journals intended for publication. Lewis contracted yellow fever during his second return trip to England and, as Lord Byron succinctly observed, "died a martyr of his new riches."[6] *Journal of a West India Proprietor* was not published until decades later, in 1834, as emancipation was nigh.

Lewis inherited and visited his plantations between the abolition of the slave trade in 1807 and the 1833 Slavery Abolition Act. Evelyn O'Callaghan notes, Lewis "record[ed] a colonial encounter between slave-holder and slaves at a significant and potentially explosive historical moment."[7] In the genre of the Romantic "suffering traveler," Lewis represented himself as an enlightened, "humane" enslaver who worked diligently to ameliorate the conditions of enslaved people on his estates.[8] The *Journal* must then be read both against and with the grain because it fluctuates between Lewis's casual dismissal of the arduous work of enslaved people and his intense interest in learning about and recording their lives and cultures. Generations of scholars have noted the *Journal*'s value for its detailed descriptions of enslaved people's practices and life experiences. For example, Kamau Brathwaite argues that, although he was an enslaver, Lewis "got as close, perhaps, as it was possible to get, to a personal description" of enslaved people.[9] The *Journal* recorded the names and experiences of at least 50 of the 250 enslaved people on his Cornwall estate. Since Lewis was interested in amelioration, he actively listened to and recorded complaints. By recording complaints about plantation life and labor, Nicole N. Aljoe argues, Lewis's *Journal* integrated individual "testimonies" of enslaved people's experiences. These testimonies illustrated how "complaint is also a form of resistance and a means for asserting a modicum of power."[10] Building on Aljoe's insights about the substance of enslaved people's complaints, this chapter argues that Lewis also repeatedly recorded collective complaints and negotiations for more access to the provision grounds. While these collective complaints do not provide insight into individual lives, they confirm Wedderburn's assertion of the centrality of the provision grounds as a source of communal freedoms that challenged plantation logics.

The next part of this chapter explores Lewis's first visit to Jamaica, when negotiations about the provision grounds persuaded Lewis that these grounds were "a matter of right." The second part of the chapter analyzes Lewis's growing awareness that provision grounds, beyond providing an alternative to plantation work and schedules, also cultivated dangerous multispecies insurrectionist plots. Rodrigo C. Bulamah argues, "human-animal alliances were crucial to the new life-worlds forged inside the provision grounds," and these human-animal alliances cultivated a "materiality of freedom that inspired broad demands for liberty."[11] Lewis vividly depicted how human–animal collaborations among enslaved people gave them power. He needed to buy pigs and cattle from the provision grounds, so these animals became sources of independent revenue for the people he enslaved, and, at times, the animals were strategically deployed to destroy sugar cane fields. Finally, this chapter concludes by exploring the impact of the provision grounds on Lewis's beliefs about slavery. He contemplated manumitting the people he enslaved through land reparations, and his last act before departing from Jamaica imposed "strict Agrarian law" on the provision grounds to regulate their productivity. Lewis's *Journal* testified to British colonizers and enslavers' constant, unsuccessful struggle to contain the abundant agriculture and markets of New World Black communities.

Negotiating the Grounds

When Lewis arrived at his Cornwall plantation, the enslaved people on his estate immediately began negotiating for more time at their provision grounds. While recording this request, Lewis described the location and function of the provision grounds for his anticipated English readership. He explained:

> For although their cottages are always surrounded with trees and shrubs, their provision grounds are kept quite distinct, and are at a distance among the mountains. Of course, I made no difficulty of acceding to their request, but upon condition, that they should ask for no more holidays till the crop should be completed. For the purpose of cultivating their provision-grounds, they are allowed every Saturday; but on occasion of my arrival, they obtained permission to have the Saturday to themselves, and to fetch their week's provisions from the mountains on the following Monday. All the slaves maintain themselves in this manner by their own labour. (*Journal* 81–2)

Lewis's description of the provision grounds evoked traces of the Black geographies that Wedderburn championed. The entreaty "to have tomorrow to themselves," particularly on a workday like Monday, resisted the commodity plantation both in time and space. Even more foreboding, the request uncannily conjured the early days of the Haitian Revolution, when, as Michel-Rolph Trouillot documents, "rebelling slaves did not ask for an end to slavery, but merely for additional days to cultivate their plots."[12] The provision grounds were not only a place for creating and controlling diet. They were also associated with rebellions plotted in mountain areas far from plantation discipline and surveillance.

Lewis's initial negotiations hinted at a more significant ongoing conflict in Jamaica between labor for the plantation economy and work toward everyday subsistence. The Consolidated Slave Act of 1792 stipulated that enslaved people must be allowed one day every other week to cultivate the provision grounds. Lewis noted that every other Saturday for the provision grounds was a custom in place at Cornwall when he arrived. Enslaved people on his estate were negotiating for even more time, and in his eagerness to be a "good" enslaver, Lewis readily assented to the request for every Saturday at the provision grounds.[13] While these negotiations hardly seem revolutionary, Wedderburn's theorization of the provision grounds suggested that such tensions are a precursor to overt rebellion. Wedderburn prophetically warned, "the slaves of Jamaica, are ready now to demand a day of their masters, in addition to the day and a half that was allowed before, being taught by the methodists that it is a crime to labour on the sabbath day; and it is the opinion of many, that they will have it" (*Axe* 1.11). For Wedderburn, the demand for more time on the provision grounds was a reliable indicator that "the island of Jamaica will be in the hands of the blacks within twenty years" (1.12). Joseph Albernaz argues that Wedderburn's admonition to request an additional day illustrated a politics that drew upon the "inner connection between work refusal and revolution."[14] Wedderburn's reading of the provision grounds exposes the revolutionary potential within the seemingly friendly negotiations during Lewis's first visit to his Cornwall estate, which, incidentally, was located just a few miles away from James Wedderburn's estates in the Westmoreland parish.

Scholars have noted that Lewis's *Journal* recorded the everyday resistances of enslaved people. Roberto del Valle Alcalá argues, "in their [enslaved people's] obstinate refusal of labour, in the (sometimes elaborate) performativity of idleness, and in Obeah, the transitivity of traditional forms of resistance such as marronage is replaced by a constituent openness."[15] Resistance to work on the plantation produced an openness within plantation power structures. However, Lewis also registered geographical and ecological resistance. Monique Allewaert points out, "Lewis not only made visible the terrain he meant to call forth but also evoked traces of other terrains, entirely different inhabitations of territory that cannot simply be overlaid onto his own mappings of the plantation zone."[16] Lewis evoked the trace terrains of the abolitionist geographies of the provision grounds. Recent archival work by Elizabeth Maddock Dillon confirms the importance of provisions as a material form of freedom in her analysis of an African-Jamaican song from the eighteenth century. "Guinea Corn" celebrated all aspects of planting, harvesting, and eating corn. As labor is lyrically and intimately connected to culture and community, the song serves as a performative commons that, Dillon argues, "performs food sovereignty in the unlikely site of the plantation, ground zero of the destruction of food sovereignty, ground zero of racial capitalism and the long history of uncommoning."[17] In this light, enslaved workers' requests to spend more time at the provision grounds demonstrated a significant refusal of and an alternative to the plantation economy.

Lewis's explication of the provision grounds for his European readers noted the spatial arrangement of his plantation: The provision grounds are "quite distinct" from the plantation and located up to ten miles away in "mountains," land unsuitable for commodity crops like sugar. Situated in a liminal space outside the cultivated plantation and next to inaccessible mountains, provision grounds limited the space commercial plantations

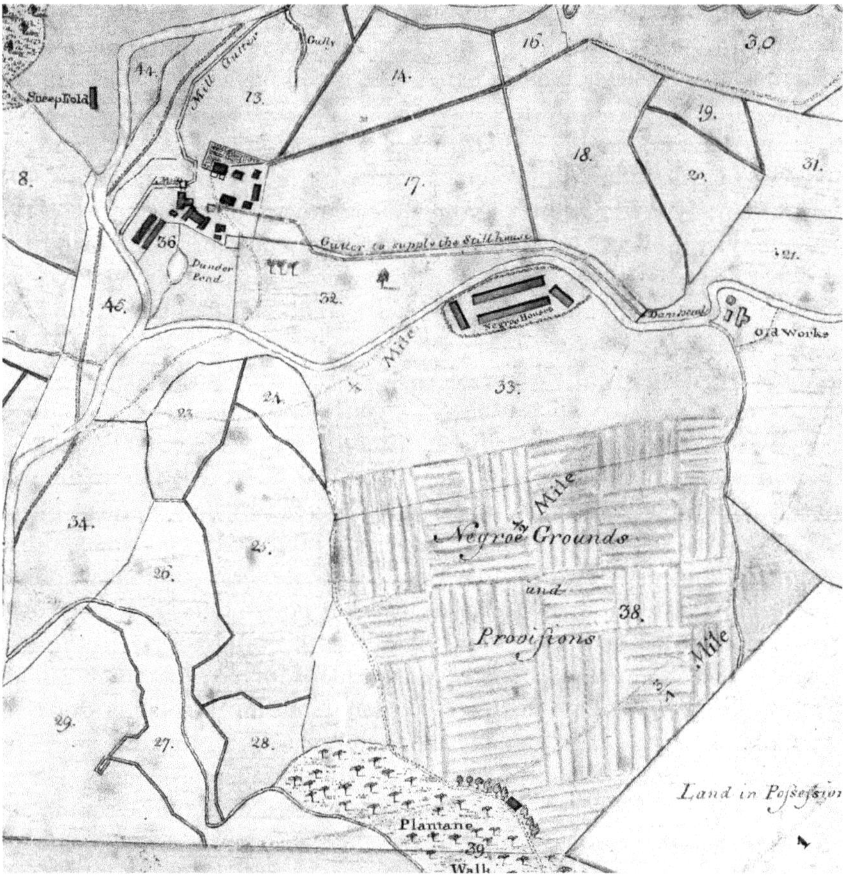

Figure 4.1 Detail from a plan of Edward Long's Lucky Valley Estate. By James Blair, 1769.
Courtesy of the British Library.

could occupy, similar to Maroon villages and territories, as argued in Chapter 5. For example, the survey of Edward Long's Lucky Valley Estate (1769) documented that planters reserved a large part of the estate for provision grounds: 385 acres were planted in sugar cane, while 145 acres were set aside for provision grounds (Figure 4.1). Since provision grounds were located next to the mountains, John H. Parry argues, they often provided food and shelter for self-emancipated individuals as they fled the plantations and became a meeting place for enslaved people actively fighting against plantation slavery.[18]

Proslavery writer Bryan Edwards documented the independent productions of the provision grounds in *The History, Civil and Commercial, of the British Colonies in the West Indies* (1793). He noted that the provision grounds were worked once every other week, and the superabundance of produce from the grounds created internal markets that drew approximately 10,000 enslaved people to Kingston every Sunday.[19] Robert Charles Dallas's *History of the Maroons* (1803) provided more detail about the biodiversity of the grounds and the internal markets of Jamaica:

> Every proprietor is compelled by law, to cultivate ground provisions (of course indestructible by hurricanes)[,] one acre for every ten negroes; besides the allotment of negro territory. To cultivate this allotment, one day in every fortnight belongs to the slaves, exclusive of Sundays and holidays. Thus they raise vegetables, poultry, pigs, or goats, which they consume, bestow, or sell. While some raise provisions, others fabricate coarse chairs, baskets, or common tables. These are bartered at market for salted meat, or pickled fish, utensils, or gaudy dresses; of which they are fond. Their right of property in what they thus acquire, is never questioned; but seems completely established by custom.[20]

Dallas documented that goods from the provision grounds were distributed in three ways – consumed, bestowed, or sold – outlining the development of local markets alongside the global plantation economy. The mixed local economy included "bestowing," a gift economy in which kinship and other relationships were built and maintained through the superabundant produce and crafts cultivated on the provision grounds. While some food and crafts were sold in the internal markets, these items retained use value for subsistence and community-building. Descriptions of fertile provision grounds and flourishing markets are designed to reassure their English readers that slavery was a humane institution. At the same time, Dallas's report on the provision grounds illustrates why Wedderburn championed them as a form of freedom: Enslaved Africans creatively managed the allotment to produce an immense amount of items for their subsistence as well as for the Jamaican internal markets, which, as argued in Chapter 3, distributed revolutionary ideas alongside fruits and vegetables and functioned independently from the global economy. Dallas's description further enumerates the diversity of food cultivated for production: ground provisions such as yams and taro, vegetables, and various animals. Orlando Patterson affirms that on the provision grounds, enslaved people "diversified their crops, the three staple foods being yams, plantains, and cocos. In addition, there were pumpkins, bananas, achee, "catalue" or calalue and many others."[21] Moreover, a veritable arts and crafts movement grew alongside the provision grounds, with enslaved people using time and natural resources to create baskets and furniture.

While Dallas suggested that rights to property earned through the provision grounds were "never questioned," it should be emphasized that the customary rights of the provision grounds did not transcend the law that made enslaved people and everything they accumulated the property of their enslavers. Edwards acknowledged instances in which enslaved people who had acquired significant personal property were seized, along with their wealth, and sold to pay their enslaver's debts.[22] An additional barrier to understanding the abolitionist ecologies of the provision grounds was how proslavery writers, like Edwards, actively celebrated them. Picturesque images of the wealth and health of enslaved people due to the tropical environment were used to justify the horrific violence of slavery. This chapter aims to proceed cautiously, aware of proslavery motivations for romanticizing the provision grounds while following Wedderburn's assertion that they were necessary for freedom from slavery.

By the middle of his first visit to Cornwall, Lewis gave enslaved people an extra day to visit their provision grounds every week. He recorded this decision using the language of English common right: "I therefore granted them as a matter of right, and of which no person should deprive them on any account whatever, *every* Saturday to cultivate their grounds" (*Journal* 191–92). By using the language of English "gentry-crowd reciprocity" to frame his understanding of the provision grounds, Lewis assuaged his conscience, making himself believe slavery was no worse than England's moral economy. However, in the English moral economy, laborers and landlords are "the prisoners of each other."[23] In contrast, chattel slavery in the West Indies made laborers the property of the planters. Lewis's decision to establish a common right to the provision grounds by comparing it to the English moral economy elided the violence of plantation slavery. Even worse, as Keith Sandiford proposes, "he implies that slaves and nature constitute a moral economy that has the potential to redeem the Creole slavocracy from total degeneracy."[24] On the one hand, Lewis's attention to provision grounds arose from his ameliorative position on slavery, yet on the other, it raised the intractable question that haunts the *Journal*: How can people who are considered to be property have rights to the land as well as the produce and income earned from that land?

While seemingly untroubled by other decisions that attempted to ameliorate the conditions of the people he enslaved, such as forbidding the use of whips, Lewis repeatedly equivocated between anxiety about the potential danger associated with the provision grounds and his desire to facilitate more access to them. For example, Lewis recorded an evening drive where he saw people bringing food down the mountain. He noted that the provision grounds benefited him because enslaved people "grow habitually much attached" to the land and did not want to flee the plantation. The abundance of provisions, moreover, saved money by preventing the need "to beg a supply from the master's storehouse." Nevertheless, at the same time, he complained that the abundant produce from the grounds allowed enslaved people to become "so thoughtless and improvident" because their abundance drew "wandering higglers" who sold alcohol in exchange for their produce (*Journal* 83). Lewis's paternalistic and condescending concerns displayed a curious amnesia that the laborers on the Cornwall estate – far from "thoughtless" – had shrewdly negotiated for extra time. Moreover, the agency and influence of "wandering higglers" haunted Lewis. He recorded anxiety about the independence arising from African-Jamaican women and the internal markets, which traded in, according to Hilary McD. Beckles, a "rebellious commercial culture [that] was linked to a complex network of social relationships on the estates."[25]

Access to provision grounds allowed African traditional ecological knowledge and food cultures to thrive alongside the commodity plantation. Judith Carney and Richard Rosomoff call them the "botanical gardens of the dispossessed," where:

> Africans realized an alternative botanical vision to the plantation export commodities that were vested with the dehumanizing practices of the plantocracy. Here, slaves organized cultivation for their own purposes, selecting plants that improved their diet, healed their bodies, and provided them spiritual succor in the liturgical practices of Africa-based religions.[26]

Throughout the text, Lewis noted the diverse productions of the provision grounds with as much or even more interest than the sugar produced on his plantation.[27] While Lewis failed to acknowledge the expertise required to manifest the provision grounds' alternative botanical vision, he nonetheless marveled at their diverse and abundant produce:

> The provision-grounds of the negroes furnish them with plantains, bananas, cocoa-nuts, and yams: of the latter there is a regular harvest once a year, and they remain in great perfection for many months, provided they are dug up carefully, but the slightest wound with the spade is sufficient to rot them. Catalue (a species of spinach) is a principal article of their pepper-pots. (*Journal* 105–6)

When enslaved people on Lewis's plantation negotiated for the right to weekly access to their provision grounds, it facilitated a host of other freedoms in diet, medicine, kinship, and religion, most of which was left unrecorded by Lewis. Elizabeth DeLoughrey argues that yams in particular were significant provisions for New World Africans: "The yams location in the provision grounds outside of the plantation complex (often out of view), as well as its subsistence underground (where it collects nutrients for the community), underlies its significance as an invisible resource, one that must be physically and imaginatively sought, cultivated, and excavated in terms of both time and space."[28] While DeLoughrey makes this argument about the continuing legacy of yams in contemporary Caribbean writing, such as Edna Brodber's *The Rainmaker's Mistake*, her assessment of the material, cultural, and spiritual importance of yams reveals the significance of Lewis's documentation of them. Lewis never mentioned visiting the provision grounds himself, so their establishment as a place haunted the margins of his more extensive deployment of picturesque aesthetics.

Lewis expressed wonder and admiration at the house gardens of enslaved people, a prime example of the "planter-painter perspective," in which, Evelyn O'Callaghan contends, "African slave labour disappears, and a sugar plantation is depicted as a harmonious little town in which there is an intimate connection between 'everything that grows and everything that labours.'" [29] Lewis writes, "I never witnessed on the stage a scene so picturesque as a negro village … and if I were to decide according to my own taste, I should infinitely have preferred their habitations to my own" (*Journal* 107). In this description, Lewis elided the burdensome work of enslaved people. Then, in a typical proslavery formulation, he then contrasted the scarcity of provisions for the British lower classes with enslaved people in Jamaica:

> Not such gardens as those belonging to our English cottages, where a few cabbages and carrots just peep up and grovel upon the earth between hedges, in square narrow beds, and where the tallest tree is a gooseberry bush; the vegetables of the negroes are all cultivated in their provision-grounds; these form their *kitchen*-gardens, and these are all for ornament or luxury, and are filled with a profusion of oranges, shaddocks, cocoa-nuts, and peppers of all descriptions. (*Journal* 108)

Lewis's interpretation of these gardens speciously emphasized that there was beauty and even luxury within West Indian slavery, appealing to a picturesque mode that, in Elizabeth Bohls's words, deployed "landscape aesthetics to reimagine the traces of trauma in the form of aesthetic appeal."[30] While writers and painters were motivated to depict plantations as beautiful to elide the cruelty of plantation slavery, at the same time, Lewis's detail of the fruit trees and peppers demonstrated that he also misread and dismissed the complexity of the gardens, which existed for supplementing provisions in addition to their beauty. Lewis's description, moreover, unintentionally demonstrated that the cultures and disruptions of African-Jamaican self-sufficiency wandered from the provision grounds in the mountains onto the plantation itself.

Although the provision grounds were a point of resistance to slavery, they also required additional hard work during "leave" from plantation labor. Ashton Warner, enslaved on St. Vincent's Island, argued that additional work on the provision grounds was cruel: "They are obliged to work on these days at the provision grounds, if they wish ever so much for a holiday."[31] In addition to the labor of subsistence gardening, the distance to the provision grounds created a burden. According to the abolitionist Zachary Macaulay, retrieving food from the provision grounds was "a labor which is often aggravated by the distance of these provision-grounds from the homestall of the plantation, – a distance often extending to six, and sometimes even to ten miles." However aggravating the distance was, Macaulay's writing was also highly motivated: He was frustrated by the provision grounds and internal marketing system because they prevented enslaved people from attending Sunday church services.[32] While Macaulay advocated for Sunday to become a day of rest free from labor in gardens and markets, he also wanted to attenuate the provision grounds' Afrocentric culture, which resisted missionary and church authority, just as it opposed the plantation.[33]

Productions of the Provision Grounds: Poisons and Pigs

Because of Lewis's attention to the lives of enslaved people, he documented the insurrectionary energy emerging from the provision grounds even as he facilitated more access to them. Lewis's "cultivation of a picturesque surface" for his Cornwall estate, according to Bohls, was disrupted by numerous theatrical encounters with the people he enslaved.[34] Enslaved people's multispecies alliances with plants and animals also repeatedly disrupted Lewis's picturesque surface. Although he never directly argued that Black agricultural practices resisted plantation slavery, at several crucial moments in the *Journal*, he juxtaposed the provision grounds with the potential for violent rebellions against plantations. For example, on February 2, 1817, Lewis recorded an entire entry on various poisons that could be grown or otherwise sourced in Jamaica. Poisoning was a substantial and ongoing concern of planters, and he noted the provision grounds were a source:

> Another means of destruction is to be found (as I am assured) in almost every negro garden throughout the island: it is the arsenic bean, neither useful for food nor ornamental in its appearance; nor can the negroes, when questioned, give any reason for affording it a place in their gardens; yet there it is always to be seen. (*Journal* 330)

Provision gardens not only allowed partial independence from the plantation but also grew poisons that could be employed in rebellion. Lewis's description of otherwise verbose enslaved people refusing to discuss their reasons for growing arsenic beans while "it is always to be seen" signaled his awareness that African-Jamaican botanical knowledge was a continual threat to his plantation. The *Journal*'s concerns about poison align with Susan Scott Parrish's observation that "a perceived African expertise became troubling for the white population – especially after black majorities were established – in the area of mineral and, especially, plant poisons."[35] Lewis's concerns about poison were more explicitly addressed during his conflicts with Adam, an enslaved man accused of poisonings and other disruptions. These disruptions were so threatening that Lewis took the rare step of prosecuting Adam legally. Diana Paton argues, "Adam's prosecution for obeah, Lewis's *Journal* reveals, took place only after Lewis had seriously considered prosecuting him for poisoning."[36] Lewis blamed the poisonings on isolated instances of obeah, even though he documented the poisonous plants' ubiquitous growth on provision grounds.

Although he never directly addressed the connection between Black geographies and abolition, Lewis recorded two significant dangers cultivated on the provision grounds – poison and fire – which were uncannily associated with slave rebellion. The danger of fire was associated with preparing the provision grounds, as Lewis recorded, "clearing their grounds by fire is a very expeditious proceeding, consequently in much practice among the negroes; but in this tindery country it is extremely dangerous, and forbidden by the law." Although illegal, clearing grounds by fire was still "in much practice" (*Journal* 386–87). On April 5, 1817, Lewis discovered that while enslaved people were burning their grounds, a strong wind carried the fire's reach out of human control. The fire slowed down enough to be extinguished only after encountering a morass of water. Of the event, Lewis stated, "I own I was heartily frightened" (*Journal* 387). Clearing the land with fire had horticultural purposes, as Sidney Mintz records, "it is known that the slave cultivators burned off the land they were preparing to plant."[37] At the same time, the provision grounds' fire threatened the plantations' highly flammable sugar cane. As with poison, fires on the provision grounds resembled the tactics of slave revolts and created fear among British planters.

While using fire or poison to resist enslavement was so commonplace as to be expected, Lewis also documented a surprising form of insurrection from the animals of enslaved people. The provision grounds became a toolbox of material and multispecies resistance to plantation ecologies.[38] Lewis explained: "They keep a large stock of poultry, and pigs without number; which latter cost their owners but little, though they cost me a great deal; for they generally make their way into the cane-pieces, and sometimes eat me up an hogshead of sugar in the course of the morning" (*Journal* 112). Lewis's description of the livestock – pigs without number – hinted at a frighteningly out-of-control animal population. With the ability to consume an entire cane field in just one morning, these animal provisions were as destructive as a fire unleashed against the plantation.[39] More importantly, conflict with the pigs had become so commonplace as to be "generally" expected. At this moment, Lewis's planter picturesque shifted into an abolitionist grotesque, in which the cultivations of enslaved people grew rapidly and threatened to overtake plantations. Scott Hess argues that the Romantic picturesque was tied to ownership: "Focusing the entire landscape on a single point of view also confers a sense of imaginative ownership, supporting a form of possessive individualism."[40] In the abolitionist grotesque, that viewpoint is scattered over many different pigs going in diverse directions for unknown reasons, thus undermining the picturesque visuality that confirms the ownership of land and people.

Lewis's *Journal* disclosed several examples of enslaved people tactically deploying animals against plantation ecologies. For example, Lewis recorded a day when unpenned cattle ruined one of his best cane fields: "Although they were perfectly aware of the detriment which the cattle were doing to my interests, not a negro could be prevailed upon to rouse himself and help to drive them out" (*Journal* 207). Despite the destruction, Lewis persistently interpreted animal invasions as the result of incompetence instead of strategic resistance. Not long after, another escape happens, "the cattle were at length replaced in their pen, but not till the cane-piece had been ruined irretrievably" (*Journal* 322). Lewis's record of animal resistance provides an additional viewpoint on the paintings of William Berryman, an English artist who visited Jamaica between 1808 and 1815. Berryman is most well-known for his paintings of enslaved people, which have been called dignified "ethnographies of labor."[41] Nathan K. Hensley

Figure 4.2 William Berryman, *Croptime – Cutting Pieces of Cane – Cattle Feeding in Stubble*, c. 1808–1816. Watercolor on paper.
Courtesy of the Library of Congress, Washington, DC.

argues that Berryman's paintings "bear witness, from within the vocabulary of white supremacist visual representation, to shards of life that will not be contained by language."[42] Berryman's paintings bore witness to the labor and lives of enslaved people in Jamaica, moreover, by emphasizing African–Jamaican relationships with animals and land. *Croptime* illustrates a herd of cattle feeding on the stubble left after harvesting sugar cane. Only one watchman is vastly outnumbered by at least twenty-four cattle, and the line of uncut cane, where captive laborers are still working, lingers in the background (Figure 4.2). While this scene seems peaceful and controlled, reading Berryman's painting through Lewis's observation that enslaved people "were perfectly aware of the detriment cattle were doing to my interests" allows new insights: The numerous cattle might soon wander into the uncut cane, filling their appetites while reducing the work for enslaved people and destroying plantation profits. Another painting, *Two Chickens, Two Pigs, and Huts*, suggestively places pigs with their faces hidden among the residences of enslaved people (Figure 4.3). The secretiveness of Berryman's pigs may suggest that alliances with animals were a secret weapon against the plantation because, as Ron Broglio points out, "we don't anticipate the multiplication of animals in swarms, mobs,

Figure 4.3 William Berryman. *Two Chickens, Two Pigs, and Huts*, c. 1808–1816. Watercolor and ink on paper.
Courtesy of the Library of Congress, Washington, DC.

troops, teams, colonies, and gangs." [43] Hence, keeping "pigs without number" facilitated forms of resistance beyond food sovereignty. Best of all, multispecies rebellions provided plausible deniability, remaining in plain sight with their faces hidden, like Berryman's pigs.

Pigs and cattle were simultaneously necessary to the functioning of the plantation and constantly undermining its profitability. Lewis's final moments at Cornwall described a new tactic in his ongoing battle with enslaved people's pigs:

> On my return from Hordley [Lewis's other plantation], I was told that the negroes suffered their pigs to infest the works and grounds in the immediate vicinity of the house in such numbers, that they were become [*sic*] a perfect nuisance; nor could any remonstrance prevail on them to confine the animals within the village. An order was in consequence issued on a Saturday, that the first four pigs found rambling at large after two days should be put to death without mercy. (*Journal* 406–7)

In this dramatic response, Lewis anthropomorphized the pigs as human trespassers who were "rambling at large" and should be "put to death without mercy." Ron Broglio argues that Romantic-era aesthetics negotiated the "mutual vulnerability" between humans and animals. In particular, "animal death would remind the worker of his or her own expendability."[44] A threat to "execute" the pigs, then, was also a threat, beyond the loss of livestock, to the lives of enslaved laborers as well. The implicit doubling of animal and human bodies in trespassing and boundary crossing further recalls John Clare's sentiments about seeing the "little mouldywharps hang sweeing to the wind," executed moles on private property. His "Remembrances" allied the human and mole experiences of the total expropriation of former commons, when "traps are set to kill / The homeless little miners."[45] Clare suggested enclosure's violent repression and criminalization of commoning practices involved disciplining or removing both human and nonhuman bodies that took their nourishment from the land.[46] Likewise, on Lewis's liberalized plantation, animals that crossed property lines were classified as criminals and threatened with execution.

As a former member of Parliament, Lewis was certainly aware that "the 'swinish multitude' serves as a figure for life in excess of population."[47] However, in the context of Jamaica, other revolutionary ideas are layered onto the image of unruly pigs. Bulamah has argued that pigs were essential to the freedom practices of the African diaspora across the Caribbean: "Pigs as well as other beings, with their own intentions and projects, played a crucial role in the technogenesis of these agrarian landscapes and in the ontogenesis of modern ideas such as freedom."[48] Thus, pig freedom and human freedom mutually reinforced resistance to the plantation system. Moreover, the origin of the word Maroon is *cimarron*, a Spanish word for "wild," which was initially used to describe escaped livestock.[49] Pigs were also associated with the Jamaican Maroons' food culture. During his first visit, Lewis rejoiced over finally having pork made in "true maroon fashion." Of all the Jamaican dishes, he observed, there is "none so excellent as this" (*Journal* 151). This much-coveted dish evoked, then and now, Black food sovereignty through its very presence, which facilitated the political sovereignty of the Maroons. After his dramatic threat to execute the pigs, Lewis recorded that they were immediately contained within their enclosures. However, without their execution, the "pigs without number" waited to be strategically rereleased to do more destruction to the plantation.

Provision grounds grew poisons, unleashed fires, and harbored crowds of destructive animals. Moreover, they finally cultivated another potentially revolutionary crowd when they served as places of respite for self-liberated New World Africans. Bessie, whom European doctors could not cure, repeatedly voiced her wish, finally granted, to see a black doctor "in the mountains" (*Journal* 150–51).[50] Marcia and Richard Fuller "pulled foot" because they could find a "hiding-place in the mountains" (*Journal* 109, 117).[51] Furthermore, Lewis recounted concerns that the provision grounds were a haven for self-liberated people to take rest and nourishment, thus facilitating petit marronage: "My agent was informed that a negro of very suspicious manners and appearance was harbored by some of my people on the mountain lands" (*Journal* 95). These notes suggested that the provision grounds not only allowed settlement but also enabled freedom of movement for African Jamaicans unconnected with Lewis's plantation. As Nihad M. Farooq argues about fugitive farms in Colson Whitehead's *The Underground Railroad*: They were "not an actual utopian space for black workers but a vital layover" for unfree people "who knew they had to keep moving on."[52] Lewis recorded this dialectic between freedom and movement in the Black abolitionist geographies on the margins of his plantation, demonstrating that provision grounds grew more than food; they grew, according to Davis et al., "innovative practices of resistance and kinship."[53] Lewis's *Journal* inadvertently documented the abolitionist botanical and animal ecologies of the provision grounds, which enabled a potentially insurgent social and political world that Lewis's final actions in Jamaica sought to regulate.

"Strict Agrarian Law": Food Sovereignty and Freedom

Midway through his first visit, Lewis granted weekly access to the provision grounds as a matter of "right." By the end of his second visit, Lewis faced the consequences of increased access to the provision grounds. The superabundance of provisions, along with higglering and the internal markets, generated property among the people he enslaved. Lewis attempted to solve the issue of unequal accumulation of property before leaving Jamaica:

> Thus the negroes were in the practice of bequeathing their houses and grounds, by which means some of them were become [*sic*] owners of several houses and numerous gardens in the village, while others with large families were either inadequately provided for, or not provided for at all. I made it public, that from henceforth no negro should possess more than one house, with a sufficient portion of ground for the family. (*Journal* 405–6)

With no acknowledgment that his position as a plantation owner and enslaver facilitated an even more violently inequitable economy, Lewis restructured Cornwall's burgeoning provision-ground economy. Imposing "an entire new distribution according to the most strict Agrarian law," Lewis equally divided the land and possessions among the people he enslaved, a final act that left him with a sense of accomplishment before departing from his ameliorated plantation (*Journal* 406). Lewis's decision to redistribute land recalls the radical agrarianism of Thomas Spence, who advocated for land redistribution in England, and further resonates with Wedderburn, who argued that in a post-slavery society, "you are not told to hold it [the land] as private property, but as tenants at will to the sovereignty of the people" (*Axe* 1.6).[54] However, a notable difference is that Lewis was the sovereign in this case. He retained ownership of all the land and, worse, all the people on the land. By eliminating an internal system of kinship and inheritance, Lewis's supposedly equitable redistribution resonated with other spatial forms of control initiated at Cornwall, such as building a new hospital with solitary confinement. Maureen Harkin argues that "the most distinctive elements of his attempt at a reform program are the means he establishes for regulating and policing space and the gaze on the plantation."[55] Although Harkin does not mention the provision grounds, Lewis's imposition of "agrarian law" reiterated two central conflicts in his narrative: the "common right" to the provision grounds and whether people considered to be property could own property.

By imposing agrarian law, Lewis attempted to harness and control the superabundance of Black agricultural production. Lewis's awareness of the provision grounds on his estate led to his belief, like Wedderburn's, that food sovereignty was inextricable from emancipation from slavery. Lewis's biographer, D. L. MacDonald, records that between his two visits to

Jamaica, Lewis corresponded with William Wilberforce to ask for advice about freeing the people he enslaved. Perhaps due to his many negotiations over the provision grounds during his first visit, Lewis's plan for manumission included land reparations that ensured continued communal access to housing and food. Lewis pondered:

> Shall I leave all of them their liberty? Then they must have a provision made for them; and I could allot to them a certain portion of my land, giving them also their huts, provision grounds, and working implements . . . As to my nephews [and heirs], the mere ties of blood can have no force in a question like this: whether ten white individuals shall be able to afford two courses at [the] table instead of one, or 600 blacks and their descendants be secured against the possibility of future ill treatment, is not a question to discuss for two moments. But if I set them free, how can I be certain that the consequences may not be dangerous to the island and to its white inhabitants?[56]

When Lewis contemplated freeing the people he enslaved, he implied that freedom must include reparations through continued use of the provision grounds. Remarkably, he further noted that kinship among white heirs amounted to an unjust and excessive intergenerational wealth transfer. Barbara Lalla argues that since Lewis recorded African-Jamaican stories and songs, the *Journal* preserved "the expression of a peasant voice, black, poor, and untutored," which "is itself a romantic development and a stroke for freedom."[57] The empowered peasant voice also survives in Lewis's records of collective negotiations for more time on the provision grounds.

Lewis listened to the people he enslaved enough to know that freedom from slavery must include access to the provision grounds. His plans for manumission had uncanny similarities to Wedderburn's prophetic representation of Miss Campbell in his *Axe Laid to the Root* (1817), written during the same time Lewis recorded his journal. When Miss Campbell freed the people she enslaved, she resolved "to resign to you your natural right in the soil on which you stand" (*Axe* 4.57). As discussed in Chapter 1, the magistrate viewed Miss Campbell's plans as dangerous and refused to register the manumissions or property transfer. Lewis's letter to Wilberforce oscillates wildly between a vision of freedom like Miss Campbell's and the magistrate's fear that providing land reparations would be "dangerous to the island." By evoking the danger associated with Black sovereignty, Lewis employed what Raphael Hoermann calls the "Haitian Gothic," an aesthetic and political mode that "makes excessive use of tropes of horror and terror in narrations of Haiti" and other slave rebellions in the West Indies.[58] It is unknown what Wilberforce replied, but since

Lewis instead returned to his estate to enact more reforms, he must have decided his plan for emancipation was too threatening to other estates in Jamaica.

Lewis's *Journal* finally concluded with the white abolitionist talking points that "there cannot be more tractable or better-disposed persons" than the people he enslaved at Cornwall. He declared this while the masses of pigs awaited another delicious raid on the sugar cane, and the thriving internal markets in Jamaica would continue to allow property accumulation among enslaved people. Emancipation in 1838 revealed the significance of this tension. Sidney Mintz argues, "the freedman's most important means for establishing independence was by repudiating his previous status as an estate laborer and becoming a peasant, that is, an agriculturalist who produced, wholly or mainly from his land, the bulk of his own food needs and a surplus for sale."[59] From this perspective, the seeds of liberation had already been sown on Lewis's estate, regardless of his attempt to control and direct the outcome of those abolitionist geographies. Édouard Glissant argues that the Caribbean plantation was characterized by "technical irresponsibility" in its pursuit of profit through mechanization. However, enslaved people and their descendants were an exception to this irresponsibility because their "habitual economy of bits and scraps" in the provision grounds and internal markets arose "because of their own need to guarantee daily survival on the edges of the system."[60] This counter-planation system produced Black geographies that locate freedom in an "ecological vision of Relation."[61] Lewis's journal recorded this ecological vision of relation, which was far removed from the abolitionist position of William Wilberforce and others. His journal revealed that plantations were terrorized, not by overt rebellion or lazy ineptitude, but rather by the *success* of the Black ecological vision. The botanical and animal ecologies of the provision grounds were anticipatory abolitionist commons that enabled an entirely different social and political world, one that was cultivated to its fullest extent in Maroon villages, as I argue in Chapter 5.

CHAPTER 5

Maroon Settlements as Abolitionist Commons
Nanny of the Maroons, R. C. Dallas's *History of the Maroons*, and J. G. Stedman's *Narrative of a Five Years' Expedition*

When Wedderburn wrote about Black abolitionist geographies for his London-based, lower-class audience, he held out the Jamaican Maroons' ecological and agricultural knowledge as a model for resistance. As discussed in Chapter 1, Wedderburn suggested the Maroons won and retained their freedom by cultivating food sovereignty: "Their weapons are their bill-hooks; their store of provision is ever were [*sic*] in abundance; you know they can live upon sugar canes, and a vast variety of herbs and fruits, – yea, even on the buds of the trees. You cannot cut off their supplies" (*Axe* 1.12).[1] By evoking Jamaican Maroons using the tools for harvesting sugar cane to revolt against plantations, Wedderburn demonstrated how, as Michael Morris argues, "the source of Atlantic wealth and the tools to harvest it become the means of pursuing anti-imperial revolt."[2] However, bill hooks were not the only weapon wielded against the British. Reappropriated sugar cane and foraged fruits were formidable weapons, creating a "store of abundance" that enabled continued independence from plantation slavery. The British could not defeat the Maroons because they could not "cut off their supplies." Wedderburn's emphasis on the Maroons' food sovereignty goes against the grain of contemporary scholarly arguments that associate the Maroons primarily with "flight."[3] This chapter follows Wedderburn's description of the Maroons' freedom practices – their grounded settlement through independent food production – to reread British Romantic military and natural history. Histories of European warfare against the Maroons acknowledged that the Maroons' flight from slavery was short. In contrast, their skilled, grounded resistance to the colonial plantation system generated decolonial reterritorializations of the Caribbean that have endured to the present day.

Evidence to support Wedderburn's assertion about the ecological basis of Maroon warfare can be found in early eighteenth-century accounts of the Jamaican Maroons, such as the anonymously penned *History of the Maroons*, which described the Windward Maroons as:

> well acquainted with the most difficult and almost inaccessible places of the Blew [*sic*] Mountains where their love of liberty induced them to settle or rather hide themselves for I am well informed they there lived innocently for many years and as they were not interrupted they planted in several places and by the plenty of Wild Hogg and fish which the Mountains and rivers supplied them with they were well contented and as they had some women multiplyed [*sic*] fast.[4]

The writer's equivocation about the Maroons' relationship to land, in which their need for freedom "induced them to settle or rather hide," pinpointed the difficulty British writers encountered when recording the Maroons' radical challenge to colonial property. If the Maroons were described as "settling" the land, they would be no different from white settlers. In the same sentence, the writer quickly corrected himself and criminalized Maroon settlements as mere attempts to "hide" from British authority. Yet, the writer's documentation of the Maroons' extensive ecological and material grounding provided evidence of settlement. The Maroons "planted in several places" while hunting and building a thriving community on Jamaica's most inaccessible land. Alex A. Moulton argues that the geographic study of Maroon habitations indicates they were "not only symbolic sites of resistance but material sites that instantiate a counter-hegemonic spatial-ecological logic to the colonial order."[5] The Jamaican Maroons, then, not only fled from plantations but also established alternative, abolitionist commons, dwelling communally and claiming territory by gardening, hunting, and fishing.

This chapter moves backward in time to trace the Maroons' decolonial relationship with the environment, starting with Queen Nanny, a leader of the Jamaican Windward Maroons, and a present-day National Hero of Jamaica. Narratives of Nanny's warfare against the British noted that her fight included growing pumpkins in the rugged terrain of the Blue Mountains. The chapter then turns to a critically neglected Romantic-era text, Robert Charles Dallas's *The History of the Maroons* (1803). Although primarily a military history, Dallas repeatedly admired the Maroons' communal "superabundance" and recorded how ecological and agricultural knowledge was imbricated with Maroon guerrilla warfare. For example, countering the assertion that Maroon communities were dangerous to settlers, Dallas testified that Jamaican Maroons "produced a stock not only sufficient for their own use, but so superabundant as to enable them to supply the neighbouring settlements."[6] Dallas's admiration of Maroon agriculture provoked outrage, even from the ostensibly antislavery *Edinburgh Review*. The last part of this chapter then turns to a text more familiar to Romanticists, John Gabriel Stedman's *Narrative of a Five Years' Expedition against the Revolted Negroes of Surinam* (1796), accompanied by illustrations engraved by William Blake. Although describing Maroon settlements in Surinam rather than Jamaica, Stedman's narrative and Blake's engravings resonate with Wedderburn's insistence that the Maroons cultivated viable, sustainable counter-planation societies as an alternative to plantation capitalism.

Queen Nanny's Pumpkins

Stories of the Jamaican Maroons' communal land rights often begin with the early eighteenth-century figure of Queen Nanny of the Maroons, who is now a National Hero of Jamaica.[7] Mentions of Nanny are scarce in narratives written by European colonists, whose patriarchal bias led them to focus on male leaders. A British expedition leader against the Windward Maroons in the First Maroon War (1728–40), Philip Thicknesse briefly described Nanny as a powerful obeah woman who killed white men:

> The old *Hagg*, who passed sentence of death upon this unfortunate man [who tried to negotiate a treaty], had a girdle round her waste, with (I speak within compass) nine or ten different knives hanging in sheaths to it, many of which I have no doubt, had been plunged in human flesh and blood.[8]

Thicknesse's description of Nanny as a brutal killer encircled by implements of violence bears minimal resemblance to oral stories of the Windward Maroons in the Jim Crow Mountains of Jamaica. Although written descriptions were few, colonial maps of Jamaica, even one "produced at an extended moment of intellectual ferment and optimism," recorded "Nanny Town," demonstrating unprecedented British acknowledgment of a self-liberated Black woman's reterritorialization of the colony of Jamaica[9] (Figure 5.1). The mapping of Maroon towns reveals, Alex Moulton argues, "the Maroons had not simply hindered the expansion of settler-colonialism, they curtailed the expropriation of 'good land' and took possession of good land for themselves."[10] Following Nanny, the Maroons' combined food and land reclamation became an established model of communal freedom in contrast to European models of individualist freedom.

After Jamaica's Independence from Britain (1962), Kamau Brathwaite advocated for establishing Nanny as a National Hero because her story demonstrated that "at the very beginning of Jamaica's history, there was an active, complex and highly successful, even victorious opposition to the

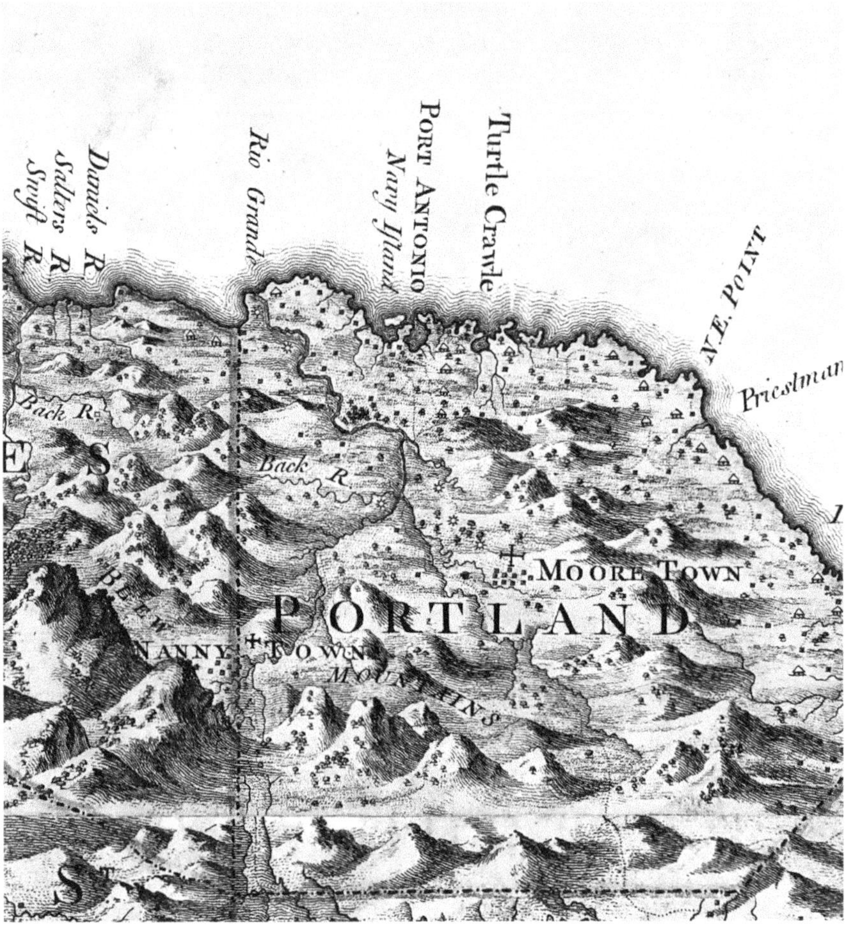

Figure 5.1 Detail of Windward Maroon Towns, designated with a cross. Map of the Island of Jamaica from actual surveys. T. Craskell and J. Simpson, 1763. Courtesy of the Library of Congress.

Euro-plantation."[11] However, coherent historical documents about Nanny's life do not exist. In her survey of representations of Nanny from the colonial period to present-day Jamaica, Jenny Sharpe concludes, "the story of Nanny is the story of contending forms of knowledge: written versus oral histories, colonial versus national cultures, institutional versus popular ways of knowing."[12] Building on Sharpe's archival work, my argument acknowledges the limitations of the contending stories of Nanny and, more generally, of the Maroons. Frances Botkin also details the difficulty of writing about Black Romantic-era freedom fighters in her book about Three-Fingered Jack. Her method combines attentiveness to three categories of sources: Romantic-era historical documents, the stories of present-day Jamaican Maroons, and the interpretations of contemporary Black poets and artists. Botkin argues, "when applied to research, these methods, improvisational as they might be, make way for counternarratives; they open up new possibilities for the production of knowledge."[13] Using Botkin's method and adding Wedderburn's insights about the Maroons' ecological knowledge, this chapter emphasizes that Nanny's role as a fighter and leader was intrinsically connected to agriculture. In other words, Nanny's opposition to the plantation system and slavery was accomplished both through overt military resistance to the British and by cultivating independent food production for her people.

Wedderburn's insistence on the Maroons' ecological and food-based resistance to slavery resonates with the stories of Nanny recorded by Colonel C. L. G. Harris, a twentieth-century leader of the Moore Town Maroons. During the establishment of Nanny as a National Hero of Jamaica, he published a series of articles in the *Jamaica Gleaner* that argued Nanny's many roles as "the person, the tactician, the mystic, and 'generalissima' par excellence—nemesis of her foes" emerged from deep environmental knowledge gained by working with the formidable terrain of the Jamaican Mountains.[14] One of the places about which Nanny cultivated deep environmental knowledge was "Watch Hill," a place that provided a clear view of British soldiers entering Maroon territory. Behind Watch Hill lies "Pumpkin Hill," an area of equal tactical importance. Harris explains the origin of Pumpkin Hill:

> Because of an unexplained shortage of food Nanny contemplated giving up the struggle; but in the dead of night she heard a voice calling, "Nanny, Nanny", it said, "don't give up; plant the pumpkin seeds." She looked up but there was no one, neither did she hear the voice again; but she did have a packet of dried pumpkin seeds. On the morrow she planted them on the hill and in a few days they had grown covering acres of virgin land. They remained, so it is said, for many, many years bearing fruit incredible in numbers and sizes.[15]

In Harris's account, Nanny was a prophet whom the creator had advised to prioritize feeding her people by planting pumpkin seeds. Significantly, the pumpkins provided subsistence for her people, and as the vines grew abundantly, they claimed acres of territory for the Maroons. Nanny's pumpkins demonstrated that bodily health was inextricable from territorial claims; pumpkins nourished the Maroons so they could continue fighting.

The supernatural quickness with which Nanny's pumpkins matured and thrived was also interpreted as a divine message that the Windward Maroons were destined to establish themselves in Jamaica outside of the British plantation economy. Kenneth M. Bilby has transcribed many of the Maroons' oral stories, and he contends that Pumpkin Hill endures as a "topographic monument" that reminds present-day Maroons they were chosen by the Creator to live in the Blue Mountains.[16] If, as Sylvia Wynter argues, Caribbean plantations "planted" people as well as crops, then Nanny's supernatural gardening allowed the "planting" of her people both within and beyond colonizer geographies.[17]

Nanny's pumpkin reterritorialization aligned with Wedderburn's interpretation of Maroon warfare as a more-than-human alliance against plantation ecologies. Mutually vulnerable and vibrant, the entanglement of people and plants in Nanny's story allows the significant achievement of continued cultural survival outside plantation monocultures, demonstrating, as Sophie Chao suggests, "fugitive seeds and bodies became literally and figuratively entangled in marronage."[18] The significance of Nanny's pumpkins can be usefully illuminated by scholarship on the work of plants in colonial and decolonial projects. Nicholas Blomley argues that during the late eighteenth- and early nineteenth-century enclosures of the commons in Great Britain, "the hedge did important practical work. Most immediately, it made it difficult for human and nonhuman bodies to move as they had done in the past."[19] If plants, such as hedges and sugarcane, were employed to do the work of enclosure and dispossession, then Nanny's pumpkins accomplished repossession for commoning futures. Nanny's pumpkins function as a synecdoche for the Maroon's larger ecological project of reterritorialization through what Bev Carey describes as "hundreds of acres of plantains, yams, potatoes, pumpkins, corn and lentils."[20] Nanny's pumpkins marked not only a war with the British but also the rise of global plantation capitalism more generally. As Maroon communities persisted, British colonizers associated subsistence with pumpkins with Black independence from wage labor for colonial sugar plantations, an enduring representation that reemerges forcefully in Thomas Carlyle's "Discourse on the Negro Question" (1849), discussed in Chapter 6.

Reading Nanny's obeah as a supernatural gift for agriculture counters the British colonial representation of Nanny as a violent "old hag," which evoked stereotypical Romantic-era fears of obeah.[21] Although he does not mention Nanny, Alan Richardson argues that Romantic-era representations of obeah "symbolically exorcise the threat of black self-determination, equating its pursuit with the empty display of a barbaric and vulnerable superstition."[22] Contrary to British representations of obeah, the Maroons interpret Nanny's obeah along the lines of "oracular wisdom."[23] The Maroons' story of Nanny's reterritorialization of Pumpkin Hill and feeding her people through miraculous pumpkin-growing can be usefully understood as what Dipesh Chakrabarty calls a "subaltern past," which includes the "agency of supernatural beings" in its history.[24] There is no historical "proof" for the pumpkins, but they can be partially understood as the insurgent productions of traditional ecological knowledge that arose through what Karla Gottlieb describes as "close communication with the ancestors."[25] Nanny's role as the grower of pumpkins facilitated the African diaspora's physical and cultural survival in the Maroon towns of Jamaica.

The longevity and fertility of Nanny's pumpkin rebellion can be inferred from its continued retelling by Black Caribbean artists and poets. Angelita Reyes argues that "Nanny's identity in history and collective memory" underwrites a sense of communal mothering that inspires and affirms "island women's lucrative contributions to history and traditions."[26] Lorna Goodison, a Jamaican poet with just such lucrative contributions, reimagined Nanny's childhood in Africa as a training ground that strategically elided ecology and warfare.[27] In the poem "Nanny," her training entailed schooling in traditional ecological knowledge: "I was schooled in the green-giving ways / of the roots and vines." The "green-giving ways" nourished her power for "healing acts" (lines 9–11).[28] Nanny's African ecological education also facilitated her navigation of "the rhythms of the forest" and her ability to "sense and sift / the footfall of men" (lines 16–18). After her training, Nanny was intentionally sold into slavery, where she survived as a Trojan horse transported to Jamaica:

> And when my training was over
> they circled my waist with pumpkin seeds
> and dried okra, a traveler's jigida,
> and sold me to the traders
> all my weapons within me
> I was sent, tell that to history.
>
> (lines 30–35)

In Goodison's retelling, Nanny's weapons were African seeds to be planted in the West Indies. These seeds originated the counter-plantations that contested British plantation slavery. Goodison's rendering of Nanny's story resonates with Wedderburn's location of the success of Maroon warfare in a supply of food that British troops cannot entirely obstruct.

Goodison's "Nanny," according to Jahan Ramazani, "revalorises and remythologises a gendered resistance against colonial oppression" while refusing to place her legacy within "an exclusively nationalist vision."[29] The accomplishment of representing a National Hero of Jamaica without nationalism occurs, in part, through emphasizing the way Nanny's persona unsettled European gender roles. Most stories of Nanny, including Goodison's, represent her as straddling masculine (military) and feminine (caretaking) roles, which leads Ronald Cummings to argue that Nanny can be understood as a neglected example of Caribbean "female masculinity."[30] This is undoubtedly true when reading Nanny through the lens of contemporary theories of gender identity. Yet Nanny also reflects the expansive roles that women played in African society as warriors and leaders. Stella Dadzie explains that Akan culture has "a long-standing reputation for female military prowess and communal survival strategies in which women played an active, sometimes central role."[31] Stories of Nanny's insurgent pumpkin farming are at odds with European binaries between food and weaponry and masculine and feminine gender roles.

Nanny's complex combination of agricultural and military strategy pervades Jamaican-American artist Paul Lewin's painting, *Nanny and the Pumpkin Seeds* (Figure 5.2). Part of his more extensive oeuvre of visual art inspired by Jamaican folklore, his painting draws on stories his Jamaican mother told him about Nanny while growing up.[32] The painting centrally features Nanny, who looms large with a sword, knife, and abeng, the traditional weapons of war, around her waist. While these weapons resonate with Thicknesse's description of Nanny's girdle full of knives, Lewin prevents any lingering focus on violence by overshadowing the weapons with an enormous caretaking hand. The hand is nearly two-thirds the size of her lower body, and the uneven proportions of Nanny's physical form suggest the difficulty representing the convergence of her dual positions as pumpkin farmer and military fighter to a contemporary audience influenced by Western gender roles. Flanked by a warrior on the left side and a mother with children on the right, Lewin's Nanny resides within a liminal space between genders, a hero who participates in an ethics of care as a fierce warrior. Signaling the consequence of Nanny's pumpkins to every figure around her, the foreground of the painting displays two giant pumpkins, one on the caretaking and the other on the fighting side of Nanny. Lewin's painting then suggests that Nanny's pumpkins exist as both weaponry and communal care, and the painting shifts our perspective toward Nanny's legacy as a revolutionary grower of pumpkins.

Figure 5.2 Paul Lewin, *Nanny and the Pumpkin Seeds*, 2014. Acrylic paint on canvas, 24 in × 30 in. Private Collection.

Contemporary representations of Nanny by Goodison and Lewin foreground that traditional ecological knowledge and military strategies were intrinsically connected, as Wedderburn argued about the Jamaican Maroons to his London audience in 1817. Nanny's pumpkins were the material means through which the Maroons reterroritalized British space. Nanny was the only Black woman to whom the British government officially granted land, and stories about her have left an enduring claim on that land: the Maroons tell outsiders that they cannot visit old Nanny Town or Pumpkin Hill because Nanny's spirit presides over them.[33] In this way, Nanny's legacy prevents tourists and other neocolonialists from seeing and exploiting these sites, and her story continues to facilitate Maroon-led cultural and ecological preservation.[34] While stories of Nanny, Nanny Town, and Pumpkin Hill both predate (Thicknesse) and postdate (Harris, Goodison, and Lewin), the Romantic-era military narratives discussed in the remainder of this chapter, her story similarly represented traditional ecological knowledge and food sovereignty as formidable weaponry against the European plantation system.

"The Superabundance of the Maroons" in R. C. Dallas's *History*

The critically neglected military history, Robert Charles Dallas's *The History of the Maroons, from Their Origin to the Establishment of Their Chief Tribe at Sierra Leone* (1803), was written as a part of a larger conversation in Great Britain about how to understand the intractable, ongoing existence of Maroon societies in the West Indies.[35] Dallas's introduction notes that he wrote the history as a "rebuttal to the hostile and inaccurate descriptions" of the Maroons in the proslavery writer Bryan Edwards's *Proceedings of the Governor and Assembly of Jamaica, in Regard to the Maroon Negroes* (1796). Dallas warned readers that he has not "caught the zeal of Edwards, in painting these people as tygers [*sic*]," while at the same time stating he does not want to be misunderstood as an "apologist for the rebellion."[36] Despite his equivocal stance on Maroon sovereignty, Dallas sought to correct Edwards's dehumanization of the Maroons by documenting that their independence stemmed from cultivating "superabundance" in the Jamaican mountains.

Dallas's information about the Jamaican Maroons was collected during long conversations with his friend, William Dawes Quarrell, who served in the Second Maroon War (1795–96) and went to Cuba to acquire the dogs used to subdue the Maroons.[37] Subsequently, Quarrell was appointed Principal Commissary and supervised the removal of the Trelawney

Maroons to Nova Scotia.[38] Living under the same roof, they had many detailed discussions about Quarrell's experiences. Dallas also gathered additional information for his *History* from the cartographer William Robertson, who served in the Second Maroon War and drafted the first map of Jamaica's Cockpit Country, the formidable territory of Leeward Maroons. In the introduction, Dallas introduced the topic of the Second Maroon War by comparing it to the American and French Revolutions. He acknowledged that the late eighteenth century had seen "the revolution of empires, the destruction of states, the extinction of whole classes of men, the alteration of established customs, the sacrifice of millions of lives." Dallas then challenged his readers to shift from contemplating the sublime changes wrought by the oceanic "unbounded expanse" of European revolutions to considering the "streamlet" of the Second Maroon War. While the comparison may have minimized the breadth of the Maroons' fight against British imperial power, it also surprisingly implied that state power might again be overthrown, this time by New World Black communities "long-established" in the West Indies.[39]

Although not an abolitionist, Dallas's emphasis on the humanity and culture of the Maroons challenged his British audience's perceptions. *The Edinburgh Review* met this challenge with impassioned criticism. Writing ostensibly from a liberal, antislavery point of view, the reviewer Henry Brougham objected to Dallas's assertion that Jamaican Maroons even *have* a history because any events connected to them were "very short and simple, not necessarily connected with any other branch of West Indian politics." The review further argued that Dallas "aggravates the meanness of the subject" by including names, descriptions, and statements of individual Maroons: Brougham complained, "his negroes are always chattering." Worst of all, Dallas's *History* "positively denies the dangers of an independent negro commonwealth being allowed to grow up in the West Indies.[40] Due to the Haitian Revolution, Michael Craton notes, the continuing independence of Nanny Town and other Maroon towns was understood as "a dangerous anomaly."[41] Since Dallas's *History* was published during the Haitian Revolution, the reviewer's fears of an "independent negro commonwealth" would have been shared by most British people, whether for or against slavery in the West Indies. While his text replicated British assumptions about cultural superiority and the necessity of empire, Dallas nonetheless represented the "dangerous anomaly" of Maroon towns as orderly communities that functioned independently of the British economy by employing traditional ecological and agricultural practices.[42]

In his preface, Dallas stated his goal was to counter Bryan Edwards's testimonies that the Jamaican Maroons lacked agricultural knowledge and skill. Edwards insisted, "they had no inclination for the pursuits of sober industry. Their repugnance to the labour of tilling the earth was remarkable. In some of their villages I never could perceive any vestige of culture."[43] In refuting Edwards, Dallas's *History* outlined the contours of what Michael Craton calls the Maroons' "rival version of creolization" that was "deeply inimical to the slave plantation nexus."[44] Disputing the widespread belief that the Maroons were thieving and ransacking plantations for food, Dallas asserted the reverse: White settlers in Jamaica depended on the "superabundance" of the Maroons' provision grounds to supplement their diets, which put the Maroons' culture on equal footing or perhaps even above other colonists' settlements. Dallas's *History* provided ample, detailed evidence of the Maroons' agricultural successes:

> Their provision grounds consisted of a considerable tract of unequal land, from which was produced a stock not only sufficient for their own use, but so superabundant as to enable them to supply the neighbouring settlements. Plantain, Indian corn or maize, yams, cocoas, toyaus, and in short all the nutritious roots that thrive in tropic soils, were cultivated in their grounds. In their gardens grew most of the culinary vegetables, and they were not without some fine fruits: . . . they had some valuable fruit-trees, among which the Avocado, or Alligator-pear, ranked foremost. Mammees, and other wild but delicious fruits, were at their hand, and pine-apples grew in their hedges. They bred cattle and hogs, and raised a great quantity of fowls. When to this domestic provision of good and wholesome food, we add the luxuries afforded by the woods, the wild boar, ring-tail pigeons, and other wild birds, and the land-crab, which some esteem the greatest dainty in the West Indies, we may doubt whether the palate of Apicius would not have received higher gratification in Trelawny Town than at Rome.[45]

The sheer diversity of different fruits and vegetables, also noted in Stedman's description of the Maroons of Surinam, discussed later in the chapter, starkly contrasted with the monocultures of commodity plantations. As with the provision grounds of enslaved people, the grounds of the Maroons demonstrated a remarkably diverse polyculture. At the end of the description, Dallas compared the Leeward Maroons' food culture to Roman gourmet cuisine. Although this flourish was intended to be hyperbolic, at the same time, Dallas radically argued that the food culture of the Maroons was just as advanced as that of the West, thus countering the idea that the Maroons were stuck in a less developed time of hunting, foraging, and thievery, as Edwards asserted.

Black geographies, such as those of the Maroons, resemble what Anna Tsing has called the "latent commons," those "fugitive moments of entanglement in the midst of institutionalized alienation" that exist in the margins or ruins of industry. These commons are latent because "while ubiquitous, we rarely notice them." Tsing calls for developing the "arts of noticing" to discern the fugitive entanglements of the latent commons.[46] In the following passage, Dallas criticized Edwards for failing to develop the art of noticing when he testified that Maroon villages and agricultural land were "always in a shocking state of neglect and ruin."[47] Dallas recorded an explicit retort to Edwards's description:

> It has been said, that the Maroons let their provision-grounds, both those belonging to themselves, and those they held on sufferance, go to ruin, and trespassed on the provision-grounds of the settlers in the mountains. I am informed that the fact was otherwise; that those of the settlers were often insufficient, their negroes being employed in different labour, and that they purchased the superabundance of the Maroons. Their grounds, after the corn was cut down, might, for a length of time, appear to the eye in a ruinous state; while under the surface a large stock of nutritive roots were growing to maturity. These roots were their surest support at the period when a scarcity was most to be apprehended, after a long-continued succession of dry weather. In the course of time these patches of land were cleared and replanted, and they again gradually assumed the appearance of being neglected; it is no wonder, therefore, that the eye of a casual visitor should have been deceived, and that he should have been led to declare, "that he perceived no vestige of culture."[48]

Describing Edwards's superficial reading as the "eye of a casual visitor," Dallas argued that the Maroons intentionally worked with mountain ecologies by intercropping, planting several crops in the same field. Moreover, reading the landscape of the Maroons further required attending to their underground ecologies: while their land appeared to be neglected, "under the surface a large stock of nutritive roots were growing." To understand Maroon agriculture, Dallas suggested, one must know how to interpret their gardens accurately. Edwards failed to see or acknowledge yams and other cultivations of the Maroons because he evaluated their land through the lens of European plantation monocultures.

Dallas's account critiqued plantation ecologies when he argued that white settlers cultivated an "insufficient" amount of food for survival because they were "employed in different labour," the labor of the monoculture commodity plantation. Instead of stealing from plantations, the Maroons' "superabundance" contributed to the success of the nearby plantations by growing sustainable, diverse crops that allowed people to thrive. The idea that Maroons grew a superabundance of produce that supported sugar plantations suggests some complicity with slavery. At the same time, Maroon agriculture amounted to another "plot" or narrative of freedom through kinship with the land, plants, and animals. As Alex A. Moulton argues, "the yam – and other plot crops – suggests epistemologies and ontologies that are denied or obscured in trans-Atlantic histories centering the plantation."[49] Dallas's *History* directed attention to an agricultural and ontological underground hidden in plain sight. The Maroons' nutritive roots under the surface, barely discerned by most Europeans, amounted to a synecdoche, like Nanny's pumpkins, for subsistence as resistance among the African diaspora in Jamaica.

The superabundance of the Maroons' agriculture further facilitated resistance to plantation slavery because excess provisions were sold at the internal markets, where Maroons were able to mix unnoticed with enslaved people engaged in "market marronage," trading not only in provisions but also talk of resistance and liberation.[50] Dallas pointed out, "a Maroon himself might, by carrying a few fowls and a basket of provisions on his head, pass unnoticed and unknown through the immense crowd of negroes frequenting the markets in the large towns."[51] Here is yet another iteration of a "higgler" who can traverse boundaries unnoticed, like Wedderburn's grandmother, Talkee Amy, discussed in Chapter 3. The extent of exchange between Maroons and enslaved African Jamaicans cannot be traced; as Kathryn Benjamin Golden points out, "we can never fully grasp the extent of these enslaved-maroon networks of freedom, since an unquantifiable amount of subversive relationships remained undetected and unmolested by white authority."[52] Dallas's description of the markets as meeting places resonates with an unpublished manuscript, *History of the Maroons*, which argued that Maroons and enslaved people frequently met in the markets, with a potentially dangerous outcome: "The Rebels not only become more daring but plantation Slaves also become more insolent."[53] The internal markets were Black geographic sites where food and money were exchanged alongside talk of insurrection.

The Maroons' settlements in Jamaica's mountainous interior also resisted the plantation, whether in the Cockpit Country of the Leeward Maroons or the Blue Mountains of the Windward Maroons. The rugged and almost inaccessible Blue Mountains and Cockpits are examples of what Willie Jamaal Wright calls "unruly landscapes," natural environments, overlooked or discarded by colonial governments and capitalist enterprise, where "marginalized, hunted, and exploited people … have taken a desire for liberation and merged it with an ignored and undervalued environment to gain liberties in opposition to repressive administrations."[54] Dallas described the unruly landscape of the Jamaican mountains in military terms, wherein "nature had secured the flanks of her own fortification."[55] The inaccessibility of the Jamaican mountains created a place for thriving Maroon communities. Dallas's *History* included the first European map of one of these unruly landscapes, the Cockpit Country of the Leeward Maroons.[56] While the Cockpit map intended to maintain European superiority by asserting knowledge of Black geographies, at the same time, this map acknowledged the Maroons' territory, as with the recording of Nanny Town on colonizer maps. The Maroons' geographies exceeded these maps; an entire system of secret roads that enabled mobility around the island was absent. [57] Vincent Brown records, "numbering in the thousands by the early eighteenth century, the Leeward and Windward Maroons established pathways through the island quite distinct from those of the colonists."[58] Wedderburn referred to these secret roads as a military tactic in *Axe Laid to the Root* when he noted that Maroons "want no turnpike roads" when they engaged in battle against the British and instead used place-based knowledge for navigating terrain (1.12).[59]

The Cockpit Country maps were unable to convey that Maroons developed other tactical uses for these inaccessible places.[60] Dallas documented how the rocky cliffs facilitated a communication system by using acoustics and sounds from conch shells or abengs (cow horns):

> They communicated with one another by means of horns; and when these could scarcely be heard by other people, they distinguished the orders that the sounds conveyed. It is very remarkable, that the Maroons had a particular call upon the horn for each individual, by which he was summoned from a distance, as easily as he would have been spoken to by name, had he been near.[61]

While Dallas noted that Jamaican Maroons developed subtle, imperceptible communication, James Knight's *History* described a cacophony that was used to mislead and distress the colonizing armies: "When They Engaged They constantly kept blowing Horns, Conch Shells, and other Instruments, which made a hideous and terrible Noise among the Mountains in hopes of terrifying our Parties, by making them imagine Their Number & strength much greater than it really was."[62] The Maroons' strength was "much greater" than it appeared because they fought with the environment itself, using even the rocky mountains and chasms to their advantage. Ecological knowledge made their fighting more potent than the British, even though their numbers were far fewer. Beyond the Maroons' agricultural abundance, then, even the more traditionally depicted methods of Maroon warfare were accomplished through what John Favini identifies as the "principle of ecological immersion."[63]

Recently, Rinaldo Walcott has expressed concern about the "need to be more critical of Nanny and Quilumbo and refuse the romance story that they are quickly becoming in some forms of political theory." As Walcott notes, holding up Maroon communities' resistance may also elide the painful fact that they are "the outcome of an encirclement of unfreedom."[64] Walcott's caution provides an opportunity to pause and acknowledge that while Wedderburn and Dallas represented the Maroons' traditional ecological knowledge as a version of freedom, it was not uncomplicated. The Maroons were not only encircled by unfreedom; they also were not entirely free from British compulsion. Ruma Chopra foregrounds that "the treaties turned the Maroons into an internal police force that prevented new outlaw communities from emerging in the interior."[65] Morris argues that in championing marronage, Wedderburn problematically "ignores the ambivalent legacy of the Maroons as hunters of runaway slaves, foregrounding instead a remarkable inversion of symbols of colonial power."[66] However, Wedderburn acknowledged the complicated and compromised freedom of the Maroons when he wrote about Black self-emancipation: "The slaves are not so ignorant as the Maroons were, when, after they had gained their own liberty, became instruments to guard the woods from being a harbour for other runaway slaves" (*Axe* 6.96). Wedderburn contended that the Maroons' ecological and land-based resistance could be a model for emancipation without repeating the obligations enshrined in the British-drawn treaties.[67]

J. G. Stedman's "Inconceivable Astonishment"

The final section of this chapter turns to a text more familiar to Romanticists, John Gabriel Stedman's *Narrative of a Five Years' Expedition against the Revolted Negroes of Surinam, from the Year 1772 to 1777*. Stedman was a mercenary soldier hired by the Dutch States-General to assist local troops fighting against self-emancipated New World Africans in the South American colony of Surinam.[68] While on the military campaign, Stedman kept extensive diaries detailing his relationships with other people, various military strategies and engagements, and numerous accounts of landscape, flora, and fauna. Consulting these notes ten years after the military campaign, Stedman wrote the *Narrative*, which was published in 1796 by Joseph Johnson, the prominent radical publisher for Mary Wollstonecraft and William Godwin.[69] William Blake notably engraved sixteen images for the printed edition, and scholarship about this text has unsurprisingly focused on Blake's provocative engravings, which, as Debbie Lee argues, were "the most epically disturbing ones Blake himself would ever design" because they "bring the full horror of slavery to the British eye, to bring the self face-to-face and into responsible proximity with the other." Saree Makdisi further emphasizes that the images reflect "Blake's tendency to de-exoticize as much as possible many of the images of otherness in his work."[70] A second stream of scholarship about *Narrative of a Five Years' Expedition* analyzes Stedman's highly publicized and romanticized "marriage" with Joanna, the enslaved daughter of a white plantation owner. Nicole N. Aljoe suggests that Joanna's story is an example of embedded fragmentary "Caribbean slave narratives within colonial archives."[71] Joanna's story was excerpted and republished several times in the Romantic period.

By reading Stedman's *Narrative* through Wedderburn's arguments about the Jamaican Maroons, a substantially different account emerges: The Maroons' agricultural practices cultivated food and freedom from plantation economies. When Stedman wrote his narrative, depictions of unstable, violent Maroons in Surinam had been in the news in Europe for almost 100 years because "Marronage plagued the colony from its earliest years, as slaves escaped into the rain forest that grew up almost to the doorsteps of the plantations."[72] Stedman stepped into the ongoing European debates about marronage in Surinam from his dual roles as soldier and naturalist, which meant, Elizabeth Bohls argues, that he "was uniquely positioned to represent natural history's complex imbrication with colonialism."[73] While the *Narrative* repeated the colonial justification that the Maroons must be subdued because they were raiding and stealing from plantations, at the same time, Stedman documented that knowledge of the natural world was also imbricated with fighting for freedom from plantation slavery. The primary method of warfare against the Maroons involved the destruction of their advanced forms of subsistence agriculture since it was impossible to win through military advances alone. Stedman's *Narrative* then described what Rachel B. Herrmann calls "victual warfare," a form of colonial violence that aimed to conquer indigenous and Black people in the Americas by destroying or controlling their food supply.[74] At one point in the text, Stedman documented that, in response to Colonel Fourgeoud's strategy of victual warfare, the Maroons used conch shells and other noise as a distraction while they were "preparing warimboes or hampers filled with the finest rice, yams, and cassava" before the troops invaded. Much to the troops' consternation, "they had only Left us the Chaff, and Dregs for our Contemplation And to our Great And inconceivable Astonishment."[75] Stedman's "inconceivable astonishment" evoked extreme cognitive dissonance about the military campaign: He waged a "war of civilization" against people whose lives were more orderly, productive, and peaceful than his own. Although he was not an abolitionist, Stedman's documentation of his astonishment at the civilization of Maroon villages and agriculture blatantly contradicted European colonial arguments for warfare against them.

For example, after finding an abandoned Maroon village, Stedman recorded that he encountered "the most beautiful Oblong Square field with Rice in full ripeness that ever I saw in my Life."[76] Stedman expressed surprise at finding the Maroons growing rice, a commodity crop from European plantations. Yet the Maroons were not engaging in plantation monoculture; Stedman marveled that the Maroon villages were also abundantly "Stock'd With Cassava, Yams, Plantains, Maise, Pistachio Nuts, And Pidgeon Peas," along with fruit resembling strawberries and plums.[77] Like Dallas, he documented many valuable items crafted through a resourceful foraging of the forests, including pistachio butter, palm tree wine, clay pots, soap, gourds, candles, brooms, and ropes. Instead of confirming the European assumption that the Maroons' habitations were filled with European items stolen from the surrounding plantations, Stedman expressed wonder at the order of their villages, the abundance of their agriculture, and their artisan crafts. Judith Carney and Richard Rosomoff argue, "Stedman's catalog of crop destruction, however, is also a document of maroon achievement. It reveals unmistakably how Africa's botanical legacy had taken deep root in tropical America."[78] As with Nanny's pumpkins, the gardens of the Maroons cultivated thriving abolitionist commons.

The Maroons' productive abundance was inextricable from maintaining healthy environments and bodies, which contrasted starkly with the starving degeneration Stedman witnessed in his troops and with the excessive and unhealthy gluttony of the European planters. Descriptions of illness, particularly in white soldiers, recur in Stedman's *Narrative*. Alan Bewell contends the text made significant "contributions to growing public concern, during the 1790s, about the epidemiological cost of colonialism."[79] Emily Senior also argues that bodily health was a central theme of the *Narrative*: "Bodies – human, animal and vegetable – are decaying, dissected, dismembered, opened up and pieced apart."[80] European military and planter bodies were diseased and decayed; however, the Maroons and their environments were healthy. Stedman verified and recorded the Maroons' tranquility and health, horrifically, by inspecting bodies of those who had been murdered:

> Where in a State of *Tranquility* they Seemed as they had Said to us Want for Nothing – Being Plump and Fat at Least Such we found those that had been Shot – For instance *Game* and *fish* they Catch in Great Abundance by Artificial Traps and Springs, And Which they Preserve by Barbacuing, While with *Rice, Cassava, Yams, Plantains* and so on, theyr [*sic*] fields are ever over Stoked [*sic*][81]

The *Narrative* repeatedly juxtaposed the moral and physical sicknesses of living European colonizers with the violent, unnecessary deaths of healthy and tranquil New World Africans. Moreover, in this passage, Stedman represented the physical health of the Maroons as inextricably connected to their "ever overstocked" fields and their communal "tranquility."

While Stedman documented the thriving abolitionist commons and physical health of the Maroons, he inadvertently argued for their work ethic. At one point, he even vividly illustrated how difficult it was for European troops to do the same subsistence work:

> While it was no bad Scene to See 10 or 20 of us, with heavy Wooden Pestles beating the Rice, Like so many Apothecarys [*sic*], in a Species of Mortar, Cut All Along the trunk of a Level'd Purper hart Tree for that purpose ... This Exercise was nevertheless Very Painful & Verified the Sentence Pronounced on the Descendents of *Adam* that they Should Eat Bread by the sweat of their Brow, Which trickled Down my Forehead in particular like Deluge.[82]

This comedic scene documented the technology of the Maroons – a mortar carved in a tree that facilitated the strenuous task of threshing rice – for which the troops were grateful because they were starving and wanted supplies. The deluge of sweat when applying to this task, even though he was a mercenary soldier acclimated to physically strenuous conditions, indicated, as Bohls notes, "the Maroons exemplify a relationship to tropic nature that radically diverges from both the planters' commodity agribusiness and the colonial soldiers' out-of-placeness, their miserable vulnerability."[83] Threshing rice elicited Stedman's "inconceivable astonishment" again, this time during an embodied realization that the Maroons' superabundance did not simply spontaneously erupt from the West Indies' "waste fertility," in Thomas Carlyle's coinage, which is discussed in Chapter 6. Instead, the superabundance of the Maroons was the product of both agricultural expertise and arduous labor. Like Wedderburn,

Stedman's *Narrative* recognized that Black ecological knowledge and labor created ecologically and socially ordered counter-plantation modernities.

Several of Blake's engravings also noted Stedman's astonishment at Black abolitionist geographies, although the extensive scholarly discussion of William Blake's engravings for Stedman's *Narrative* often foregrounds his representations of the violence done to enslaved people.[84] However, Susan Scott Parrish argues that Blake's engravings "portray this alternate, and even resistant, territorial experience and nature-knowledge of New World Africans."[85] Parrish locates that challenge to colonial territorial mastery in *March Thro' a Swamp or Marsh in Terra-Firma*, which depicts New World Africans helping European soldiers navigate treacherous swamps. Insurgent environmental experience and expertise was also implied by the abundant food production detailed in *Family of Negro Slaves from Loango* (Figure 5.3). Blake designed the plate to illustrate Stedman's apparently proslavery talking point that contended for "benevolent" slavery: Stedman wrote, "I Will introduce a Negro Family in that State of Tranquil Happiness to Which they are all entitled When they are Well treated by their Owners."[86] However, Blake's engraving, notably, did not depict a benevolent enslaver but rather a representation of food sovereignty, which, as in both Dallas and Stedman's depictions of the Maroons, drew direct associations between food superabundance, physical health, and independence from European colonial logics.[87]

Blake's illustration of an enslaved family's "tranquil happiness" might be usefully interrogated by Lily Gurton-Wachter's provocative question about slavery in Blake's work: "Might happiness, rather than consenting to atrocity or proving that there is no injury, serve as a placeholder for the unnamable feeling of agency and accusation Blake sought to illustrate?"[88] In Blake's *Family*, perhaps part of this unnamable agency arises from food. The male figure balances grain and a basket of fish and eels on his head while carrying a giant fish on a line, "All Caught by Himself."[89] The female figure balances a basket of diverse fruits and root vegetables on her head while spinning cotton and tending to her children. Did Blake's reading of Stedman's *Narrative* lead him to associate agency with food sovereignty?[90] If so, Blake's detailed images of food and cottage industry gesture toward the thriving presence of Black geographies outside the engraving. Planting and harvesting, fishing and foraging, and even reappropriating colonizer crops such as cotton are forms of what Moulton calls "plot-work": "the place-epistemologies and relations of communities who are forging worlds through plots against [the] apocalypse" of slavery and dispossession.[91] It is impossible to state with certainty exactly what Blake

Figure 5.3 William Blake. *Family of Negro Slaves from Loango* from John Gabriel Stedman, *Narrative of a Five Years' Expedition against the Revolted Negroes of Surinam*. London: Printed for J. Johnson, 1796.
Courtesy of the Huntington Library, San Marino, California.

intended. Still, if he had familiarity with the entirety of the *Narrative*, which was overshadowed by Stedman's cognitive dissonance at the military strategy of Colonel Fourgeoud, who sought "to Destroy the Surrounding Harvest" of the Maroons' rice, cassava, and yams, then perhaps Blake's *Family* pointed toward self-emancipation through Black geographies created by the extensive agricultural and ecological knowledges of Black people in the Caribbean.[92]

The Maroons' agricultural and culinary "superabundance," documented by Dallas, Stedman, Blake, and Wedderburn alike, supplies an additional context for the Romantic trope of a solitary walker communing with nature. Malcom Ferdinand juxtaposes Maroon communities with Romantic solitary walkers. He contends, "faced with the solitary walking man, the Maroon demonstrates another relationship to nature imbued with a desire for the world . . . this figure points to ecological practice as a condition for emancipation."[93] Ferdinand suggests that the Maroons' decolonial ecological practices amounted to another form of the Romantic relationship with nature that critiqued mainstream European society. The Maroons' establishment of sovereign, counter-plantation economies, then, reveals the limits of Jean Jacques Rousseau, William Wordsworth, and Henry David Thoreau's imaginations of the radical and transformative possibilities for solitude in nature. Wedderburn evoked the legacy of Nanny's pumpkin revolution and the insurgent Black geographies documented by Dallas, Stedman, and Blake when he held out marronage as an exemplary liberation practice with potential insights for radicals in England. By shifting attention away from the Maroons' flight to their agricultural knowledge, Wedderburn opened up possibilities for locating underground insurgent Black geographies in Romantic-era texts and, perhaps, their migration into radical thought in Britain.

CHAPTER 6

Emancipation as the Enclosure of "Waste Fertility"

Thomas Carlyle's Rage against Pumpkins

The Slavery Abolition Act, passed in 1833 and enacted on August 1, 1834, legally ended chattel slavery in the British West Indies, freeing more than 800,000 enslaved people. While legally "free," formerly enslaved people in Jamaica were required to continue working on the estates of their enslavers as apprentices until Emancipation in 1838. While Wedderburn first outlined Black abolitionist geographies in 1817, this chapter moves forward into the 1830s and 1840s, arguing that the stakes of his radical, place-based politics emerged vividly during the transition from slavery to wage labor. For example, the letters of Thomas McNeil, overseer of Lord Holland's Friendship Estate in Westmoreland, Jamaica, documented how Black geographies troubled and even contested British conceptions of freedom after abolition.[1] In 1839, Lord Holland attempted to introduce a new policy for formerly enslaved laborers residing on his estate. They were told to pay one-sixth of their wages to rent their provision grounds. McNeil complained to Holland about the workers' resistance to the transition: "During the time they have withheld so much labour from the estate they have devoted much labour to improve their cottages, and increase the extent of their provision lands."[2] After Emancipation, instead of prioritizing labor for wages on the sugar plantation, free Black people on the Friendship Estate set out doing precisely what Wedderburn had recommended, keeping hold of their provision grounds. Even more, they were expanding their boundaries, sending out tendrils and taking over colonized space like Nanny's pumpkin vines. In this way, newly freed Black people all over Jamaica challenged the plantocracy by stubbornly staying put and using their new freedoms to expand the boundaries of their communal grounds.

Wedderburn had anticipated that British emancipation would proceed via the dispossession of enslaved people's common rights to the provision grounds. In his last pamphlet, *An Address to the Right Honourable Lord Brougham and Vaux*, he warned, "should the slaves ever obtain their freedom . . . the landholders will demand rent of them."[3] As Wedderburn predicted, after emancipation, enslavers became landlords who demanded that formerly enslaved people pay rent for their homes and provision grounds, which, in many cases, had been cultivated and cared for by families through generations of enslavement. Laborers on the Holland estate refused to pay rent, as McNeil complained:

> They declare they will not pay any rents whatever until they see "the Queen's Law" to say they must do so, that their parents before them, had possession of the land and had houses where theirs now are, before Lady Holland was born and that they cannot think of paying any rent whatever and work for the estate also.[4]

McNeil's letter indicated that formerly enslaved African Jamaicans understood the land as a common inheritance gleaned through long-established intergenerational care and not through the lens of individual property ownership. McNeil's observation that "they cannot think" of paying rent, beyond its intended condescension, demonstrated that the provision grounds cultivated a "semiautonomous moral and social order" that was incommensurate with the ideologies of plantation capitalism.[5] During and after emancipation, antislavery and proslavery writers were united in their goal of detaching Black Jamaicans from the land because, as Malcom Ferdinand observes, it was "an abolition of slavery on the condition that the colonial plantation continues." Ferdinand calls this an "abolition without ecology," which arose from a "truncated understanding of slavery [that] resulted in thinking about antislavery and abolition in a way that dissociated them from colonial inhabitation and its consequences for ecosystems."[6] For commodity plantations to continue to thrive after the end of slavery, the place-based freedoms built and inhabited by Black Jamaicans needed to be enclosed.

Instead of embracing British liberal individualism, Black Jamaicans understood freedom as the ability to participate freely in cultivating intergenerational, place-based communities. Ruth Wilson Gilmore argues that "freedom is not simply the absence of enslavement as a legal and property form. Rather, the undoing of bondage – abolition – is quite literally to change places: to destroy the geography of slavery by mixing their labor with the external world to change the world and thereby themselves."[7] The formerly enslaved people on the Holland estate "cannot think" of paying rent because they were busily engaged in the abolitionist project of expanding their grounds. Refusing to recognize the long-established Black geographies of the provision grounds, Lord Holland continued, without success, to demand that laborers pay rent. His overseers began "ejectmants" for non-payment of rent the same year, and the village was soon deserted. Although the outcome of this conflict was finally land dispossession, at the same time, McNeil's letter documented traces of the Black geographies that Wedderburn championed.[8]

After emancipation, Catherine Hall documents, "rents charged for every member of a family, summary eviction, and the destruction of crops which had been carefully cultivated were powerful incentives to break local attachments."[9] The task of McNeil and other plantation managers, who were seeking to enclose Black geographies in the wake of slavery, was made significantly more manageable when the Jamaica Assembly passed the Ejectment Act in 1840, which allowed the eviction of Black Jamaicans from land they had held for generations. Tim Barringer argues that the Ejectment Act was "a parallel to the eviction of squatters under the Enclosure Acts that had transformed rural life in England and the Scottish Highland clearances."[10] George Beckford and Michael Witter cite the additional enactment of vagrancy laws and heavy land taxes, which were also intended to force Black Jamaicans off the land and into wage labor on plantations.[11] Such laws resonate with enclosure in Great Britain, in which J. M. Neeson notes, "dependence through reliance on a wage was to identify the new structure of agrarian society and ensure the authority of farmers over labourers."[12] Thus, emancipation from slavery in Jamaica was experienced as the enclosure of intergenerational, communally held land and culture.

The remainder of this chapter explores how the Jamaican provision grounds became sites of resistance to exploitative wage labor and plantation capitalism after the abolition of slavery. The following section analyzes Joseph Sturge and Thomas Harvey's *The West Indies in 1837*. Although written from an antislavery, humanitarian perspective, they made several recommendations for severing newly freed Black Jamaicans from the land. Then I trace similar arguments in Thomas Carlyle's notorious "Occasional Discourse on the Negro Question" (1849). Although perhaps best known for coining the term "dismal science," this chapter argues that the essay's most significant coinage was "waste fertility," which was illustrated by Carlyle's racist depiction of "Quashee" surrounded by pumpkins, a synecdoche for independent Black people who cultivated abundant provisions alongside freedom from wage labor. In Carlyle's imagination of post-emancipation Jamaica, the planter picturesque transformed into an abolitionist grotesque: an environment of proliferating, uncontrollable plants and animals swarming around free Black people unwilling to relinquish their relationship with the land and each other. As pumpkins were represented as a viable threat to the British empire, Carlyle inadvertently illustrated the liberatory power of the Black geographies outlined by Wedderburn.

"Humanitarian" Enclosures after Emancipation

The Quaker antislavery activist Joseph Sturge visited Jamaica during the apprenticeship period between the abolition of slavery in 1834 and emancipation in 1838. After abolition, the British West Indies imposed an apprenticeship system that forced formerly enslaved people to work for their enslavers without compensation. Written with Thomas Harvey, Sturge's *The West Indies in 1837* documented and deplored the excessive violence of the apprenticeship system in Jamaica. The narrative also recorded a veritable war on the provision grounds. They lamented, "the negros have either been generally deprived of these allowances, now called with bitter truth, 'the indulgences of slavery,' or their partial continuance has been made the pretext of extorting a far more than equivalent value in extra labor."[13] Although criticizing the planters' brutal exploitation of Black Jamaicans' attachment to their provision grounds, their solution did not support workers' common right to the land they had already cultivated. Instead, Sturge and Harvey implored planters to pay a higher wage. While higher wages would undoubtedly be welcome, a wage increase differed significantly from the independence achievable through land reclamation. Sturge believed higher wages would enable laborers' wives to stay home, which would, in turn, motivate workers to remain on the estates and pay rent. Based on the norms of the European patriarchal nuclear family and private property, this proposal aptly demonstrates how the colony of Jamaica, according to Hall, "became a site for acting out white visions of how black people should live."[14]

Although a humanitarian emancipationist text, *The West Indies in 1837* was also actively engaged in the "war of representation" in print about whether formerly enslaved people would work for wages.[15] Richard Huzzey concludes that Sturge "supported sugar protection and government regulation in pursuit of a harmonious, hierarchical freedom in the West Indies, a position quite similar to that of government ministers."[16] Sturge's belief in upholding the racial hierarchy was evident in both his writing and actions. For example, on his return trip to England, Sturge brought along the apprentice James Williams, because Williams's testimony about the abusive apprenticeship system would support the campaign for complete emancipation. When Williams failed to obey the details of Sturge's mission in England, he was sent back to Jamaica, where he returned to an apprenticeship, in which, Sturge wrote, he would be "compelled to labour for his bread."[17] Christopher Taylor surmises that "Sturge's treatment of Williams reproduces the very structures of Apprenticeship that Williams's *A Narrative of Events* indicted."[18]

Maintaining a managerial and hierarchical version of emancipation, Sturge advocated for enclosing and destroying Black geographies in the provision grounds and internal markets. While lamenting the abuse and violence of the apprentices' unfree laboring conditions, which included the destruction of provision grounds in retaliation for not providing enough labor, *The West Indies in 1837* articulated fears "that the negroes will be tempted, by the abundance and fertility of the waste lands, to become small settlers, and independent cultivators."[19] Sturge and Harvey's insistence that formerly enslaved people must labor on commodity plantations instead of becoming "independent cultivators" pointed toward the colonial managerial strategy of using access to food to enforce labor discipline.[20] The provision grounds cultivated resistance to the landowners' biopolitical control of laborers by providing food sovereignty and marginal independence from wages.

Fearing that formerly enslaved people might become "independent cultivators" of the land instead of dutiful laborers on Britain's sugar estates, Sturge and Harvey recommended enervating the internal Jamaican markets by importing cheap provisions from Haiti. If the provision grounds were no longer profitable, the policy would destroy the Sunday markets and detach Black people from the land.[21] Sturge's commitment to the liberal economy and global free market led him to recommend using the strategy of cheap imported provisions to coerce Black Jamaicans into cheap labor. This approach bears out Raj Patel and Jason Moore's argument that within plantation capitalism, "cheap is a strategy, a practice, a violence that mobilizes all kinds of work – human and animal, botanical and geological – with as little compensation as possible."[22] By importing cheap food for purchase with wages, the British government devalued the produce of the provision grounds, a strategy that anticipated the later scheme of importing cheap labor through the Indian indenture system.

As activists who advocated for improving Black lives after slavery, Sturge and Harvey also resisted the idea that more laws should be passed to prevent the purchase of land by Black people. They argued: "In a country of mountain fastness, the negroes can only be prevented from squatting on crown lands, by being suffered to acquire them honestly by purchase."[23]

The term "mountain fastness" denotes how the harsh mountainous geography of Jamaica historically excluded white settlers. While advocacy for free Black people to buy mountain land may appear humanitarian, it was also motivated by an urge to enclose, privatize, and control impenetrable "mountain fastness," the domain of Maroon communities, as discussed in Chapter 5. Allowing free Blacks to "acquire them honestly" under British rule might prevent the emergence of more unruly, independent Maroon towns with uncertain boundaries. Moreover, this scheme transformed the practice of communal provision grounds into individual property ownership, thereby weakening a culture of solidarity among formerly enslaved people.

At the end of the narrative, Sturge and Harvey noted that Black people in Jamaica were considered more "unintelligent and degraded" than those in Antigua or Barbados. They argued that this prejudice existed because, instead of being fed by rations, African Jamaicans have always grown their own food, making them less "modern" but also cultivating a "firmness and self-reliance" that should be respected.[24] The alternating dismissal and admiration of the Jamaican provision grounds and internal markets in *The West Indies in 1837* signaled that the text was written and received in conversation with James Phillippo, the Baptist missionary who helped to found Jamaica's free villages.[25] The free villages were another humanitarian land-based movement that sought to partially eradicate Black geographies and culture in the wake of British slavery.[26] Marcus Wood argues that within such British antislavery rhetoric, "Black resentment, violence, traumatic memory, sexuality, and above all agency are ruthlessly locked out of this version of events. Controlled, yet contented, happy to choose a state of continued servitude, this black laboring population not only suggests that it will continue to produce sugar, but implied that it was always happy under a benevolent patriarchy."[27] Sturge's plans for Black freedom after emancipation similarly elided traumatic memory and sought to inculcate continued servitude in a tractable Black proletariat; his antislavery, humanitarian recommendations for curtailing Black-led land use uncannily resonated with Thomas Carlyle's decidedly proslavery sentiments.[28]

Thomas Carlyle's Rage against Pumpkins

From an unapologetic proslavery perspective, Thomas Carlyle's 1849 essay, "Occasional Discourse on the Negro Question," explicitly sought to undermine public faith in humanitarian political views like Sturge's, which he condensed metonymically under the term "Exeter Hall," referring to the 1840 meetings, organized by Sturge, of the World Anti-Slavery

Society. Carlyle described antislavery philanthropists as "bleating and braying" a "broadbrimmed form of Christian sentimentalism" that was dangerous to the stability of the colony of Jamaica.[29] Despite his refutation of Sturge's work, Carlyle's essay articulated concerns remarkably similar to Sturge's apprehension that formerly enslaved people in Jamaica "will be tempted, by the abundance and fertility of the waste lands" to create agricultural and economic independence from British sugar plantations.[30] Although notorious for its virulent racism, particularly its trope of a Jamaican "Black Quashee" surrounded by pumpkins, scholars have argued that the essay was a performance about "black" Ireland or mere antagonistic prose "to create a strongly antipathetic reaction" rather than engage in a straightforward argument.[31] However, this reading builds on Gretchen Gerzina's suggestion that the essay should be read as the culmination of "a whole intellectual industry of justifying slavery" that began with Edward Long's *History of Jamaica* (1774).[32]

By using the figure of "Black Quashee" as a metonym to describe free Black people in Jamaica, Carlyle evoked the name's history as a derogatory term used by Europeans to describe people of African descent as evasive, deceptive, and childlike.[33] Carlyle's Quashee was evasive and rebellious precisely because he was a skilled agriculturalist:

> Sitting yonder, with their beautiful muzzles up to the ears in pumpkins, imbibing sweet pulps and juices; the grinder and incisor teeth ready for every new work, and the pumpkins cheap as grass in those rich climates: while the sugar-crops rot round them uncut, because labour cannot be hired, so cheap are the pumpkins.[34]

While Carlyle intended to dehumanize African Jamaicans with animal imagery, he also revealed British anxieties about Black agricultural knowledge and capabilities. In other words, Carlyle's image of prolific pumpkins referred metonymically to African-Jamaican food sovereignty and the freedom it provided from the compulsion to work on sugar plantations. Although Carlyle articulated this anxiety in shockingly racist terms, the concern about Black food sovereignty was shared by Sturge and other antislavery advocates.

Throughout the Atlantic world, Black food sovereignty was imagined as threatening, particularly post-emancipation. For example, in the United States, watermelons, another prolific vine fruit, were perceived as menacing by white people due to their power as a cash crop. The response in the United States was to ridicule growing watermelons by animalizing the Black farmers associated with them.[35] The derisive representation of farming pumpkins and watermelons after abolition strengthened colonial state power, which, as Jean Casimir points out, "worked hard to invent their [formerly enslaved people's] lack of history and tradition and, on this basis, to assert the incapacity of those assigned to this infra-world to produce their own autonomous knowledge, or to be sovereign in any way."[36] Carlyle's essay was part of this colonial work toward discrediting autonomous Black economic and agricultural networks. By using pumpkins as the metonymy for Black agriculture that allowed independence from labor on sugar plantations, Carlyle further evoked the much older story of Nanny of the Maroons, who, as Chapter 4 outlined, waged a successful guerrilla campaign against the British by growing pumpkins. Although Carlyle's essay was written more than 100 years after the First Maroon War, his fear of the proficiency of Black agriculture demonstrates how Black abolitionist geographies were a long-established tradition that, J. T. Roane argues, "created possibilities for survival, connection, and insurgency through the strategic renegotiation of the landscapes of captivity and dominion."[37] Such insurgency was revealed by how Nanny and Quashee's multispecies alliances with proliferating pumpkins signified rebellion against colonial, carceral plantation geographies, both before and after emancipation.

In addition to being notorious for its open racism, "Occasional Discourse" is well-known for its coinage of the phrase "dismal science" to describe economics. However, a Carlylean coinage in "Occasional Discourse" worth more consideration is "waste fertility." Carlyle argues, "West India Islands, still full of waste fertility, produce abundant pumpkins; pumpkins, however, you will please to observe, are not the sole requisite for human wellbeing."[38] Alan Rice argues that "waste" is central to Carlyle's essay, where African Jamaicans are represented as the creators of waste in a land that should be growing sugar.[39] By insisting that communal food sovereignty was "waste fertility," Carlyle enunciated a principle that continues to justify the enclosures of agricultural capitalism. Wendell Berry, for example, notes that a central mechanism of global agribusiness is to depict "fertility as waste," which allows the monoculture commodity farm to be understood as redemptive of that fertility.[40] Walden Bello similarly argues that contemporary agribusiness proceeds via "depeasantization," a process that includes representing small farms and indigenous subsistence agriculture as inefficient to justify making "the countryside a more congenial site for intensive capital accumulation."[41]

Somewhat predictably, then, Carlyle's sweeping agricultural history of Jamaica amounted to a blatant fantasy of depeasantization through British domination and supremacy.[42] In his view, the West Indies were entirely dormant until the "white Enchanter" came along and woke the islands to commerce: "Before the West Indies could grow a pumpkin for any Negro," a great deal of "European heroism had to spend itself in obscure battle."[43] European sugar plantations arose after many heroic battles with the "waste savageries" of indigenous people, who produced nothing more than "reeking waste and putrefaction." Therefore, only the descendants of the white Enchanters have any right to land in the West Indies. Carlyle then contrasted the image of heroic, conquering Europeans with African Jamaicans depicted as "indolent two-legged cattle" who needed the "beneficent whip." Carlyle's rhetoric was shockingly extreme even in an era when open racism was commonplace. According to Hall, Carlyle's essay "marked the moment when it became legitimate for public men to profess a belief in the essential inferiority of black people."[44] Wood adds that another disturbing legacy of this essay was that "dehumanizing mechanisms for attacking the blacks in popular culture become humorous; the race joke becomes a standard white bonding experience."[45]

More than that, Carlyle's representation of Black "waste fertility" reinforced and naturalized the racial hierarchy of land ownership in the West Indies. Transforming European representations of Jamaica's climate, which historically had been blamed for causing physical and moral decline in white settlers, Carlylean "waste fertility" suggested, quite differently, that the tropical climate degenerated British plans for the colony precisely because it was so healthy and productive that Black Jamaicans were not easily sickened and starved into wage labor. Carlyle complained that Black people in Jamaica had too many natural resources: "Strong sun supplies itself gratis, rich soil in those unpeopled or half-peopled regions almost gratis; these are *his* 'supply;' and half an hour a-day, directed upon these, will produce pumpkin[s] which is his 'demand.'"[46] Using the economic language of supply and demand, Carlyle accused Black laborers of using free soil and sun (upon which all farmers, whether of commodities or subsistence crops, rely alike). By suggesting that Jamaica's healthy soil and climate were solely responsible for successful Black agricultural projects, Carlyle sought to erode any suggestion that formerly enslaved people possessed scientific knowledge and skill.[47] In this endeavor, Carlyle was hardly original. The Romantic-era proslavery writer Bryan Edwards, whose minimization of the Maroons' agricultural success was discussed in Chapter 5, similarly argued: "The most industrious of Negroes do not, I believe, employ more than sixteen hours in a month in the cultivation of their own provision-gardens (leaving all further care of them to the beneficence of nature)."[48] Even Matthew Lewis, with all his attention to the rebellious productions of the provision grounds, indulged this delusion that denied the labor and knowledge of New World Africans. He wrote, "whether I chose to enter life anew as an English labourer or a Jamaica negro, I should have no hesitation in preferring the latter . . . for here nobody appears to work at all."[49] Assertions that Jamaica's fertile climate eliminated the need for agricultural labor when slavery existed to provide cheap labor on European plantations were laughably disingenuous.

Diminishing or outright denying the labor of the propertyless, however, was already a well-established strategy of dispossession in Britain. As Raymond Williams observed:

> Locke produced a defence of private property based on the natural right of a man to that with which he has mixed his own labour, and many thousands of people believed and repeated this, in periods when it must have been obvious to everybody that those who most often and most fully mixed their labour with the earth were those who had no property, and when the very marks and stains of the mixings were in effect a definition of being propertyless.[50]

Enclosure and land expropriation, both in Great Britain and its colonies, operated by discrediting the labor of commoners as minimal and merely physical, even animal, to justify the existing landowner's right to the property. When deployed in the sugar plantations in Jamaica, this belief became further entrenched in the racial regime of property. Thus, Carlyle's assertion that Jamaica's climate created "waste fertility" made the oxymoronic argument that the apparent abundance and success of independent Black agriculture and markets should be dismissed in favor of growing commodity crops, or "things far nobler than pumpkins." The repeated minimization and sabotage of Black labor and agricultural proficiency by both antislavery and proslavery advocates further led to the enduring consequence that the British colonial government had an "inability to even conceive of an alternative economy based on black initiative and enterprise."[51]

Carlyle denounced Jamaica's "waste fertility" because it failed to provide the disciplinary scarcity that would force Black people to work on sugar plantations. When Carlyle argued that the British government should refuse "to permit the Black man any privilege whatever of pumpkins till he agree for work in return," he drew on Thomas Malthus's political economy in *An Essay on the Principle of Population* (1803).[52] Malthus naturalized the necessity of wage labor when he concluded, "no person has any claim of right on society for subsistence if his labour will not purchase it."[53] Malthusian logic supported the institution of private property; as David Collings notes, "in this view of the world, those who held property and power did so unconditionally; their property was indeed theirs, rather than a social debt which, in situations of crisis, they owed to others."[54] In his arguments for the provision grounds, Wedderburn wrote specifically against Malthus, arguing that private property amounted to nothing less than a violent war against the poor: "What would the difference be, whether these starving wretches were sent to heaven by an invader, or the land holders, though Malthus has said, to please the rich, that the superabundant population is doomed to perish by the laws of nature, which are laws of God."[55] Wedderburn's concern that those in power manipulated the "laws of nature" was realized after emancipation, when, as Sturge documented, planters sometimes would burn provision grounds and kill animals to create food scarcity to discipline and punish intractable African-Jamaican laborers.[56] Like the planters who decimated Black intergenerational ecologies, Carlyle argued that the British government of Jamaica should reinforce the artificially created environment of scarcity in which Malthusian "natural laws" would continue to coerce laborers after the end of slavery.[57]

Although gardening hardly seems a radical act of resistance, the provision grounds and the idea of Black food sovereignty originating outside European capitalism and knowledge remained intimidating after emancipation. Carlyle outrightly declared that Black gardening should be illegal. In an address to Black Jamaicans, he raged, "the State has plenty of waste soil; but the State will religiously give you none of it on other terms. The State wants sugar from these Islands, and means to have it."[58] He even conflated Black Jamaicans with pumpkins to suggest the destruction of formerly enslaved people and their gardens at once, arguing that if laborers are unwilling to work, the British state "will sheer him out, by and by, like a lazy gourd overshadowing rich ground."[59] While the suggestion that "lazy" Black people should be "weeded" out of the colony was shockingly racist and inhumane, it also revealed that Carlyle understood the potential insurgency of Black geographies. As he predicted, the contest between British colonial land possession and Black farmers continued. For example, the Morant Bay Rebellion in 1865 was a revolt "sparked off by the unjust treatment of a small free farmer accused of 'squatting' on land he had already bought."[60]

When Carlyle argued that subsistence agriculture and local markets were fundamentally animal and not cultural relationships with the land, he strategically erased the traditional ecological knowledge cultivated and passed down through generations of enslaved people. Even J. S. Mill's well-known "enlightened" response to Carlyle's essay did not acknowledge the work or knowledge of the African diaspora. He explicitly decried slavery in the British West Indies, countering Carlyle's myth of the "white enchanter," when he asked, "how many hundred thousand African men laid their bones there, after having had their lives pressed out by slow or fierce torture?"[61] While Mill argued that the abolition of slavery was necessary humanitarian progress, like Sturge, he also appealed to the capitalist free market to reorganize the West Indian economy after abolition. Mill argued, "if labor is wanted, it is a very obvious idea to import laborers and if negroes are best suited to the climate, to import negroes."[62] Thus, Mill merely recommended another, somewhat more humanitarian version of unfree labor. Moreover, Lisa Lowe points out that Mill believed in the necessity of state despotism in the colonies "not as a counter to liberty, but the very condition out of which liberty arises and the condition to which it is integral and bound."[63] Sturge and Harvey had likewise turned to liberal economic principles when they suggested lifting the ban on Haitian provisions to decimate the internal markets in Jamaica. These antislavery "allies" may not have contributed to the discourse of biologized forms of racism. Still, they were aligned with overt racists like Carlyle in seeking to control whether and on what terms Black people would be allowed to occupy land and participate in food production.

African Jamaicans cultivated the provision grounds in relationship with land, animals, and plants, which became more-than-human alliances against the extractive and destructive ideology of the plantation. Carlyle's essay vividly illustrated that, after the end of slavery, a racialized hierarchy continued as the foundational structure of the commodity plantation system. During this post-abolition surge to enclose Black abolitionist commons, the lands of the Maroons were also targeted. The Maroon Lands Allotment Act of 1842, passed just four years after emancipation, did not, as the name suggests, allot more lands to the Maroons. Instead, the law was implemented, Kenneth M. Bilby argues, "by dividing the communally owned Maroon lands and parceling them out to individual owners."[64] The surge toward enclosing communal Black geographies in the West Indies supports Alex A. Moulton's argument that "the ecologies of white supremacy, therefore, were realized not simply through the expansion of plantations, but through the destruction of Black residential infrastructures, food systems, and botanical heritages."[65] Wedderburn had anticipated that emancipation would proceed via enclosure and dispossession, at which point the landholders would have the unstoppable power to "cause famine, or create abundance" (*Axe* 1.9). Carlyle's description of food-sovereign Black people with such outrageous dehumanization demonstrates that Wedderburn's political theory of Black freedom through the provision grounds continued to threaten the British empire even after the end of slavery.

Conclusion
Wedderburn's Last Word – Abolition with Pigs, Pumpkins, and Yams

Although Black geographies of the provision grounds are still underrepresented in scholarly readings of radicalism and resistance in the Romantic period, they figured heavily within the early nineteenth-century political "war of representation" about whether Black people in the West Indies would be willing to work for wages after emancipation. As Catherine Hall notes, by 1823, it was becoming clear that emancipation was on the horizon, so proslavery propagandists published pamphlets and articles promoting biologized racism, insisting that Black people were naturally lazy and must continue to be coerced into labor. Antislavery activists, on the other hand, argued that emancipation was a moral and economic "great experiment" through which the British government would "construct a successful free-labour economy with black labour."[1] A significant obstacle to this experiment was that many enslaved people in the West Indies had their own vision of liberation from slavery: They would keep and expand their provision grounds and continue to trade within already flourishing internal markets. As Michael Craton argues, "the freedom sought seems to have become that of an independent peasantry, a way of life about which the slaves had quite clear notions and of which, in most areas, they already had considerable experience."[2] Wedderburn's last known pamphlet, *An Address to the Right Honourable Lord Brougham and Vaux* (1831), contributed to the ongoing debate about the future of Black labor in the West Indies. Unlike other antislavery activists, Wedderburn, like the contemporary abolitionist Ruth Wilson Gilmore, insisted that abolition "starts from the homely premise that freedom is a place."[3]

Written when Wedderburn was sixty-nine years old and serving a second jail sentence, the pamphlet distinctively advocated for emancipation through Black abolitionist geographies. Ryan Hanley discovered the pamphlet, and he justifiably points out Wedderburn's bafflingly idyllic representation of slavery, describing it as "an unsettling, even disappointing departure from his earlier work."[4] For example, Wedderburn recorded a conversation with a fellow Black Londoner who claimed he "felt happier at home [in Jamaica], enjoying his house, land, and a pig in the stye, than to be here as a poor mechanic."[5] The suggestion that "wage slavery" in England was worse than chattel slavery in the West Indies alarmingly resonated with racist working-class and proslavery arguments.[6] Yet, Wedderburn was not making a proslavery argument but rather anticipated the limitations of liberal freedom, in which, as Lisa Lowe outlines, "abstract notions of individual rights neither removed social barriers nor included the material means necessary to fulfill the promised freedoms."[7] From this perspective, Wedderburn was not idealizing slavery but rather making sure that the door stayed open to the "material means" of liberation. If, as Malcom Ferdinand suggests, scholars "take the Caribbean world as the scene of environmental thinking," then further attention can be directed to the material things evoked by Wedderburn's anonymous Black Londoner – a house, land, and pig in Jamaica – which together conjure the Black abolitionist geographies explored throughout this book.[8] Wedderburn's vision of dwelling on the land with pigs, pumpkins, and yams outlined a nuanced, speculative abolitionist and decolonial future.

Wedderburn's pamphlet was written in anticipation of a top-down emancipation administered by British colonial power. Wedderburn argued: "Now, as slaves, they are landholders; but when free, they will be dispossessed of this necessary foundation of human happiness: three free men will be by necessity compelled to do the work of five slaves: the other two will be obligated to rob for subsistence."[9] For many formerly enslaved people, Diana Paton argues, freedom from slavery was experienced immediately as policing and restriction: "In this period former slaves, now known as apprentices, came into regular and direct conflict with representatives of the imperial state at precisely the moment when that state claimed to be responsible for their liberation."[10] Therefore, freedom from slavery was often experienced as a transition to policing by the state. Although idealizing the condition of slavery as "landholders," Wedderburn enunciated a prophetic concern about what Katherine McKittrick calls "plantation futures," racialized futures that continue to criminalize and incarcerate dispossessed Black people.[11] Wedderburn wrote the *Address* during his second prison sentence as a "free" man in England, so he was keenly aware that poverty and prison followed the plantation, even for Black people who had escaped to the London metropole.

As emancipation drew near, Wedderburn may not have been idealizing slavery so much as thinking pragmatically, like Matthew Lewis, who, when contemplating freeing the people he enslaved, argued that "they must have a provision made for them," meaning that he would need to "allot to them a certain portion of my land, giving them also their huts, provision grounds, and working implements." In other words, even an enslaver like Lewis understood that the foundation for a just liberation from slavery must include land reparations so that formerly enslaved people would be "secured against the possibility of future ill treatment."[12] Wedderburn's final pamphlet balked at immediate abolition because he anticipated Sylvia Wynter's insight: Abolition employed a "liberal *Free Trade* rhetoric" that "compensated the masters and set the slaves free in a world dominated by market relations, to fend naked for themselves."[13] Through this lens, it is clear that Wedderburn rejected emancipation as it was imagined by middle-class antislavery activists, such as Joseph Sturge, whose advocacy for the end of slavery was accompanied by plans to ensure that formerly enslaved people would become tractable, dependent wage laborers.[14] After all, as the subtitle of Wedderburn's last pamphlet stated, he desired "an equitable plan for the emancipation of slaves" that insisted on the rights of Black people in the West Indies to refuse continued land dispossession and to claim their intergenerational provision grounds, along with their communal diasporic cultures, as reparations for slavery.[15] For Wedderburn, liberation was cultivated through what Édouard Glissant calls "relation identity," which "does not think of land as a territory from which to project towards other territories but as a place where one gives-on-and-with rather than grasps."[16] Black abolitionist geographies differed from British antislavery's goals because they were established through ethical and material relationships with land and people in the West Indies. Furthermore, they transformed the affect of abolition from the individualized "grateful slave" begging for release, which produced a "binding obligation" to continued subordination, into a demand to allow independent Black communities to flourish without European colonial intervention.[17]

As an alternative to being free to participate in the global wage labor economy, Wedderburn suggested continuing to allow enslaved people to work their provision grounds to buy land and freedom simultaneously. He argued:

> Strange as this may appear to Europeans, they can do all this without any expense, as the country is ever green, and the Indian corn is produced in about three months, on the same land and at the same time with the yams, which take nine months to bring the latter to perfection. With the exception of a very few, all the produce which is consumed in the times, is the property of the slaves. On sugar estates, the slaves may also be allowed, without any injury to their masters, to grow cotton, coffee, ginger, and pimento.[18]

Wedderburn admitted that his abolitionist geographies would appear "strange" to Europeans. Indeed, they are still strange because they do not fit neatly with the European understanding of freedom through possessive individualism. Yet Wedderburn's version of a just apprenticeship was to work, not for wages, but for keeping hold of intergenerational and communal lands. His plan was remarkably similar to the one deployed by the newly freed workers on Lord Holland's estate, discussed in Chapter 6, when, after emancipation, they withheld labor from the plantation and instead "devoted much labour to improve their cottages, and increased the extent of their provision lands."[19] Black independence produced with and alongside an "ever green" Jamaica amounted to the same threatening "waste fertility" that enraged Thomas Carlyle eleven years later.

Wedderburn's last pamphlet reiterates this book's overarching argument: Wedderburn's Black geographies were "ever green." Scholarship about the Haitian revolution resonates with Wedderburn's view. Michel-Rolph Trouillot argues, for example: "In Haiti, the acquisition of family land and the laborer's right to the product of the labor on such land were the terms under which freedom was first formulated."[20] Jean Casimir also notes that Haitian provision grounds enunciated a politics of emancipation: "From the moment the captives took control of their gardens and provision grounds and demanded more free days in the wake of the general insurrection, the counter-plantation system and the institutions through which it was articulated were put into place."[21] Yet how many Romanticist readings of the Haitian Revolution interpret it through the lens of the American and French Revolutions instead of through Black abolitionist geographies? Can the grand narratives of the Romantic revolutionary age be opened to accommodate a revolution that starts in a garden with pigs and pumpkins? Wedderburn's insistence on land-based freedom sought to establish and formalize counter-plantations like the ones noted by Casimir and Trouillot. This book attempts to add Wedderburn's Black and Green Romanticism to the era's radical and revolutionary spirit.[22]

Wedderburn advocated for Black abolitionist geographies to his working-class London audiences during the turbulent post-Waterloo years. The impact of Black West Indian political thought on British radicalism has only begun to be explored, but in 1817, George Cruikshank put Wedderburn on the same table as Robert Owen.[23] Like Owen's utopian factory community New Lanark, Wedderburn's Black geographies cultivated alternative forms of freedom and community in opposition to unfettered capitalist enterprise.[24] Wedderburn's thought resonates with Stefano Harney and Fred Moten's idea of a Black "undercommons" functioning in the "surround" of the plantation system and settler cartographies. Like Harney and Moten, he believed "it is recourse to self-possession in the face of dispossession … that represents the real danger."[25] Wedderburn rejected British emancipation as self-possession and instead points toward liberation in African-Jamaican undercommons. This book began by examining Wedderburn's vision of an expansive, transatlantic undercommons: Black people in Jamaica reading Cobbett's *Political Register* while discussing the Haitian Revolution. His vision of William Cobbett's English cottage garden in dialogue with Black abolitionist geographies cultivated in the West Indies challenges scholarly perspectives on significant aspects of the Romantic period, including the abolition of slavery, the British Empire in the Caribbean, and nineteenth-century radical politics.[26] Although they do not fit easily within established Romanticist paradigms, my hope is that this book begins to grapple with how Wedderburn's Black geographies might redefine Romantic-era struggles for freedom.

Notes

Introduction

1 The italics are Peter Linebaugh's in *Stop, Thief! The Commons, Enclosures, and Resistance* (Oakland, CA: PM Press, 2014), 13. Linebaugh, along with Marcus Rediker, argued that Wedderburn "asserted a proletarian version of jubilee that had its modern origins in the written and practical work of Thomas Spence on the one hand, and in the anonymous oral tradition of African American slaves on the other." *The Many-Headed Hydra: Sailors, Slaves, Commoners, and the Hidden History of the Revolutionary Atlantic* (Boston: Beacon Press, 2000), 291.

2 Robert Wedderburn, *Axe Laid to the Root, or a Fatal Blow to Oppressors, Being an Address to the Planters and Negroes on the Island of Jamaica*, no. 1–6 (London: A Seale, 1817). Hereafter parenthetically cited as *Axe*, issue, and page number. Due to active repression by the British government, the only remaining copies of Wedderburn's 1817 publications are in the British Library, the Senate House Library at the University of London, and the British Home Office Records.

3 Nadine Hunt documents this information in "Remembering Africans in Diaspora: Robert Wedderburn's 'Freedom Narrative.'" In *Slavery in Africa and the Caribbean: A History of Enslavement and Identity since the 18th Century*, edited by Olatunji Ojo and Nadine Hunt (London: I. B. Tauris, 2012), 178.

4 Thomas Spence died in 1814, yet the Spencean Philanthopists continued under his name after his death. The leader, Thomas Evans, was arrested and held after the suspension of habeas corpus in 1817.

5 David Worrall notes that "Wedderburn's Hopkins Street Chapel was a device conjured up by a mature phase of wholly artisan London ultra-radicalism." See David Worrall, *Radical Culture: Discourse, Resistance and Surveillance, 1790–1820* (Detroit: Wayne State University Press, 1992), 131.

6 Iain McCalman, *Radical Underworld: Prophets, Revolutionaries, and Pornographers in London, 1795–1840* (Cambridge: Cambridge University Press, 1988), 113.

7 By referring to the Haitian revolution, Wedderburn further called on the politics of Black self-emancipation. Raphael Hoermann argues that in an era when white writers commonly used the "Haitian Gothic" to strike fear in their readers, Wedderburn uniquely "casts the Haitian Revolution as the primal scene of transatlantic emancipation." See Raphael Hoermann, "'A Very Hell of Horrors'? The Haitian Revolution and the Early Transatlantic Haitian Gothic," *Slavery & Abolition* 37.1 (2015): 197.

8 The spy report, located in the Home Office Records, was transcribed by Iain McCalman in *The Horrors of Slavery and Other Writings by Robert Wedderburn* (Princeton, NJ: Marcus Wiener, 1991), 116.

9 Iain McCalman, "Introduction," *The Horrors of Slavery and Other Writings by Robert Wedderburn* (Princeton, NJ: Marcus Wiener, 1991), 22.

10 *Trial of the Rev. Robt. Wedderburn*, edited by Erasmus Perkins (London, 1820), 19–20.

11 Ryan Hanley, *Beyond Slavery and Abolition: Black British Writing, c.1770–1830* (Cambridge: Cambridge University Press, 2018), 207.

12 McCalman, *Radical Underworld*, 161.

13 Hanley, *Beyond Slavery and Abolition*, 218.

14 Eric Pencek, "Intolerable Anonymity: Robert Wedderburn and the Discourse of Ultra-Radicalism," *Nineteenth-Century Contexts* 37.1 (2015): 72.

15 My methodological reasoning here follows Ryan Hanley, who proposes, "however, since he was the subject of numerous spy reports, examples of his spoken discourse have been preserved and can be compared against the texts published under his name. As a result, it is possible to gauge the extent to which any particular text was subject to editorial intervention, since Wedderburn's written style, like Cugoano's, tended to reflect his oratory rather than grammatical convention." Hanley *Beyond Slavery and Abolition*, 208.

16 Ian Haywood, *Romanticism and Caricature* (Cambridge: Cambridge University Press, 2013), 2. Haywood proposes that Cruikshank, James Gillray, and Thomas Rowlandson were the three major caricaturists of the Romantic period.

17 By mentioning his mother, Sue Thomas observes, Wedderburn is "calling on the authority of his birth to identify him to a knowing audience." See Thomas, *Telling West Indian Lives: Life Narrative and the Reform of Plantation Slavery Cultures 1804–1834* (New York: Palgrave Macmillan, 2014), 103. Joseph Albernaz argues that Wedderburn's "maternal devotion" spurred many of his political views. See Albernaz, "Abolition, Ultra-Radicalism, and the Generation of the General Strike," *Critical Times: Interventions in Global Critical Theory* 5.3 (2022): 550.

18 Morris documents that Owen opposed emancipation in the colonies even as he advocated for improving working conditions in England. See Morris, "The Problem of Slavery in the Age of Improvement: David Dale, Robert Owen and New Lanark Cotton." In *Cultures of Improvement in Scottish Romanticism, 1707–1840*, edited by Alex Benchimol and Gerard Lee McKeever, 111–31 (London: Routledge, 2018), 127.

19 Robert Wedderburn, *The Forlorn Hope, or a Call to the Supine, to Rouse from Indolence and Assert Public Rights* (London: C. Jennison, 1817), 1.16. This journal was co-published with fellow radical Charles Jennison. See McCalman, *Radical Underworld*, 126.

20 Growing up in Jamaica, Wedderburn would have seen the worst excesses of enclosure. Vandana Shiva explains that "the 'enclosure' of biodiversity and knowledge is the final step in a series of enclosures that began with the rise of colonialism. Land and forests were the first resources to be 'enclosed' and converted from commons into commodities." These ecological changes had immense consequences for indigenous and enslaved people, for whom "the transformation of common property rights into private property rights, implies the exclusion of the right to survival for large sections of society." See Shiva, *The Enclosure and Recovery of the Commons: Biodiversity, Indigenous Knowledge, and Intellectual Property Rights* (New Delhi: Research Foundation for Science, Technology, and Ecology, 1997), 9, 11.

21 Wedderburn's views on Wilberforce would have been influenced by his West Indian background. According to Hilary McD. Beckles, William Wilberforce was viewed by enslaved people in the West Indies as a "constrained ally" who could not advance the cause of abolition. This view "affirmed their political thinking that it was necessary to take up arms in order to secure abolition and emancipation." See Beckles, "The Wilberforce Song: How Enslaved Caribbean Blacks Heard British Abolitionists," *Parliamentary History* 26.4 (2007): 118.

22 McCalman, *Radical Underworld*, 127.

23 Bakary Diaby, "Feeling Black, Feeling Back: Fragility and Romanticism," *Symbiosis* 23.1 (2019): 134. Attending to Wedderburn's thought might also help Romanticists start to respond to Paul Youngquist's rhetorical question: "What about Romanticism remains uncongenial to black freedom?" in "Black Romanticism: A Manifesto," *Studies in Romanticism* 56.1 (2017): 4.

24 Manu Samriti Chander, "Romantic Diversitarianism: Problems and Promises," *European Romantic Review* 31.3 (2020): 296. Chander also challenges the field in an earlier book exploring the literary work of "Brown Romantics" who adapted "the Romantic cult of the author" toward their own anticolonial projects, which were "perplexed" and "fraught with contradictions." Although he is discussing poets in Britain's colonies, my project has similar investments. See Manu Samriti Chander, *Brown Romantics: Poetry and Nationalism in the Global Nineteenth Century* (Lewisburg: Bucknell University Press), 12.

25 When Wedderburn evoked the African-Jamaican provision grounds or Maroon settlements in his writing and speeches, these ideas were already circulating among his audiences in England. As David Scott argues, "the 'contact zones' uppermost in the English imagination were the slave plantations of the West Indian 'sugar islands.'" See Scott, *Conscripts of Modernity: The Tragedy of Colonial Enlightenment* (Durham: Duke University Press, 2004) 59–60. Catherine Hall also notes, "it was through the lens of the

Caribbean, and particularly Jamaica, that the English first debated 'the African,' slavery and antislavery, emancipation and the meanings of freedom; and Jamaica occupied a special place in the English imagination between the 1780s and 1860s on these grounds." See Hall, *Civilising Subjects: Metropole and Colony in the English Imagination, 1830–1867* (Chicago: University of Chicago Press, 2002), 11.

26 Malcolm Chase, *The People's Farm: English Radical Agrarianism, 1775–1840* (Oxford: Clarendon Press, 1988), 181. Chase further explains that the People's Farm "drew upon an attenuated but nevertheless lively concept of communal ownership. Opposition to enclosure, through this period always near the head of radical grievances, was one vehicle which kept concepts of communality very much alive."

27 McCalman, "Introduction," *Horrors of Slavery*, 18. McCalman also documents that *Axe Laid to the Root* was a significant publication because its "sale and distribution at Mulberry Tree meetings helped keep Spencean ideas alive against the rival claims of radicals such as Wooler, Burdett, Hunt, and Cobbett." See McCalman, *Radical Underworld*, 127.

28 Michael Scrivener, *Seditious Allegories: John Thelwall and Jacobin Writing* (University Park: Pennsylvania State University Press, 2001), 155.

29 Worrall, *Radical Culture*, 128. McCalman also stresses the influence of Wedderburn's oral performances at Hopkins Street Chapel: "Twice a week for six months Wedderburn's chapel attracted 200 or more of the most extreme and impoverished radicals in London." See McCalman, *Radical Underworld*, 127.

30 Alan Rice, *Radical Narratives of the Black Atlantic* (New York: Continuum, 2003), 11–12.

31 Helen Thomas, *Romanticism and Slave Narratives: Transatlantic Testimonies* (Cambridge: Cambridge University Press, 2000), 271.

32 Thomas, *Telling West Indian Lives*, 99.

33 Michael Morris, *Scotland and the Caribbean, c. 1740–1833: Atlantic Archipelagos* (New York: Routledge, 2015) 174.

34 Hanley, *Beyond Slavery and Abolition*, 203.

35 Raphael Hoermann, "'Fermentation Will Be Universal': Intersections of Race and Class in Robert Wedderburn's Black Atlantic Discourse of the Transatlantic Revolution." In *Britain's Black Past*, edited by Gretchen H. Gerzina, 295–314 (Liverpool: Liverpool University Press, 2020), 297.

36 Manisha Sinha, *The Slave's Cause: A History of Abolition* (New Haven, CT: Yale University Press, 2016), 198.

37 Elizabeth Bohls, *Slavery and the Politics of Place: Representing the Colonial Caribbean, 1770–1833* (Cambridge: Cambridge University Press, 2014), 8.

38 C. L. R. James, *The Black Jacobins: Toussaint L'Ouverture and the San Domingo Revolution* (New York: Vintage, 1989), 305.

39 Eric Williams, *Capitalism and Slavery*, 3rd Edition (Chapel Hill: University of North Carolina Press, 2014), 24. Sugar plantations in the West Indies also led to an extractive ecological relation that was more like mining than farming. Williams contends, "from the standpoint of the grower, the greatest defect of

slavery lies in the fact that it quickly exhausts the soil. Planters did not rotate crops but rather moved on when the soil was degraded." See Williams, *Capitalism and Slavery*, 7.

40 Sidney Mintz, *Sweetness and Power: The Place of Sugar in Modern History* (New York: Penguin Books, 1986) 47.

41 Robert Wedderburn, *An Address to Lord Brougham and Vaux* (London: John Ascham, 1831). I am using Ryan Hanley's transcription of the tract in "A Radical Change of Heart: Robert Wedderburn's Last Word on Slavery," *Slavery & Abolition* 37.2 (2016): 433–34.

42 Sylvia Wynter, "Novel and History, Plot and Plantation," *Savacou* 5 (1971): 99.

43 Ibid., 100.

44 Alex A. Moulton and Inge Salo, "Black Geographies and Black Ecologies as Insurgent Ecocriticism," *Environment and Society: Advances in Research* 13.1 (2022): 160. Wedderburn's Black geographies of the provision grounds also resonate with Stephanie M. H. Camp's theory of "rival geography," place-based "alternative ways of knowing and using plantation and southern space that conflicted with planters' ideals and demands." See Stephanie M. H. Camp, *Closer to Freedom: Enslaved Women and Everyday Resistance in the Plantation South* (Chapel Hill: University of North Carolina Press, 2004), 7. In his geographical account of plantation slavery in Jamaica, B. W. Higman argues, "there were two competing attitudes to space and its organization. One, derived from the European frame of mind, sought to create a rigidly ordered, geometric landscape. The other, with its roots in Africa, places a greater value on fluid, natural lines." See B. W. Higman, *Jamaica Surveyed: Plantation Maps and Plans of the Eighteenth and Nineteenth Centuries* (Kingston: Institute of Jamaica Publications Limited, 1988), 291.

45 Katherine McKittrick, "Plantation Futures," *Small Axe: A Caribbean Journal of Criticism* 17.3 (2013): 5.

46 Alex A. Moulton, "Towards the Arboreal Side-Effects of Marronage: Black Geographies and Ecologies of the Jamaican Forest," *Environment and Planning E: Nature and Space* 6.1 (2023): 8.

47 Rachel Goffe, "Reproducing the Plot: Making Life in the Shadow of Premature Death," *Antipode* 55.4 (2023): 1042.

48 Ruth Wilson Gilmore, *Abolitionist Geography: Essays towards Liberation* (London: Verso, 2022), 475. Gilmore further explains, "abolitionist critique concerns itself with the greatest and least detail of these arrangements of people and resources and land over time."

49 Judith Madera, *Black Atlas: Geography and Flow in Nineteenth-Century African American Literature* (Durham, NC: Duke University Press, 2015), 3. Although Madera is writing specifically about African American novels, her approach is useful for thinking about Wedderburn's cheap political periodicals and pamphlets.

50 John Barrell, *The Idea of Landscape and the Sense of Place 1730–1840: An Approach to the Poetry of John Clare* (Cambridge: Cambridge University Press, 1972), 84.

51 Bohls, *Slavery and the Politics of Place*, 82. Jill Casid notes similar aesthetics in what she refers to as the "colonial picturesque": "By translating terrain into an established compositional type, the picturesque, as a way of seeing, transformed land into landscape." See Jill Casid, *Sowing Empire: Landscape and Colonization* (Minneapolis: University of Minnesota Press, 2004), 45.

52 The first quotation is from Tim Barringer, "Picturesque Prospects and the Labor of the Enslaved." In *Art and Emancipation in Jamaica: Isaac Mendes Belisario and His Worlds*, edited by T. J. Barringer, Gillian Forrester, and Barbaro Martinez-Ruiz, 41–63 (New Haven, CT: Yale University Press, 2007), 41. The second quotation is from Bohls, *Slavery and the Politics of Place*, 19.

53 Evelyn O'Callaghan, "Caribbean Picturesque from William Beckford to Contemporary Tourism." In *Caribbean Literature in Transition, 1800–1920*, edited by Evelyn O'Callaghan and Tim Watson, 67–84 (Cambridge: Cambridge University Press, 2021), 67.

54 Nathan K. Hensley, "Landscape with Storm (Unfinished)," *Victorian Review* 47.1(2021): 35–6.

55 James Hakewill, *A Picturesque Tour of the Island of Jamaica* (London: Hurst and Robinson, 1825).

56 Orlando Patterson, *The Sociology of Slavery: An Analysis of the Origins, Development and Structure of Negro Slave Society in Jamaica* (London: Fairleigh Dickenson University Press, 1969), 7.

57 Elizabeth DeLoughrey, "Yams, Roots, and Rot: Allegories of the Provision Grounds," *Small Axe* 15.1 (2011): 63.

58 B. W. Higman notes that in eighteenth- and nineteenth-century Jamaica, the word "mountain" often meant "provision ground" because most provision grounds were allocated to steep slopes unsuitable for growing sugar. See Higman, *Jamaica Surveyed*, 265.

59 Barrell, *The Idea of Landscape and the Sense of Place*, 84.

60 Hakewill, *A Picturesque Tour*, 6.

61 Judith Ann Carney and Richard Nicholas Rosomoff, *In the Shadow of Slavery: Africa's Botanical Legacy in the Atlantic World* (Berkeley: University of California Press, 2011), 123.

62 Carlyle's post-emancipation rage against pumpkins was remarkably similar to the racist depictions of freed Blacks farming and eating watermelon in the United States. For information about the history of watermelon farming in the American South, see William R. Black's "How Watermelons Became Black: Emancipation and the Origins of a Racist Trope," *Journal of the Civil War Era* 8.1 (2018): 64–86.

63 Italics are in the original text. Malcom Ferdinand, *Decolonial Ecology: Thinking from the Caribbean World.* Translated by Anthony Paul Smith (Cambridge: Polity, 2022), 121.

64 Scott, *Conscripts of Modernity*, 62, 106.

65 Italics are in the original text. Ferdinand, *Decolonial Ecology*, 148.

66 Jenny Sharpe, *Ghosts of Slavery: A Literary Archeology of Black Women's Lives* (Minneapolis: University of Minnesota Press, 2003), xv.

67 Saidiya Hartman, *Scenes of Subjection: Terror, Slavery, and Self-Making in Nineteenth-Century America* (Oxford: Oxford University Press, 1997), 55. The book also aspires to draw on the work of Marisa J. Fuentes, who encourages "employing a methodology that purposely subverts the overdetermining power of colonial discourses." See Marisa J. Fuentes, *Dispossessed Lives: Enslaved Women, Violence, and the Archive* (Philadelphia: University of Pennsylvania Press, 2018), 4.

68 The depiction of William Wilberforce and other white abolitionists as heroic actors feeds into an overall sense of white supremacy and British superiority. By evoking Wilberforce, Catherine Hall argues, "there was a selective forgetting; only parts of the past were to be remembered. The triumph of abolition would screen the horrors and violence of the Middle Passage and the plantation." See Hall, "Rewriting the Past: Imperial Histories of the Antislavery Nation." In *Victorian Jamaica*, edited by Tim Barringer and Wayne Modest, 263–78 (Durham, NC: Duke University Press, 2018), 266.

69 Vincent Brown, *Tacky's Revolt: The Story of an Atlantic Slave War* (Cambridge: Harvard University Press, 2020), 242.

Chapter 1

1 The unstamped cheap weekly pamphlet was "built around a lead 'editorial essay,' often signed and invested with the personal authority of the editor." These weekly papers "took advantage of a legal loophole that exempted periodicals containing nothing more than commentary on the news from taxes meant to keep political information out of the hands of the poor." See Kevin Gilmartin, *Print Politics: The Press and Radical Opposition in Early Nineteenth-Century England* (Cambridge: Cambridge University Press, 1997), 77–8.

2 Helen Thomas, *Romanticism and Slave Narratives: Transatlantic Testimonies* (Cambridge: Cambridge University Press, 2000), 261. Italics in the original.

3 Matthew 3:10; Thomas Paine, *The Paine Reader*, edited by Michael Foot and Isaac Kramnick (New York: Penguin Books, 1987), 213; this proverb has many forms. This one is Bob Marley's formulation in "Small Axe" on *Burnin'* (1973).

4 Marcus Rediker and Peter Linebaugh, *The Many-Headed Hydra: Sailors, Slaves, Commoners, and the Hidden History of the Revolutionary Atlantic* (Boston: Beacon, 2000), 289. They also argue that Wedderburn's transatlantic experiences "disinclined him to think of white, male, propertied citizenship as a means to a revolutionary end" (324).

5 Sylvia Wynter, "Novel and History, Plot and Plantation," *Savacou* 5 (1971): 99.

6 John H. Parry argues Jamaica was not merely the location of sugar monoculture: "Their economic history, in particular, should be the story of yams, cassava, and salt fish, no less than of sugar and tobacco." See John H. Parry, "Plantation and Provision Ground: An Historical Sketch of the Introduction of Food Crops into Jamaica," *Revista de Historia de América* 39 (June 1955): 1.

7 Katherine McKittrick, "Plantation Futures," *Small Axe: A Caribbean Journal of Criticism* 17.3 (2013): 2, 11.

8 According to Malcolm Chase, Spence advocated for a "people's farm" because "continued access to the countryside was hence an important element in workers' attempts to retain control over their environment and general quality of life." See Malcolm Chase, *The People's Farm: English Radical Agrarianism, 1775–1840* (Oxford: Clarendon Press, 1988), 14.

9 Thomas Spence, *The Restorer of Society to Its Natural State* (London: J. Smith, 1801), 11.

10 Thomas Spence, *The Giant-Killer; Or Anti-Landlord* (London, 1814), 14. Both Wedderburn and Spence see land and food as central to freedom. Michael Scrivener argues that Spence's theories are deeply connected to food: "Spence sees his own land ownership plan as carrying the 'moral economy' of the food riots to its logical conclusion." See Michael Scrivener, *Seditious Allegories: John Thelwall and Jacobin Writing* (University Park: Pennsylvania State University Press, 2001), 142.

11 Iain McCalman, "Introduction," in *The Horrors of Slavery and Other Writings* (Princeton, NJ: Marcus Wiener, 1991), 25. Although this quotation is dismissive of Wedderburn's political theory, in another publication, McCalman argues, "most of this was adapted from standard Spencean ultra-radical theory, but Wedderburn also included some novel suggestions derived from his experience as a slave offspring, sailor, and underworld artisan. His vision of reform was sometimes more akin to the 'proto-peasant' aspirations of Jamaican slaves than to Spence's rental-based plan." See Iain McCalman, "Anti-slavery and Ultra-Radicalism in Early Nineteenth-Century England: The Case of Robert Wedderburn," *Slavery & Abolition* 7.2 (1986): 108.

12 Ryan Hanley, *Beyond Slavery and Abolition: Black British Writing, c.1770–1830* (Cambridge: Cambridge University Press, 2018), 209. David Worrall likewise concludes that "Wedderburn's views must have been expressed with Spence's ideas in mind." See David Worrall, *Radical Culture: Discourse, Resistance and Surveillance, 1790–1820* (Detroit: Wayne State University Press, 1992), 130.

13 Raphael Hoermann, "'Fermentation Will Be Universal': Intersections of Race and Class in Robert Wedderburn's Black Atlantic Discourse of the Transatlantic Revolution," in Gretchen H. Gerzina, ed., *Britain's Black Past* (Liverpool: Liverpool University Press, 2020), 308. Along these lines, Michael Morris argues that Wedderburn used the "pugilistic vernacular discourse drawn from his youth in Jamaica" to address the radical movement in Britain. See Michael Morris, *Scotland and the Caribbean, c.1740–1833: Atlantic Archipelagos* (New York: Routledge, 2015), 178. Alan Rice is also attentive to the complex combination of Caribbean and British perspectives in Wedderburn's work. He argues that Wedderburn's writing was actively "combining a vernacular Caribbean perspective with a demotic metropolitan dynamic to create a truly unique political discourse." See Alan Rice, *Radical Narratives of the Black Atlantic* (London: Continuum, 2003), 12.

14 For example, Spence argues, "have not the foxes holes, and the birds of the air nests, and shall the children of men have not where to lay their heads?" See Thomas Spence, *The Rights of Infants* (London, 1797), 5.

15 Thomas Evans, *Christian Policy, the Salvation of the Empire* (London: Seale and Bates, 1816), 25. Unfortunately, Evans problematically equated English laborers with enslaved people in the Caribbean. He argues in the same publication: "I have lived long enough to witness the effect of enclosure after enclosure, and tax after tax; expelling the cottager from gleaning the open fields, from his right of the common, from his cottage, his hovel, once his own; robbing him of his little store, his pig, his fowls, his fuel; thereby reducing him to a pauper, a slave. A slave! Aye, more a slave than the poor African in the plantations" (17). Perhaps that is why Wedderburn and Evans had a falling out soon after. A broadside advertising Wedderburn's Hopkins Street Chapel, "A Few Lines for a Double-Faced Politician," referred to Evans as an "apostate son." Iain McCalman identifies Evans as the apostate in *Radical Underworld*, 131.

16 J. M. Neeson, *Commoners: Common Right, Enclosure, and Social Change in England, 1700–1820* (Cambridge: Cambridge University Press, 1993), 3, 15.

17 Although it is possible that *Axe Laid to the Root* could have made its way to the West Indies via informal networks, Hanley argues, "in fact, no evidence has emerged to suggest that a single copy of the *Axe* was ever read in Jamaica." See Hanley, *Beyond Slavery and Abolition*, 211. McCalman surmises that *Axe Laid to the Root* was locally distributed through "sale and distribution at Mulberry Tree meetings [in London]." See McCalman, *Radical Underworld*, 127.

18 Marcus Wood argues, "the 'wage slavery' of the industrial workers could not be called up without suggesting some form of comparative relations with the 'chattel slavery' of the African-American, or Caribbean slave." See Marcus Wood, *Slavery, Empathy, and Pornography* (Oxford: Oxford University Press, 2002), 355.

19 David Worrall, *Radical Culture: Discourse, Resistance and Surveillance, 1790–1820* (Detroit: Wayne State University Press, 1992), 141. Worrall also insightfullyargues, "Wedderburn's perspective as a 'foreigner' gave him a radical purchase on English politics at the beginning of the nineteenth century. For him, England must have seemed a remarkable place, breathtakingly chained beside liberty" (140).

20 Sydney Mintz argues that "because so much of the industrial processing of the cane was also carried out on the plantations, it makes good sense to view the plantations as a synthesis of field and factory." See Sidney Mintz, *Sweetness and Power: The Place of Sugar in Modern History* (New York: Penguin, 1986), 56, 47.

21 Karl Marx, *Capital, Vol. 3* in *The Marx-Engles Reader*, edited by Robert C. Tucker, 439–43 (New York: W. W. Norton, 1978), 433. Food-based enclosures took place in England and the Caribbean during the Romantic period. Michael Niblett argues, "enclosure in England and the maturation of the plantation complex in the Caribbean represent pivotal moments in the

development of the capitalist world-food-system." See Michael Niblett, "'The Landscape Heaved with Unspeakable Terror': The Weird Presence of the World-Food-System in the Cultural Imaginaries of England and the Caribbean." In *Literary and Cultural Production, World-Ecology, and the Global Food System*, edited by Chris Campbell, Michael Niblett, and Kerstin Oloff, 65–92 (Basingstoke: Palgrave Macmillan, 2021), 66.

22 Tim Barringer, "Land, Labor, Landscape: Views of the Plantation in Victorian Jamaica." In *Victorian Jamaica*, edited by Tim Barringer and Wayne Modest, 263–78 (Durham, NC: Duke University Press, 2018), 284.

23 B. W. Higman, *Jamaica Surveyed: Plantation Maps and Plans of the Eighteenth and Nineteenth Centuries* (Kingston: Institute of Jamaica Publications Limited, 1988), 291.

24 Sidney Mintz, *Tasting Food, Tasting Freedom: Excursions into Eating, Culture, and the Past* (Boston: Beacon, 1997), 41.

25 William Cobbett, "To the Radicals" in *Cobbett's Weekly Register*, 39.4 (London: C. Clement, 1821), 274.

26 Wedderburn's view of the potato differs considerably from someone like William Cobbett, who argued against eating potatoes in his *Cottage Economy* (1828). By citing the potato, Wedderburn evoked the "potato debate," in which English advocates "wanted to keep wages down by shifting the English poor off a diet of wheat bread and on to one of potatoes." See Catherine Gallagher and Stephen Greenblatt, "The Potato in the Materialist Imagination." In *Practicing New Historicism*, 110–35 (Chicago: University of Chicago Press, 2000), 119.

27 Mary Louise Pratt, *Imperial Eyes: Travel Writing and Transculturation* (London: Routledge, 1992), 35.

28 Wedderburn advised enslaved people to appoint a day when they all sleep an hour later than usual; "the universality of your sleeping and non-resistance, will strike terror to your oppressors. Go to your labour peaceably after the hour is expired; and repeat it once a year, till you obtain your liberty" (*Axe* 1.4).

29 Catherine Gallagher, *The Body Economic: Life, Death, and Sensation in Political Economy and the Victorian Novel* (Princeton, NJ: Princeton University Press, 2006), 45.

30 Peter Linebaugh, *Stop, Thief! The Commons, Enclosures, and Resistance* (Oakland, CA: PM Press, 2014), 13. Commons and commoning also challenge the idea that "work" is about social and environmental dominance and the accumulation of wealth. Peter Linebaugh further argues that "commoning is embedded in a labor process; it inheres in a particular praxis of field, upland, forest, marsh, coast. Common rights are entered into by labor." See Peter Linebaugh, *The Magna Carta Manifesto: Liberties and Commons for All* (Berkeley: University of California Press, 2008), 45.

31 Wedderburn refers directly to this biblical millennium in the next issue of *Axe Laid to the Root*: "Then shall worthless kings who thirst for human blood to support their tottering thrones, turn their swords and spears into ploughshares and pruning-hooks" (2.17).

32 Morris, *Scotland and the Caribbean*, 183. Wedderburn's references to the Haitian revolution have been outlined by Raphael Hoermann, who argues Wedderburn's writing employed "a forceful Gothic revolutionary rhetoric." See Raphael Hoermann, "'A Very Hell of Horrors?' The Haitian Revolution and the Early Transatlantic Haitian Gothic," *Slavery & Abolition* 37.1 (2015): 197.

33 Alex A. Moulton, "Towards the Arboreal Side-Effects of Marronage: Black Geographies and Ecologies of the Jamaican Forest," *Environment and Planning E: Nature and Space* 6.1 (2023): 11. Mario Nisbett would agree that Maroon communities created "autonomous zones where liberated men and women from slaveholding regimes ... implemented their vision of a self-governing community." See Mario Nisbett, *The Workings of Diaspora: Jamaican Maroons and the Claims to Sovereignty* (Lanham, MD: Lexington Books, 2021), 21.

34 Rachel B. Herrmann, *No Useless Mouth: Waging War and Fighting Hunger in the American Revolution* (Ithaca, NY: Cornell University Press, 2019), 8.

35 Ruma Chopra points out that in the Second Maroon War, "the proximity of snarling dogs accomplished what military forces had failed to do in nearly four months." See Ruma Chopra, *Almost Home: Maroons between Slavery and Freedom in Jamaica, Nova Scotia, and Sierra Leone* (New Haven, CT: Yale University Press, 2018), 47.

36 Gallagher and Greenblatt, "The Potato in the Materialist Imagination," 111.

37 "History of the Revolted Negroes in Jamaica." Long Papers, Add. Manuscripts 12431, ca. 1733–39, folio 71, British Library. This chapter retains the spelling and punctuation of the original manuscript.

38 Ajmal Waqif, "Cato Street and the Spencean Politics of Transnational Insurrection," in Jason McElligott and Martin Conboy, eds., *The Cato Street Conspiracy: Plotting, Counter-Intelligence and the Revolutionary Tradition in Britain and Ireland* (Manchester: Manchester University Press, 2019), 113. Angelita Reyes notes another aspect of the Maroons' guerilla warfare: "Jamaica was called the 'land of look-behind' because of the Maroons. This fairyland name is deceptive because its origin was in slavery and danger. British soldiers feared riding into the unknown, precarious, rocky terrain looking for fugitive slaves and Maroons." See Angelita Reyes, *Mothering across Cultures: Postcolonial Representations* (Minneapolis: University of Minnesota Press, 2001), 80.

39 Scholars have noted that it is likely that Miss Campbell is a fictional character with whom Wedderburn staged a dramatic dialogue. See Hanley, *Beyond Slavery and Abolition*, 211. This staged dialogue can be understood as an example of Gilmartin's thesis: "Radical discourse presented itself as having been shaped and misshaped from without, not organically structured from within." See Gilmartin, *Print Politics*, 89.

40 Shelby Johnson, "'The Fate of St. Domingo Awaits You': Robert Wedderburn's Unfinished Revolution," *The Eighteenth Century*, 61.3 (2020): 383. Helen Thomas similarly argues for the significance Miss Campbell's ethnicity, through which Wedderburn "endorsed the paradigm of the mullato as a radical agent of socioeconomic transformation premised upon apocalyptic stature." See Thomas, *Romanticism and Slave Narratives*, 262.

41 Frances R. Botkin, *Thieving Three-Fingered Jack: Transatlantic Tales of a Jamaican Outlaw, 1780–2015* (New Brunswick: Rutgers University Press, 2017), 13.

42 Kamau Brathwaite describes Nanny Town as "socio-politically ordered settlement with an agricultural focus." See Brathwaite, *Wars of Respect: Nanny and Sam Sharpe* (Kingston: API, 1977), 12. Michael Craton emphasizes the significance of the British concession of a land grant of 500 acres to Nanny. See Craton, *Testing the Chains: Resistance to Slavery in the British West Indies* (Ithaca, NY: Cornell University Press, 2009), 219.

43 Miles Ogborn, *The Freedom of Speech: Talk and Slavery in the Anglo-Caribbean World* (Chicago: University of Chicago Press, 2019), 229. Julius S. Scott also notes the role "in spreading rumours, reporting news, and transmitting political currents as antislavery movements and finally a republican revolution gathered momentum in Europe." See Scott, *The Common Wind: Afro-American Currents in the Age of the Haitian Revolution* (London: Verso, 2018), 75.

44 J. T. Roane, "Plotting the Black Commons," *Souls: A Critical Journal of Black Politics, Culture, and Society* 20.3 (2018): 243.

45 Édouard Glissant, *Poetics of Relation*. Translated by Betsy Wing (Ann Arbor: University of Michigan Press, 2010), 147. Wedderburn's position here also bears resemblance to Elizabeth Maddock Dillon's work. She argues, "both the theft of land enacted by settler colonialism and the strategies of racialization refined by the plantation machine are key components of a system aimed at large-scale disentanglement or uncommoning." See Dillon, "The Plantationocene and the Performative Commons: A Brief History of Uncommoning," *The Minnesota Review* 93 (2019): 85.

46 *The Forlorn Hope, or a Call to the Supine, to Rouse from Indolence and Assert Public Rights* (London: C. Jenneson, 1817), 1.16.

47 See Iain McCalman, *Radical Underworld: Prophets, Revolutionaries, and Pornographers in London, 1795–1840* (Cambridge: Cambridge University Press, 1988), 67 and J. Anne Hone, *For the Cause of Truth: Radicalism in London, 1796–1821* (Oxford: Clarendon Press, 1982), 96.

48 Eric Pencek, "Intolerable Anonymity: Robert Wedderburn and the Discourse of Ultra-Radicalism," *Nineteenth-Century Contexts* 37.1 (2015): 72, 74.

49 Hanley, *Beyond Slavery and Abolition*, 212; Sonya Posmentier, *Cultivation and Catastrophe: The Lyric Ecology of Modern Black Literature* (Baltimore: Johns Hopkins University Press, 2017), 45, 69.

50 Ibid., 69. Posmentier uses the term "provisioning" to describe Claude McKay's lyric poetry and magazines in the early twentieth century.

51 Italics in original. Jon Klancher, *The Making of English Reading Audiences, 1790–1832* (Madison: University of Wisconsin Press, 1987), 100. Klancher argues further that cheap working-class periodicals attempted to speak to and directly engage their audiences: "In stark contrast to the mass journals, where no one speaks but everyone is spoken for, the radical text is all talk, a stormy representation of one social discourse by another."

52 William Cobbett, "To the Journeymen and Labourers of England, Wales, Scotland and Ireland," *Political Register* 31.18 (November 2, 1816). Richard D. Altick describes Cobbett's cheap *Register* as utterly transformative: "Farm laborers, mill hands, miners, handloom weavers, soldiers – all who had cause to be disaffected – were reading now or listening to someone else read. They had discovered that the printed word was capable of uses far different from those with which they had come to associate it. It was not merely a soporific dose anxiously administered by clergymen and ladies: it was a means through which they found leadership and inspiration." See Altick, *The English Common Reader: A Social History of the Mass Reading Public 1800–1900* (Chicago: University of Chicago Press, 1957), 32.

53 Marcus Wood states, "Cobbett's dehumanising of blacks constitutes a formula by which black people can be evicted from the possibility of competing with the European labouring classes for intellectual recognition, or at a more basic level, emotional empathy." See Wood, "William Cobbett, John Thelwall, Radicalism, Racism and Slavery: A Study in Burkean Parodics," *Romanticism on the Net* 15 (1999): 14.

54 James Chandler, *England in 1819: The Politics of Literary Culture and the Case of Romantic Historicism* (Chicago: University of Chicago Press, 1998), 459.

55 E. P. Thompson, *The Making of the English Working Class* (New York: Vintage, 1966), 601. Ian Haywood also documents, "the turning point in the development of 'cheap' political reading in this period is undoubtedly Cobbett's decision in November 1816 to issue his *Weekly Political Register* in a reduced, two-penny format." See Haywood, *The Revolution in Popular Literature: Print, Politics, and the People, 1790–1860* (Cambridge: Cambridge University Press, 2004), 86.

56 Cobbett was not the only radical writer lauded in *Axe Laid to the Root*. In an open letter to the archbishop of Canterbury, the attorney general, and ministerial judges, Wedderburn prophetically declared, "let the stormy breath of Hone pass over their defenceless heads" (*Axe* 6.83). William Hone's *Reformist Register* then was also noted as a publication that fought British governmental abuses.

57 Gilmartin uses the term "rhetorical bricolage" to describe Cobbett's "counter-systemic" views in the *Political Register* and *Rural Rides*. See Gilmartin, *Print Politics*, 2. The second quotation is from Jon Mee, who uses bricolage to describe William Blake's work. Wedderburn similarly brings together various parts of British culture to recombine them into something new. See Jon Mee, *Dangerous Enthusiasm: William Blake and Culture of Radicalism in the 1790s* (Oxford: Clarendon Press, 1992), 3.

58 *The Politics of Language, 1791–1819* (Oxford: Clarendon Press, 1986), 1. Smith also argues, "Cobbett's grammar was written to teach labourers how to write for the specific purpose of their political defence" (246).

59 Saree Makdisi, *Making England Western: Occidentalism, Race, and Imperial Culture* (Chicago: University of Chicago Press, 2013), 22.

60 Trees held additional, sacred roles in African-Jamaican culture. Robert Connell notes, the "arboreal texture of freedom" that can be discerned in

the "trees planted to symbolize kin group continuity among the Jamaican peasantry." See Connell, "Maroon Ecology: Land, Sovereignty, and Environmental Justice," *The Journal of Latin American and Caribbean Anthropology* 25.2 (2020): 222.

61 Thompson, *The Making of the English Working Class*, 9.

62 Lee Jackson, *Dirty Old London: The Victorian Fight against Filth* (New Haven, CT: Yale University Press, 2014), 221.

63 Makdisi argues that Occidentalism was a process in which "both radicals and evangelicals sought to civilize and enlighten – en-whiten – the people of England." He further notes that controlling cheap publications was part of that effort: "I want at least to flag the significance of the potential affiliation of the ballad with the racial politics of the multitude." See Makdisi, *Making England Western, 28, 100.*

64 Worrall, *Radical Culture*, 86.

65 Elizabeth Bohls, *Romantic Literature and Postcolonial Studies* (Edinburgh: Edinburgh University Press, 2013), 56, 58.

66 Ian Haywood, *Romanticism and Caricature* (Cambridge: Cambridge University Press, 2013), 100.

67 Marcus Wood, *Blind Memory: Visual Representations of Slavery in England and America, 1780–1865* (New York: Routledge, 2000), 166.

68 Jenna M. Gibbs, *Performing the Temple of Liberty: Slavery, Theater, and Popular Culture in London and Philadelphia, 1760–1850* (Baltimore: Johns Hopkins University Press, 2014), 124.

69 Johnson, "The Fate of St. Domingo Awaits You," 380. Hoermann also acknowledges Wedderburn's place in the print, and posits that the caricature is "full of racist bile, [and] constitutes a phantasmagoric orgy of cross-racial debauchery and anarchy with a voiceless Wedderburn at its centre." See Hoermann, "Fermentation Will Be Universal," 309.

70 Johnson, "The Fate of St. Domingo Awaits You," 380.

71 Paul Gilroy, *The Black Atlantic: Modernity and Double-Consciousness* (Cambridge, MA: Harvard University Press, 1993), 16.

Chapter 2

1 Manu Samriti Chander and Patricia A. Matthew, "Abolitionist Interruptions: Romanticism, Slavery, and Genre," *European Romantic Review* 29.4 (2018): 431.

2 For example, Ryan Hanley argues, "his longest single work, *The Horrors of Slavery*, for example, was dedicated to the archly anti-radical William Wilberforce, and in terms of radical sentiment contained only a passing mention of Wedderburn's paternal grandfather's role in the Jacobite rising of 1745." See Hanley, "A Radical Change of Heart: Robert Wedderburn's Last Word on Slavery," *Slavery & Abolition* 37.2 (2016): 426. Similarly, Michael Morris suggests that *Horrors* is "consistent with Wilberforce's

abolitionism"; thus, "this text strikes a moral rather than political tone." See Morris, *Scotland and the Caribbean, c.1740–1833: Atlantic Archipelagos* (New York: Routledge, 2015), 185. The exception to this assessment would be Raphael Hoermann's argument: "Symptomatic of Wedderburn's refusal to be neatly pigeon-holed, this self-published abolitionist pamphlet breaks the mould of abolitionist literature from the onset." See Hoermann, "'Fermentation Will Be Universal': Intersections of Race and Class in Robert Wedderburn's Black Atlantic Discourse of the Transatlantic Revolution." In *Britain's Black Past*, edited by Gretchen H. Gerzina (Liverpool: Liverpool University Press, 2020), 298. Hoermann asserts that *Horrors* breaks with abolitionist literature through its anti-capitalist, working-class orientation. This chapter builds on this argument to assert that *Horrors* departed from an antislavery discourse by drawing connections between plantations and prison and championing enslaved Black women as liberators.

3 Anthony Bogues, *Black Heretics, Black Prophets: Radical Political Intellectuals* (New York: Routledge, 2003), 27.

4 Catherine Hall, *Civilising Subjects: Metropole and Colony in the English Imagination, 1830–1867* (Chicago: University of Chicago Press, 2002), 77.

5 Iain McCalman makes the distinction between lower-class "unrespectable radicals" and middle-class respectable radicals who were part of the British establishment. See McCalman, *Radical Underworld: Prophets, Revolutionaries, and Pornographers in London, 1795–1840* (Cambridge: Cambridge University Press, 1988), 8.

6 Yuri Cowan, "Sporting Periodicals." In *The Routledge Handbook to Nineteenth-Century British Periodicals and Newspapers*, edited by Andrew King, Alexis Easley, and John Morton, 307–17 (London: Routledge, 2016), 311.

7 Leah Richards and Maurice Milne, "Bell's Life in London." In *Dictionary of Nineteenth-Century Journalism in Great Britain and Ireland*, edited by Laurel Brake and Marysa Demoor (London: British Library, 2009) 46–7. Richards and Milne further argue, "typically perceived as a publication with a lower-class audience due to its low cost and its subject matter, *Bell's* was also read by members of the middle and upper classes, and was highly respected as an institution, even serving as a stakeholder for sporting bets and prizefights." Raymond Williams also cites *Bell's Life* as a significant working-class publication. See Williams, "Radical and/or Respectable." In *The Press We Deserve*, edited by Richard Boston, 14–26 (London: Routledge & Kegan Paul, 1970), 20.

8 Ryan Hanley, "Slavery and the Birth of the Working-Class Racism in England, 1814–1833," *Transactions of the Royal Historical Society* 26 (2016): 109.

9 *Bell's Life in London and Sporting Chronicle* 3.103 (February 15, 1824): 51. The italics and typography are reproduced from the original. The editor of *Bell's Life* at this time was probably W. R. Macdonald. The paper was in the process of being bought by William Clement, former publisher of Cobbett's

Register. For details about these transactions, see Stanley Morison, *The English Newspaper, 1622–1932: An Account of the Physical Development of Journals Printed in London* (Cambridge: Cambridge University Press, 2009), 246.

10 Orlando Patterson, *Slavery and Social Death: A Comparative Study* (Cambridge: Harvard University Press, 1982), 7.

11 *Bell's Life in London* 3.103, 52.

12 *Bell's Life in London* 3.105 (February 29, 1824): 68. Sue Thomas points out that the *Bell's Life* editor neglected to mention Wedderburn's credentials as an influential, published radical. He also does not mention that Wedderburn had been mocked in a March 2, 1823, *Bell's Life* report. See Thomas, *Telling West Indian Lives: Life Narrative and the Reform of Plantation Slavery Cultures 1804–1834* (New York: Palgrave Macmillan, 2014), 108.

13 *Bell's Life in London* 3.105, 68. This chapter has reproduced the original typography.

14 Hortense Spillers, *Black, White, and in Color: Essays on American Literature and Culture* (Chicago: University of Chicago Press, 2003), 221.

15 *Bell's Life in London* 3.105, 68.

16 Marcy J. Dinius makes this observation about the typography in David Walker's *Appeal to the Coloured Citizens of the World.* See Dinius, "'Look!! Look!!! At This!!!!': The Radical Typography of David Walker's 'Appeal,'" *PMLA: Publications of the Modern Language Association of America* 126.1 (2011): 56.

17 Mary Louise Pratt, *Imperial Eyes: Travel Writing and Transculturation* (London: Routledge, 1992), 97.

18 *Bell's Life in London* 3.105, 69.

19 Stefan M. Wheelock, *Barbaric Culture and Black Critique: Black Antislavery Writers, Religion, and the Slaveholding Atlantic* (Charlottesville: University of Virginia Press, 2016), 7.

20 *Bell's Life in London and Sporting Chronicle* 3.108 (March 21, 1824): 83.

21 George Boulukos, *The Grateful Slave: The Emergence of Race in Eighteenth-Century British and American Culture* (Cambridge: Cambridge University Press, 2008), 15. Moreover, Boulukos notes, "the sentimental aspect of the grateful slave trope engages an established tradition ... of using emotional response to oppression and torture as a way of distancing oneself from responsibility for such aspects of the colonial enterprise" (14). Wedderburn refused to use the trope because he wanted his audience to feel their complicity in Britain's system of plantation slavery.

22 Brycchan Carey, "Abolishing Cruelty: The Concurrent Growth of Antislavery and Animal Welfare Sentiment in British and Colonial Literature," *Journal for Eighteenth-Century Studies* 43.2 (2020): 217. Paul Youngquist likewise points out that abolitionism's "relentless attention to the plight of enslaved Africans in the colonies helped collapse the diffuse rhetoric of race into a language of black and white that set discursive terms for the emergence some years later of biologized racism." The end result is that "abolition advances racism hand in hand with freedom, or rather freedom as *a form of*

racism." See Youngquist, "Introduction." In *Race, Romanticism, and the Atlantic*, edited by Paul Youngquist, 1–22 (Farnham: Ashgate, 2013), 11.

23 Later in his life, Colvile became governor of the Hudson's Bay Company. Biographical information on Andrew Colvile can be found in "Andrew Colvile," *Hudson's Bay Company Archives*, Archives of Manitoba, 2002: www.gov.mb.ca/chc/archives/_docs/hbca/biographical/c/colvile_andrew.pdf; and the *Legacies of British Slave-Ownership database* at University College, London: www.ucl.ac.uk/lbs/person/view/24188.

24 *Trial of the Rev. Robt. Wedderburn*, edited by Erasmus Perkins (London, 1820), 7. Perkins' patronage and his drafting of Wedderburn's defense is discussed in the Introduction.

25 Morris, *Scotland and the Caribbean*, 170. For more information about the precarious futures of mixed-race children in Britain, see Daniel Livesay, *Children of Uncertain Fortune: Mixed-Race Jamaicans in Britain and the Atlantic Family, 1733–1833* (Chapel Hill: University of North Carolina Press, 2018).

26 *Bell's Life in London*, 3.108, 83. The editor of *Bell's Life* also pointed out that that Colvile had his mother's name, but Wedderburn was given the father's name, and that "many a Slave-Dealer would feel himself offended at such liberty taken with his name; and the more especially where he intended to turn him to ready money by disposing of him." See *Bell's Life in London*, 3.108, 83.

27 *Bell's Life in London* 3.109 (March 28, 1824): 99.

28 *Bell's Life in London*, 3.109, 99.

29 Elahe Haschemi Yekani, *Familial Feeling: Entangled Tonalities in Early Black Atlantic Writing and the Rise of the British Novel* (Basingstoke: Palgrave Macmillan, 2020), 205.

30 Patterson, *The Sociology of Slavery*, 5.

31 Nicole N. Aljoe, *Creole Testimonies: Slave Narratives from the British West Indies, 1709–1838* (New York: Palgrave, 2012), 94.

32 Hanley, "Slavery and the Birth of Working-Class Racism," 104.

33 Richard D. Altick, *The English Common Reader: A Social History of the Mass Reading Public 1800–1900* (Chicago: University of Chicago Press, 1957), 328.

34 *Trial of the Rev. Robt. Wedderburn*, 19–20.

35 *Horrors of Slavery* (London, 1824), 3. Hereafter the text is cited parenthetically as (*HoS*).

36 Joseph Albernaz, "Abolition, Ultra-Radicalism, and the Generation of the General Strike," *Critical Times: Interventions in Global Critical Theory* 5.3 (2022): 538–69.

37 Hoermann, "Fermentation Will Be Universal," 298.

38 Richard Carlile, "To the Christian Judge Bailey," *The Republican* 18.5 (March 3, 1822): 548–56.

39 Carlile was remarkably attuned to racialized discrimination in his criticism of Wedderburn's trial and jail sentence. However, after he published Wedderburn's "The Holy Liturgy" in *Lion* 1:12 (1828): 359–61, he allowed a response from Robert Taylor in the next issue that argued, "if Wedderburn's

measure of talent were but served up in a better-looking vessel, or some that have ten-fold his talent would but bring it forth with half his courage and honesty, we should not want rich intellectual feasts." See *Lion*, 1:13 (1828), 395. Ryan Hanley connects this review to other racist satire, including George Cruikshank's *The New Union Club*, a caricature discussed in Chapter 1. See Hanley, *Beyond Slavery and Abolition: Black British Writing, c.1770–1830* (Cambridge: Cambridge University Press, 2018), 228–29.

40 Manu Samriti Chander, *Brown Romantics: Poetry and Nationalism in the Global Nineteenth Century* (Lewisburg, PA: Bucknell University Press), 4. Although Chander is arguing about the complex influence of Romantic poetry on poets from British colonies, this essay contends that the same structure applies to Wedderburn's use of the Romantic-era periodical.

41 Thomas, *Telling West Indian Lives*, 112.

42 *Trial of the Rev. Robt Wedderburn*, 20.

43 Morris, *Scotland and the Caribbean*, 181.

44 David Scott, *Conscripts of Modernity: The Tragedy of Colonial Enlightenment* (Durham, NC: Duke University Press, 2004), 62.

45 James Olney, "'I Was Born': Slave Narratives, Their Status as Autobiography and as Literature." In *The Slave's Narrative*, edited by Charles T. Davis and Henry Louis Gates Jr. (Oxford: Oxford University Press, 1991), 153.

46 Olaudah Equiano, *The Interesting Narrative*, ed. Brycchan Carey (Oxford: Oxford University Press, 2018), 17.

47 Lisa Lowe, *The Intimacies of Four Continents* (Durham, NC: Duke University Press, 2015), 46, 17. Lowe also argues that Equiano's narrative "contains important digressions and interruptions that mark the limits of the genre for containing and resolving the contradictions of colonial slavery" (48).

48 Scott, *Conscripts of Modernity*, 62; Bohls, *Slavery and the Politics of Place: Representing the Colonial Caribbean, 1770–1833* (Cambridge: Cambridge University Press, 2014), 130. Srinivas Aravamudan also compares the two writers, arguing, "the muted challenge of Equiano's political vocabulary ... turned into an angry and violent protest in the vision of a plebeian prophet such as Robert Wedderburn." See Aravamudan, *Tropicopolitans: Colonialism and Agency, 1688–1804* (Durham, NC: Duke University Press, 1999), 269. Alan Rice similarly argues, "Wedderburn's linkage of the two horrors of wage and chattel slavery and the activism designed to end them brought him into a conflict with the authorities, which differentiated him from those black British liberal reformers of the period like Olaudah Equiano who did not take such a consistently radical class-based position or display the same class loyalty." See Rice, *Radical Narratives of the Black Atlantic* (London: Continuum, 2003), 9.

49 Thomas, *Telling West Indian Lives*, 99.

50 Morris, *Scotland and the Caribbean*, 186.

51 Hanley, "A Radical Change of Heart," 426.

52 Simon Gikandi, *Slavery and the Culture of Taste* (Princeton, NJ: Princeton University Press, 2014), 185.

53 Vincent Brown, *The Reaper's Garden: Death and Power in the World of Atlantic Slavery* (Cambridge: Cambridge University Press, 2008), 152.
54 Morris, *Scotland and the Caribbean*, 32–4. For more on the historical connections between Scotland and Jamaican sugar plantations, see Stephen Mullen, *The Glasgow Sugar Aristocracy: Scotland and Caribbean Slavery, 1775–1838* (London: University of London Press, 2022). Shara McCallum imaginatively encounters this history in her book of poetry, *No Ruined Stone* (Farmington, ME: Alice James Books, 2022).
55 Helen Thomas, *Romanticism and Slave Narratives: Transatlantic Testimonies* (Cambridge: Cambridge University Press, 2000), 267. Daniel Livesay argues, "as a mixed-race man, Wedderburn used his hybridity to advocate simultaneously for a global uprising. In so doing, he took a fairly distinctive position among nineteenth-century reformers." See Livesay, *Children of Uncertain Fortune*, 37.
56 Katherine McKittrick, "Plantation Futures," *Small Axe: A Caribbean Journal of Criticism,* 17.3 (2013): 3. Similarly, Rinaldo Walcott observes that after slavery, Black people remain "the target of mass criminalization and incarceration and all the not-so-deadly and deadly actions of modern policing and its extensions." See Walcott, *On Property* (Windsor: Canadiana, 2021), 27.
57 Ruth Wilson Gilmore, *Abolitionist Geography: Essays towards Liberation* (London: Verso, 2022), 488.
58 Lowe, *Intimacies of Four Continents*, 45.
59 Williams, "Radical and/or Respectable," 19.
60 *Bell's Life in London* 3.109, 99.

Chapter 3

1 This statement was initially published in *Bell's Life in London*, as discussed in Chapter 2. It was republished in Wedderburn, *Horrors of Slavery* (London, 1824), 22. This publication is hereafter cited parenthetically as (*HoS*).
2 Saidiya Hartman, "Venus in Two Acts," *Small Axe: A Caribbean Journal of Criticism* 12.2 (2008): 2.
3 Debbie Lee, *Slavery and the Romantic Imagination* (Philadelphia: University of Pennsylvania Press, 2002), 208.
4 For example, Ryan Hanley argues, "his longest single work, *The Horrors of Slavery*, for example, was dedicated to the archly anti-radical William Wilberforce, and in terms of radical sentiment contained only a passing mention of Wedderburn's paternal grandfather's role in the Jacobite rising of 1745." See Hanley, "A Radical Change of Heart: Robert Wedderburn's Last Word on Slavery," *Slavery & Abolition* 37.2 (2016): 426. Similarly, Michael Morris suggests that *Horrors* is "consistent with Wilberforce's abolitionism"; thus, "this text strikes a moral rather than political tone." See Morris, *Scotland and the Caribbean, c.1740–1833: Atlantic Archipelagos* (New York: Routledge, 2015), 185. The exception to this assessment would be

Raphael Hoermann's argument: "Symptomatic of Wedderburn's refusal to be neatly pigeon-holed, this self-published abolitionist pamphlet breaks the mould of abolitionist literature from the onset." See Hoermann, "'Fermentation Will Be Universal': Intersections of Race and Class in Robert Wedderburn's Black Atlantic Discourse of the Transatlantic Revolution." In *Britain's Black Past*, edited by Gretchen H. Gerzina (Liverpool: Liverpool University Press, 2020), 298. Hoermann asserts that *Horrors* breaks with abolitionist literature through its anti-capitalist, working-class orientation. This chapter and the previous one build on this argument to assert that *Horrors* departed from an antislavery discourse by drawing connections between plantations and prison and championing enslaved Black women as liberators.

5 Jenny Sharpe, *Ghosts of Slavery: A Literary Archeology of Black Women's Lives* (Minneapolis: University of Minnesota Press, 2003), 123. Moira Ferguson asks similar questions: "Was she able to encode deliberately and discreetly, customarily unnamable privations? To what extent did she acknowledge, in directing her narrative, that both sides of the slavery debate vied for control over her?" See Ferguson, *Subject to Others: British Women Writers and Colonial Slavery, 1670–1834* (New York: Routledge, 1992), 282.

6 Edlie Wong, *Neither Fugitive nor Free: Atlantic Slavery, Freedom Suits, and the Legal Culture of Travel* (New York: New York University Press, 2009), 66.

7 Neil Roberts, *Freedom as Marronage* (Chicago: University of Chicago Press, 2015), 98.

8 Hortense Spillers, *Black, White, and in Color: Essays on American Literature and Culture* (Chicago: University of Chicago Press, 2003), 217, 220. Italics in the original.

9 Following Diana Paton, I use the lower-case "o" when spelling obeah. See Paton, *The Cultural Politics of Obeah: Religion, Colonialism and Modernity in the Caribbean World* (Cambridge: Cambridge University Press, 2015).

10 Shauna J. Sweeney, "Market Marronage: Fugitive Women and the Internal Marketing System in Jamaica, 1781–1834," *William and Mary Quarterly* 76.2 (2019): 204. The term "higgler," used in the Caribbean from the eighteenth century to the present, designates a Black female entrepreneur in the internal economies of those islands. Winnifred R. Brown-Glaude suggests that through higglering in the internal markets, enslaved women "transformed themselves into economic subjects within a broader social and economic context that defined them as objects." The occupation of "higgler" carries a stigma because "the commercial savvy of the higgler . . . marked her as deviant. Blacks, enslaved and free, were not expected to exhibit this kind of capitalist know-how. For this affront, higglers were denigrated; they were represented in the public discourse as aggressive rogues who took advantage of others." Higglers have been and continue to be denigrated in public discourse in Jamaica. However, attempts to change the word to something with less stigma, such as "vendor," problematically asserts that these alternative economies should be absorbed into capitalist discourse. When using the

term higgler, I am using the historical language not to stigmatize but rather to emphasize the rebellious and transformative aspects of the alternative economies developed by Black women. See Winnifred R. Brown-Glaude, *Higglers in Kingston: Women's Informal Work in Jamaica* (Nashville: Vanderbilt University Press, 2011), 91, 97.

11 Julius S. Scott, *The Common Wind: Afro-American Currents in the Age of the Haitian Revolution* (London: Verso, 2018), 78.

12 Patricia A. Matthew, "Quilt 5: Race, Blackness, and Romanticism," *Studies in Romanticism* 61.1 (2022): 1–2.

13 Bakary Diaby, "Black Women and/in the Shadow of Romanticism," *European Romantic Review* 30:3 (2019): 252.

14 Moira Ferguson argues that abolition was an opportunity for white women to enter the public, political sphere: "Between 1823–1833, female emancipationists transformed the cultural face of England as a result of the discourse on slavery." See Ferguson, *Subject to Others*, 299.

15 Katherine McKittrick, *Demonic Grounds: Black Women and the Cartographies of Struggle* (Minneapolis: University of Minnesota Press, 2006), 121.

16 Hoermann, "Fermentation Will Be Universal," 300.

17 Saidiya Hartman, "The Belly of the World: A Note on Black Women's Labors," *Souls: A Critical Journal of Black Politics, Culture, and Society* 18.1 (2016): 171. Hartman explains further, "it has proven difficult, if not impossible, to assimilate black women's domestic labors and reproductive capacities within narratives of the black worker, slave rebellion, marronage, or black radicalism, even as this labor was critical to the creation of value, the realization of profit and the accumulation of capital. It has been no less complicated to imagine the future produced by such labors as anything other than monstrous."

18 *Bell's Life in London and Sporting Chronicle* 3.103 (February 15, 1824): 51.

19 Brycchan Carey, "Abolishing Cruelty: The Concurrent Growth of Antislavery and Animal Welfare Sentiment in British and Colonial Literature," *Journal for Eighteenth-Century Studies* 43.2 (2020): 207. Elizabeth Bohls also mentions Wedderburn's inversion: "Abolitionist propaganda often treated slaves like livestock; Wedderburn inverts the trope." See Bohls, *Romantic Literature and Postcolonial Studies* (Edinburgh: Edinburgh University Press, 2013), 76. Sue Thomas notes that this passage contests proslavery propaganda as well: "Wedderburn plays on the human/animal species boundary used by proslavery writers to justify the treatment of bondspeople." See Thomas, *Telling West Indian Lives*, 113.

20 Debbie Lee, "Black Single Mothers in Romantic History and Literature," in *Race, Romanticism, and the Atlantic*, ed. Paul Youngquist (London: Routledge, 2013), 172.

21 William Blake, *The Complete Poetry and Prose of William Blake* (New York: Anchor Books, 1988). Wedderburn has much in common with Blake's antinomian beliefs, which, according to Saree Makdisi, "could pose as much of a problem for industrial discipline (and what Max Weber would call the

Protestant work ethic) as it would for the established political order." See Makdisi, *William Blake and the Impossible History of the 1790s* (Chicago: University of Chicago Press, 2003), 74.

22 Incidentally, the John Wedderburn who provided asylum for Rosanna is the Wedderburn in the landmark Knight v Wedderburn case (1774–78). John Wedderburn brought an enslaved man, Joseph Knight, to Scotland with him. When Knight sought his freedom, Wedderburn tried to have him arrested because he was enslaved. The court case solidified freedom for formerly enslaved people in Scotland. For a fictionalized account of Knight's quest for freedom, see James Robertson, *Joseph Knight* (London: Fourth Estate, 2004).

23 Hartman, "The Belly of the World," 166. Edlie Wong points out that Rosanna negotiated "the oppressive entanglements of kinship and property under colonial slave law to insist on her unborn child's freedom as a condition of her transfer in ownership." See Wong, *Neither Fugitive nor Free*, 64.

24 Joseph Albernaz insightfully interprets Wedderburn's depiction of maternal practices as a type of general strike that should alter our understanding of the worker: "Seen through the prism of Wedderburn's life, activity, and writing, the general strike's intimacy with maternal captivity and defiance further displaces the frame of the striker as only, or paradigmatically, a waged white male productive worker." See Albernaz, "Abolition, Ultra-Radicalism, and the Generation of the General Strike," *Critical Times: Interventions in Global Critical Theory* 5.3 (2022): 551.

25 Hartman, "The Belly of the World," 171.

26 Shelby Johnson, "'The Fate of St. Domingo Awaits You': Robert Wedderburn's Unfinished Revolution," *The Eighteenth Century* 61.4 (2020): 376.

27 Miles Ogborn, *The Freedom of Speech: Talk and Slavery in the Anglo-Caribbean World* (Chicago: University of Chicago Press, 2019), 5.

28 Scott contends, "in addition to providing some unique opportunities for runaway slaves, Caribbean cities also held special attraction for free blacks and browns, the most marginal of the various groups comprising the masterless Caribbean." See Scott, *The Common Wind*, 22.

29 Olaudah Equiano, *The Interesting Narrative*, ed. Brycchan Carey (Oxford: Oxford University Press, 2018), 142.

30 Elizabeth Bohls argues that Equiano's description of Kingston reveals his skill as a travel writer. See Bohls, *Slavery and the Politics of Place: Representing the Colonial Caribbean, 1770–1833* (Cambridge: Cambridge University Press, 2014), 125–42.

31 Alex A. Moulton, "Towards the Arboreal Side-Effects of Marronage: Black Geographies and Ecologies of the Jamaican Forest," *Environment and Planning E: Nature and Space* 6.1 (2023), 10. Hilary McD. Beckles also proposes that higglers made economic decisions as a "free" persons: "By combining their work as fieldhands, artisans, domestics, or whatever with their own productive and commercial activities, female slaves made economic

decisions as 'free' persons." See Beckles, *Centering Woman: Gender Discourses in Caribbean Slave Society* (Kingston: Ian Randle Publishers, 1999), 140.

32 Sweeney, "Market Marronage," 214.

33 In England the social consequences of enclosure along with the simultaneous shift to wage labor had the direst consequences for women because they could no longer earn money through the cottage economy. See K. D. M. Snell, *Annals of the Labouring Poor: Social Change and Agrarian England, 1660–1900* (Cambridge: Cambridge University Press, 1987), 157–58.

34 Sweeney, "Market Marronage," 198. It is impossible to estimate how long the journey would have taken. However, Matthew Lewis's Cornwall plantation was located just a few miles from James Wedderburn's, and his *Journal of a West India Proprietor* recorded that the journey between Kingston and Westmoreland required navigating narrow roads over dangerous precipices and through raging rivers. It took him approximately eleven days via horse-drawn coach to make the roundtrip journey. See *Journal of a West-India Proprietor* (London: J. Murray, 1834), 157–73.

35 Michael Morris points out that Wedderburn's depiction of his father is one of many absentee Scottish fathers featured in Black Caribbean writing. See Morris, "Yonder Awa: Slavery and Distancing Strategies in Scottish Literature." In *Recovering Scotland's Slavery Past: The Caribbean Connection*, edited by Tom M. Devine, 41–61 (Edinburgh: Edinburgh University Press, 2015), 57.

36 Diana Paton states that in abolitionist literature, "concern about the flogging of women is evident from the earliest critical representations of slave punishment." See Paton, *No Bond but the Law: Punishment, Race, and Gender in Jamaican State Formation, 1780–1870* (Durham, NC: Duke University Press, 2004), 6.

37 Although Wedderburn's conflation of witchcraft and obeah problematically replicated British colonial biases, Wedderburn's description of his grandmother as a witch may have consciously intended to translate her practices into the European imagination of witches, who were "commoning" older women accused of subsisting by "magic" rather than wage labor. Silvia Federici explains, "eradicating these practices [witchcraft] was a necessary condition for the capitalist rationalization of work since magic appeared as an illicit form of power and an instrument *to obtain what one wanted without work*, that is, a refusal of work in action." See Federici, *Caliban and the Witch: Women, the Body, and Primitive Accumulation* (Brooklyn: Autonomedia, 2004), 142. Italics in the original.

38 Diana Paton, *The Cultural Politics of Obeah: Religion, Colonialism and Modernity in the Caribbean World* (Cambridge: Cambridge University Press, 2015), 18–19. Wedderburn also claimed Talkee Amy's role as a spiritual leader as his own inheritance, and during his trial for blasphemy in 1820, he went to great lengths to defend the "Witch of Endor." He argues, "Jesus Christ tells us, that no one can raise the dead but God; then the witch must have the power of God." This digression must have been against his best

interest, but he wanted it recorded, nonetheless. See *The Trial of the Rev. Robt Wedderburn for Blasphemy*, ed. Erasmus Perkins (London, 1820), 5. Michael Scrivener reads Wedderburn's discussion of the Witch of Endor as a "typical allegorical moment": "when Wedderburn tried to explain why he disputed the witch of Endor section in Samuel; the narrative about the violence against his grandmother was the new context for that story." See Scrivener, *Seditious Allegories: John Thelwall and Jacobin Writing* (University Park: Pennsylvania State University Press, 2001), 166.

39 Janelle Rodriques, "Obeah, Religion, and Nineteenth-Century Literature." In *Caribbean Literature in Transition: 1800–1920*, edited by Evelyn O'Callaghan and Tim Watson, 198–212 (Cambridge: Cambridge University Press, 2020), 199.

40 Jeffrey Cottrell, "At the End of the Trade: Obeah and Black Women in the Colonial Imaginary," *Atlantic Studies* 12.2 (2015): 213. Wedderburn's recollections of his grandmother fall in line with Emily Senior's analysis of obeah: "The obeah practitioner is one such model of an alternative 'colonial modernity'—a spectral figure identified with moments of intercultural encounter specific to the unique social complex of the plantation that brought exchange, instability, and revolution, with influence far beyond the plantation's bounds." See Senior, *The Caribbean and the Medical Imagination, 1764–1834: Slavery, Disease and Colonial Modernity* (Cambridge: Cambridge University Press, 2018), 160.

41 Helen Thomas, *Romanticism and Slave Narratives* (Cambridge: Cambridge University Press, 2000), 255.

42 Lizabeth Paravisini-Gebert, "Colonial and Postcolonial Gothic: The Caribbean." In *The Cambridge Companion to Gothic Fiction*, edited by Jerrold E. Hogle, 229–57 (Cambridge: Cambridge University Press, 2006), 235. Paravisini-Gebert also cites obeah's connection to rebellion in the British imagination: "The perception of the Caribbean as a site of terror dates back to the myriad tales of atrocities committed against white planters during the Tacky Rebellion in Jamaica in 1760 and three decades later in the gory and brutal slave rebellion that destroyed the colony of Saint Domingue in what is now Haiti" (233–34).

43 Thomas W. Laqueur, *The Work of the Dead: A Cultural History of Mortal Remains* (Princeton, NJ: Princeton University Press, 2015), 84.

44 Vincent Brown, *The Reaper's Garden: Death and Power in the World of Atlantic Slavery* (Cambridge, MA: Harvard University Press, 2008), 62. J. T. Roane also argues for the significance of funerals and graves as Black commons: "Plots for the dead signal a primary mode of organizing community, anchoring the present through the past within the grooves of a landscape." See Roane, "Plotting the Black Commons," *Souls: A Critical Journal of Black Politics, Culture, and Society* 20.3 (2018): 242.

45 *Journal of a West-India Proprietor*, 227. For a critical analysis of the "conspiracy" at the child's funeral, see Carl Plasa, *Slaves to Sweetness: British and Caribbean Literatures of Sugar* (Liverpool: Liverpool University Press, 2011), 65.

46 Lisa Lowe, *The Intimacies of Four Continents* (Durham, NC: Duke University Press, 2015), 50.

47 Wedderburn's model of Black self-liberation would have been familiar to his London audience. Gretchen Gerzina documents that slave revolts were both in the news and on the stage: "A person could read these advertisements and sensational stories of revolts on West Indian plantations quite coolly in the morning newspaper, and then shed tears that evening over similar situations presented on stage." See Gerzina, *Black London: Life before Emancipation* (New Brunswick, NJ: Rutgers University Press, 1995), 7. Ryan Hanley agrees that "Caribbean insurrections continued to make their way into the intellectual world of the London ultra-radicals well into the 1820s." See Hanley, "Cato Street and the Caribbean." In *The Cato Street Conspiracy: Plotting, Counter-Intelligence, and the Revolutionary Tradition in Britain and Ireland*, edited by Jason McElligott and Martin Conboy, 81–100 (Manchester: Manchester University Press, 2020), 93.

48 *The History of Mary Prince*, edited by Sara Salih (New York: Penguin, 2000), 3. All subsequent quotations from the *History* are taken from this text and cited parenthetically as (*HMP*).

49 Kerry Sinanan, "The 'Slave' as Cultural Artifact: The Case of Mary Prince," *Studies in Eighteenth-Century Culture* 49 (2020): 79. Debbie Lee has also grappled with the complexity of this textual history, and she argues that *History of Mary Prince* "revised the most heavily symbolic antislavery icon: that of the slave woman." See Lee, *Slavery and the Romantic Imagination*, 208.

50 McKittrick, *Demonic Grounds*, xxiv. Italics in the original.

51 Judith Madera, *Black Atlas: Geography and Flow in Nineteenth-Century African American Literature* (Durham, NC: Duke University Press, 2015), 10.

52 Although this chapter reads *The History* in light of Wedderburn's narrative, Shelby Johnson recommends reading it within a larger "literary archive" that "included seventeenth- and eighteenth-century settler portrayals of colonial expansion, as well as Indigenous and Black witnesses to the intertwined emergences of Native displacement and plantation empires." See Johnson, "Plotting the Plantationocene with *The History of Mary Prince*," *ABO: Interactive Journal for Women in the Arts, 1640–1830* 13.1 (2023), 4.

53 This chapter uses a matrifocal concept of kinship because it is the one Wedderburn proposed. However, scholars have pointed out that kinship among the enslaved in Jamaica is far more complex. For example, Colleen A. Vasconcellos argues that "a concentration on nuclear or matrifocal families oversimplifies the complex nature of life in the slave villages." See Vasconcellos, *Slavery, Childhood, and Abolition in Jamaica, 1788–1838* (Athens: University of Georgia Press, 2015), 29.

54 Neil Roberts, *Freedom as Marronage* (Chicago: University of Chicago Press, 2015), 10. Roberts further notes the political significance of petit marronage: "Although petit marronage is neither a state of war nor revolution, it can cause them. Causality and purpose are intertwined, and petit marronage is a

micropolitical causal mechanism for the macropolitics of revolution and freedom" (98).

55 What appears to be Prince's excessive grief for Mrs. Williams after her death was inseparable from their family's impending sale and separation when the estate is transferred to a new owner. On the antislavery trope of the grateful slave, see George Boulukos, *The Grateful Slave: The Emergence of Race in Eighteenth-Century British and American Culture* (Cambridge: Cambridge University Press, 2008), 15.

56 J. T. Roane, "Plotting the Black Commons," *Souls: A Critical Journal of Black Politics, Culture, and Society* 20.3 (2018): 243.

57 Spillers, *Black, White, and in Color*, 218. Italics in the original.

58 Ibid., 221.

59 Matthew Rowney, *In Common Things: Commerce, Culture, and Ecology in British Romantic Literature* (Toronto: University of Toronto Press, 2022), 113.

60 Sharpe, *Ghosts of Slavery*, 138.

61 Sweeney, "Market Marronage," 222.

62 For example, see Zachary Macaulay, *Negro Slavery, or A View of Some of the More Prominent Features of that State of Society as It Exists in the United States of America and in the Colonies of the West Indies, especially in Jamaica* (London: Richard Taylor, 1823), 38–9. George Beckford and Michael Witter argue, "the Sunday Market was a meeting place for the slaves where information concerning the various local struggles and other important news was passed on." See Beckford and Witter, *Small Garden ... Bitter Weed: Struggle and Change in Jamaica* (Jamaica: Maroon Publishing, 1982), 40. Chapter 6 discusses how infrastructure of the internal markets facilitated the rise of an independent peasantry after emancipation.

63 Sharpe, *Ghosts of Slavery*, 150.

64 Robert Dirks, *The Black Saturnalia: Conflict and Its Ritual Expression on British West Indian Slave Plantations* (Gainesville: University of Florida Press, 1987), xi. Verene A. Shepherd also notes, "Christmas, like other holidays, was not only a time for play; it was a time for opposition, as indicated by the many revolts that took place around Christmas and Easter in Jamaica." See Shepherd, "Work, Culture, and Creolization: Slavery and Emancipation in Eighteenth and Nineteeth-Century Jamaica." In *Art and Emancipation in Jamaica: Isaac Mendes Belisario and His Worlds*, edited by T. J. Barringer, Gillian Forrester, and Barbaro Martinez-Ruiz, 27–39 (New Haven, CT: Yale Center for British Art in association with Yale University Press, 2007). 34.

65 From supplementary material in *History of Mary Prince* (102). Although Sharpe does not mention the Christmas "stir-up," this would be another example of her argument that the paratext around Prince's *History* reveals more of her "troublesome character" than the narrative itself. See Sharpe, *Ghosts of Slavery*, 146–51.

66 In addition to allowing her to exit slavery, Prince's Moravian faith undergirded her willingness to tell her narrative, according to Sue Thomas, who

suggests reading Prince's narrative "intertextually in relation to oral practices and vocabularies of Moravian spiritual self-formation, and to genres of Moravian life narrative and conversion with which Prince was familiar." See Thomas, *Telling West Indian Lives*, 121.

67 Alan Bewell, "'The Stranger and the Exile Who Is in Our Land within Our Gates': Mary Prince as a Black British Immigrant," *Modern Philology* 118.2 (2020): 235, 250. Sinanan also highlights Prince's desire to return to Antigua as significant: "Prince refuses to accept freedom in pre-emancipation England as freedom, and her desire to return to Antigua insists on a future of full abolition, not just of slavery itself, but of Western humanism." See Sinanan, "Mary Prince's Back and Her Critique of Anti-slavery Sympathy," *Studies in Romanticism* 61.1 (2022): 77.

68 Elizabeth Bohls, *Slavery and the Politics of Place: Representing the Colonial Caribbean, 1770–1833* (Cambridge: Cambridge University Press, 2014), 127.

69 Vincent Brown, *Tacky's Revolt: The Story of an Atlantic Slave War* (Cambridge, MA: Harvard University Press, 2020).

Chapter 4

1 Lewis recorded numerous performances of affection on the part of the people he enslaved. Simon Gikandi argues that Lewis recognized that the affection was subversion: "The more this fawning was piled on him, the more he began to recognize that it was part of a subtle and insidious reversal of the structure of control . . . the slaves who flattered him the most were those who had transgressed in his absence or needed favors from him." See Gikandi, *Slavery and the Culture of Taste* (Princeton, NJ: Princeton University Press, 2014), 203–4.

2 All quotations cited parenthetically as *Journal* are from *Journal of a West-India Proprietor* (London: J. Murray, 1834).

3 Mary Louise Pratt, *Imperial Eyes: Travel Writing and Transculturation* (London: Routledge, 1992), 78–9.

4 Lizabeth Paravesini-Gebert, "Colonial and Postcolonial Gothic: The Caribbean." In *The Cambridge Companion to Gothic Fiction*, edited by Jerrold E. Hogle, 229–57 (Cambridge: Cambridge University Press, 2006), 230. For an extended argument about slavery and the Gothic novel, see Kari J. Winter, *Subjects of Slavery, Agents of Change: Women and Power in Gothic Novels and Slave Narratives, 1790–1865* (Athens: University of Georgia Press, 2010).

5 D. L. Macdonald, *Monk Lewis: A Critical Biography* (Toronto: University of Toronto Press, 2000), 47–8. Lewis was so invested in plantation management that he bought out a partner to have sole control over the workings of his plantations. For more details about Lewis's inheritance, see Judith Terry, "Introduction" to *Journal of a West India Proprietor*, ix–xxxiv (Oxford: Oxford University Press, 1999), xiv.

6 Letter to Thomas Moore, January 2, 1821. From *Letters and Journals of Lord Byron*: https://lordbyron.org/monograph.

7 Evelyn O'Callaghan, "Early Colonial Narratives of the West Indies: Lady Nugent, Eliza Fenwick, Matthew Lewis, and Frieda Cassin." In *Routledge Companion to Anglophone Caribbean Literature*, edited by Michael A. Bucknor and Alison Donnell, 149–56 (New York: Routledge, 2011), 151. Maureen Harkin agrees that the timing of Lewis's visits to Jamaica explain the tensions in his journal: "Lewis gives an account of the colonial slaveholder's increasingly acute sense of his own vulnerability in the period between abolition of the slave trade in 1807 and of slavery in British colonies in 1833." See Harkin, "Matthew Lewis's *Journal of a West India Proprietor*: Surveillance and Space on the Plantation," *Nineteenth-Century Contexts* 24.2 (2002): 141.

8 Carl Thompson, *The Suffering Traveller and the Romantic Imagination* (Oxford: Clarendon Press, 2007), 4. In attempting to represent himself as an "enlightened" slave owner, Lewis's narrative unreliably vacillated between self-justification and observation. Similar tensions are noted in Romantic ecological travel narratives. See David Higgins, "Stewardship and Plenitude: William Bartram, the Lake Poets, and Romantic Ecology." In *Transatlantic Literary Ecologies*, edited by Kevin Hutchings and John Miller, 42–57 (London: Routledge, 2016).

9 Kamau Brathwaite, "Creative Literature of the British West Indies during the Period of Slavery," *Savacou* 1.1 (1970): 51. More recently, Monique Allewaert agrees that "Lewis's writings became a portal through which fragments of diasporic Afro-American cultures passed into the historical record." See Allewaert, *Ariel's Ecology: Plantations, Personhood, and Colonialism in the American Tropics* (Minneapolis: University of Minnesota Press, 2013), 88.

10 Nicole N. Aljoe, *Creole Testimonies: Slave Narratives from the British West Indies, 1709–1838* (New York: Palgrave Macmillan, 2012), 89. Carl Plasa notes that Lewis also focused on health complaints, in which "'symptoms' of the slave's 'complaint' become embroiled in a conflict of interpretations – natural versus supernatural – which is never definitively resolved, remaining precisely suspended in a 'sort of doubt.'" See Plasa, *Slaves to Sweetness: British and Caribbean Literatures of Sugar* (Liverpool: Liverpool University Press, 2011), 68.

11 Rodridgo C. Bulamah, "From Marrons to Kreyòl: Human-Animal Relations in Early Caribbean." In *Global Plantations in the Modern World: Sovereignties, Ecologies, Afterlives*, edited by Colette Le Petitcorps, Marta Macedo, and Irene Peano, 35–58 (Basingstoke: Palgrave Macmillan, 2023), 50, 36.

12 Michel-Rolph Trouillot, *Haiti: State against Nation* (New York: New York University Press, 1990), 39.

13 Keith Sandiford points out that Lewis's desire to be a "humane" enslaver is better understood as his struggle "to impose on this scene of cultural conflict and political contestation an idea of romantic revolutionary ethics forged from the confident integrity of his own egotistical sublime." See Sandiford, *The Cultural Politics of Sugar: Caribbean Slavery and Narratives of Colonialism* (Cambridge: Cambridge University Press, 2000), 151.

14 Joseph Albernaz, "Abolition, Ultra-Radicalism, and the Generation of the General Strike," *Critical Times: Interventions in Global Critical Theory* 5.3 (2022): 548.
15 Roberto del Valle Alcalá, "Class Antagonism and the Limits of Utopia in Matthew Lewis and Robert Owen," *Nineteenth-Century Contexts* 43.4 (2021): 465–77.
16 Allewaert, *Ariel's Ecology*, 88.
17 Elizabeth Maddock Dillon, "The Plantationocene and the Performative Commons: A Brief History of Uncommoning," *The Minnesota Review* 93 (2019): 83.
18 John H. Parry, "Plantation and Provision Ground: An Historical Sketch of the Introduction of Food Crops into Jamaica," *Revista de Historia de América* 39 (1955): 12.
19 Bryan Edwards, *The History, Civil and Commercial, of the British Colonies in the West Indies* (London: John Stockdale, 1793), ii, 163. Edwards's proslavery "history" emphasized enslaved people's quality of life. He reassured British readers that enslaved people are given "very tolerable habitations" that "far excel the cabins of the Scotch and Irish peasants, as described by Mr. Young." This rhetorical strategy of comparing the situation of the Irish to enslaved people in the West Indies was used repeatedly in discourse of the Romantic period to justify slavery as a "humane" practice.
20 R. C. Dallas, *The History of the Maroons, from Their Origin to the Establishment of Their Chief Tribe at Sierra Leone* (London: Longman and Rees, 1803), i, cviii–cix.
21 Orlando Patterson, *The Sociology of Slavery: An Analysis of the Origins, Development and Structure of Negro Slave Society in Jamaica* (London: Fairleigh Dickenson University Press, 1969), 219.
22 Edwards, *The History, Civil and Commercial,* iii, 366–67. This story was so compelling that Maria Edgeworth retold it in her short story "The Grateful Negro." The story was retold as a great injustice because, in Great Britain, custom and common rights for subsistence served to challenge the status of absolute property. Maria Edgeworth's "The Grateful Negro" was published in her *Popular Tales*, III vols. (London: Joseph Johnson, 1804), iii, 193–240. For more information about Edgeworth's story and her views on plantation slavery, see Frances Botkin, "Questioning the 'Necessary Order of Things': Maria Edgeworth's 'The Grateful Negro,' Plantation Slavery, and the Abolition of the Slave Trade." In *Discourses of Slavery and Abolition: Britain and Its Colonies, 1760–1838*, edited by Brycchan Carey, Markman Ellis, and Sara Salih, 194–208 (Basingstoke: Palgrave Macmillan, 2004).
23 E. P. Thompson, *Customs in Common* (New York: The New Press, 1993), 71. Lewis was racked by guilt about using the word "slave," even though he never freed the people he enslaved. For example, early in his first visit, he rationalized that enslaved people at Cornwall were happy because "after all, slavery, in their case, is but another name for servitude" (*Journal* 62).
24 Sandiford, *Cultural Politics of Sugar*, 152.

25 Hilary McD. Beckles, *Centering Woman: Gender Discourses in Caribbean Slave Society* (Kingston: Ian Randle Publishers, 1999), 161.
26 Judith Carney and Richard Rosomoff, *In the Shadow of Slavery: Africa's Botanical Legacy in the Atlantic World* (Berkeley: University of California Press, 2011), 135.
27 For more on Lewis's curious lack of interest in recording specific information about sugar, see Sandiford's *Cultural Politics of Sugar*.
28 Elizabeth DeLoughrey, "Yams, Roots, and Rot: Allegories of the Provision Grounds," *Small Axe: A Caribbean Journal of Criticism* 15.1 (2011): 61.
29 The embedded quotation is from William Beckford's *A Descriptive Account of the Island of Jamaica* (London: T. and J. Egerton, 1790). See Evelyn O'Callaghan, "Caribbean Picturesque from William Beckford to Contemporary Tourism." In *Caribbean Literature in Transition, 1800–1920*, edited by Evelyn O'Callaghan and Tim Watson, 67–84 (Cambridge: Cambridge University Press, 2021), 72–3. Cassidy Picken similarly notes that Lewis was "speciously divorcing the cultural world of his slaves from the constant threat of violence under which they work." See Picken, "Annihilated Property: Slavery and Reproduction after Abolition," *European Romantic Review* 28.5 (2017): 616.
30 Elizabeth Bohls, *Slavery and the Politics of Place: Representing the Colonial Caribbean, 1770–1833* (Cambridge: Cambridge University Press, 2014), 16. As discussed in the Introduction, the planter picturesque mirrors the ideological work of Romantic picturesque aesthetics in England. Anne Bermingham argues that picturesque aesthetics in England were "an appropriate elegiac background for the laborer dispossessed by the agrarian revolution." Thus, the picturesque was used to erase the suffering of commoners during and after the enclosure of the commons: "In this respect, the picturesque represented an attempt to wipe out the fact of enclosure and to minimize its consequences." See Bermingham, *Landscape and Ideology: The English Rustic Tradition, 1760–1860* (Berkeley: University of California Press, 1986), 68, 75.
31 Ashton Warner, *Negro Slavery Described by a Negro*, edited by Susanna Strickland (London, 1831), 41.
32 Macaulay further laments, "not only is Sunday a market-day in Jamaica, but that, for the Negroes, whether as vendors of the fruit or vegetables or poultry or other articles of food they may have to dispose of, or purchases of the little necessaries or comforts they may wish to buy in return, *Sunday is the only market day*." Italics in the original. See Maucaulay, *Negro Slavery, or a View of Some of the More Prominent Features of That State of Society as It Exists in the United States of America and in the Colonies of the West Indies, Especially in Jamaica* (London: Richard Taylor, 1823), 38–9.
33 Higman notes that European bias was also applied to land use: "Planters, missionaries and surveyors shared a common view of the ideal human landscape, seeking generally to impose order wherever they saw disorder." This imposition continued after the Emancipation, when "Church-founded 'free

villages' incorporated the same geometric organizing principles." See *Jamaica Surveyed: Plantation Maps and Plans of the Eighteenth and Nineteenth Centuries* (Kingston: Institute of Jamaica Publications Limited, 1988), 279, 281.

34 Bohls, *Slavery and the Politics of Place*, 38.

35 Susan Scott Parrish, *American Curiosity: Cultures of Natural History in the Colonial British Atlantic World* (Chapel Hill: University of North Carolina Press, 2006), 273.

36 Diana Paton, "Witchcraft, Poison, Law, and Atlantic Slavery," *The William and Mary Quarterly* 69.2 (2012): 262. Although I argue Lewis's preoccupation with Adam's poisonings avoided facing the possibility of revolt being tied to provision grounds, J. Alexandra McGhee argues that Lewis's focus on Adam's poisonings individualized the potential for collective uprising: "At Cornwall, Lewis repeatedly denies the reality that both obeah and rebellion were collective practices, preferring instead to manage and quarantine individuals." See McGhee, "Fever Dreams: Obeah, Tropical Disease, and Cultural Contamination in Colonial Jamaica and the Metropole," *Atlantic Studies* 12.2 (2015):190.

37 Sidney Mintz, "The Origins of the Jamaican Market System." In *The Slavery Reader*, edited by Gad J. Heuman and James Walvin, 521–44 (London: Routledge, 2003), 525.

38 This argument also falls in line with Sophie Chao's observation that "plantations have persistently proven potent birthing grounds for the emergence of multispecies resistance and resurgence." See Chao, "Plantation," *Environmental Humanities* 14.2 (2022): 362.

39 Lewis's attention to the pigs is curious because, according to the research of Verene A. Shepherd, pigs were generally not allowed to be kept on sugar estates due to their destructive tendencies. See "Work, Culture, and Creolization: Slavery and Emancipation in Eighteenth and Nineteeth-Century Jamaica." In *Art and Emancipation in Jamaica: Isaac Mendes Belisario and His Worlds*, edited by T. J. Barringer, Gillian Forrester, and Barbaro Martinez-Ruiz, 27–39 (New Haven, CT: Yale Center for British Art in association with Yale University Press, 2007), 34.

40 Scott Hess, *William Wordsworth and the Ecology of Authorship: The Roots of Environmentalism in Nineteenth-Century Culture* (Charlottesville: University of Virginia Press, 2012), 23. Tim Barringer argues that in the colonial picturesque, "visuality implies a regime of looking that is associated with a dominant ideology, the plantation owner's view of enslaved laborers being an extreme example." See Barringer, "Land, Labor, Landscape: Views of the Plantation in Victorian Jamaica." In *Victorian Jamaica*, edited by Tim Barringer and Wayne Modest, 263–78. Durham, NC: Duke University Press, 2018), 285.

41 Tim Barringer, "Picturesque Prospects and the Labor of the Enslaved." In *Art and Emancipation in Jamaica: Isaac Mendes Belisario and His Worlds*, edited by T. J. Barringer, Gillian Forrester, and Barbaro Martinez-Ruiz, 41–63 (New Haven, CT: Yale University Press, 2007), 52–3.

42 Nathan K. Hensley, "Landscape with Storm (Unfinished)," *Victorian Review* 47.1(2021): 38.

43 Ron Broglio, *Animal Revolution* (Minneapolis: University of Minnesota Press, 2022), 88. J. Alexandra McGhee argues, Lewis "identifies the threat of obeah and the threat of yellow fever as springing from the same sources: the local environment and the crowd." Like yellow fever, the pigs are also tied to Lewis's fear of contamination from the crowd. See McGhee, "Fever Dreams," 188.

44 Ron Broglio, *Beasts of Burden: Biopolitics, Labor, and Animal Life in British Romanticism* (Albany: State University of New York Press, 2017), 37.

45 John Clare, *Poems of the Middle Period, 1822–1837*, vols. 1–5, edited by Eric Robinson, David Powell, and P. M. S. Dawson (Oxford: Clarendon Press, 1996), II.130–34, lines 36, 42–3.

46 The connection is not accidental, since, Michael Niblett argues, "enclosure and the plantation complex haunt the cultural registration of ongoing transformations in agro-food relations." See Niblett, "'The Landscape Heaved with Unspeakable Terror': The Weird Presence of the World-Food-System in the Cultural Imaginaries of England and the Caribbean." In *Literary and Cultural Production, World-Ecology, and the Global Food System*, edited by Chris Campbell, Michael Niblett, and Kerstin Oloff, 65–92 (Basingstoke: Palgrave Macmillan, 2021), 67. Donna Landry also notes that during enclosure, the discipline of animals was central: "This increasingly proprietorial relation to animals exemplifies the desacralization of nature, but also the ideological power of private property as more than a legal concept – as the representation of an imaginary, yet lived, relation to the world." See Landry, *The Invention of the Countryside: Hunting, Walking, and Ecology in English Literature, 1671–1831* (Basingstoke: Palgrave Macmillan, 2001), 8.

47 Broglio, *Beasts of Burden*, 19.

48 Bulamah, "From Marrons to Kreyòl," 54.

49 Bulamah explains the origin of the term as it is commonly accepted in Caribbean studies: "Marron (or maroon), as explained by Tardieu (2006), is a term derived from the Arawak language whose original meaning was 'fugitive,' but it was incorporated into the colonial lexicon of different empires to define native plants and animals that defied European domination both in practical and ontological terms as something external to the European order." Ibid., 40. S. J. Zhang, however, adds that scholars might attend to the use of the term *Simarrona* in Spanish colonial records from Louisiana: "*Simarrona* here indicates something you can be or do, something you can see someone else be or do, something either of you could be caught being or doing … *Simarrona* belies the etymology plot and its reified teleology of language and nation." See Zhang, "*Simarrona*: Beyond Etymologies toward a Practice of Unlearning," *Small Axe: A Caribbean Journal of Criticism* 27.2 (2023): 126–27.

50 Tim Watson argues that the demand to see a Black doctor was part of planters' "creole realism": "The primacy and legitimacy of the white West

Indian resident who has the presumed benefit of local knowledge are consistently undermined by the recurring figure of the black doctor, who combines creolised folk wisdom and the superior handling of local objects." Moreover, the tension between Black and white healing practices was constant: "Black herbalism could not in the end be allowed to challenge the supremacy of European medical methods, even though European writers were forced sometimes to acknowledge the African or indigenous American roots of much tropical medicine." See *Caribbean Culture and British Fiction in the Atlantic World, 1780–1870* (Cambridge: Cambridge University Press, 2008), 20, 22.

51 Jill H. Casid notes that "the slave garden was supposed to root the slave to the plantation" yet at the same time the provision grounds were places that facilitated self-liberation, both for *petit marronage* and for Maroons." See Casid, *Sowing Empire: Landscape and Colonization* (Minneapolis: University of Minnesota Press, 2004), 213.

52 Nihad M. Farooq, "'A Useful Delusion': Valentine Farm and the Flight for Freedom," *Utopian Studies* 30.1 (2019): 101.

53 Janae Davis, Alex Moulton, Levi Van Sant, and Brian Williams, "Anthropocene, Capitalocene, ... Plantationocene? A Manifesto for Ecological Justice in an Age of Global Crisis," *Geography Compass* 13.5 (2019): 3.

54 Thomas Spence's radical land redistribution schemes are outlined in *The Restorer of Society to Its Natural State* (London: J. Smith, 1801). Malcolm Chase documents the impact of Spence's thought, and he emphasizes that agrarianism was "not a mutant throwback to pre-industrialism." Spence's agrarianism was not premodern but rather counter-modern: "Agrarianism was very much the product of, and a response to, the increasing capitalization of industry. It sought a material platform from which industrialization might be ameliorated and directed to labour's advantage." See Chase, *The People's Farm: English Radical Agrarianism, 1775–1840* (Oxford: Clarendon Press, 1988), 179.

55 Harkin, "Surveillance and Space on the Plantation," 141. Another significantly invasive way that Lewis controlled space was through his "medical" reforms. For an analysis of those medical interventions, see Sasha Turner, "Dead Before the Ninth Day": Struggles over Neonatal Care." In *Contested Bodies: Pregnancy, Childrearing, and Slavery in Jamaica* (Philadelphia: University of Pennsylvania Press, 2017), 151–81.

56 The extract from Lewis's letter to Wilberforce is quoted from MacDonald, *Monk Lewis: A Critical Biography*, 53.

57 Barbara Lalla, "Dungeons of the Soul: Frustrated Romanticism in Eighteenth and Nineteenth Century Literature of Jamaica," *MELUS* 21.3 (1996): 7.

58 Hoermann explains that the Haitian Gothic arose because "the Haitian Revolution harboured an 'alternative modernity', which was diametrically opposed to the racialised, colonialist and capitalist North Atlantic modernity and thus had to be suppressed. The Haitian Gothic has, therefore to be considered in the light of these challenges rather than the 'natural' mode in

which to narrate a bloody and protracted slave revolution." See Hoermann, "'A Very Hell of Horrors?' The Haitian Revolution and the Early Transatlantic Haitian Gothic," *Slavery & Abolition* 37.1 (2015): 191. MacDonald would concur that Lewis was influenced by "the Gothic imagination itself, with its recurrent fantasies of domination and revolt, was presumably shaped by the contemporary debate over slavery and abolition." See MacDonald, *Monk Lewis*, 208.

59 Sidney Mintz, "The Origins of the Jamaican Market System," 541. Mary Turner agrees, "the slaves' functions as free peasants promoted the survival and development of precisely those intellectual capacities which the slave system was intended to destroy: curiosity about the world and determination to exert control over life." See Turner, *Slaves and Missionaries: The Disintegration of Jamaican Slave Society, 1787–1834* (Urbana: University of Illinois Press, 1982), 47.

60 Édouard Glissant, *Poetics of Relation*. Translated by Betsy Wing (Ann Arbor: University of Michigan Press, 2010), 65. The British West Indies were managed like extraction colonies. Colonists sought to take whatever they could and then return to Great Britain. Eric Williams notes, "from the standpoint of the grower, the greatest defect of slavery lies in the fact that it quickly exhausts the soil." See Williams, *Capitalism and Slavery* (Chapel Hill: University of North Carolina Press, 2014), 7.

61 Glissant, *Poetics of Relation*, 146.

Chapter 5

1 I have retained Wedderburn's spelling of everywhere as "ever were."

2 Michael Morris, *Scotland and the Caribbean, c.1740–1833: Atlantic Archipelagos* (New York: Routledge, 2015), 183.

3 For example, in an essay on "Black Romanticism," Paul Youngquist represents marronage as flight: "Marronage in this sense resembles what Hardt and Negri call 'exodus,' the fugitive life of the common, in flight from the carceral assemblages of Empire." See Youngquist, "Black Romanticism: A Manifesto," *Studies in Romanticism* 56.1 (2017): 10. From a Caribbean studies perspective, Malcom Ferdinand celebrates the Caribbean Maroons' accomplishment of creole ecologies of survival, yet at the same time he also emphasizes the "flight" of Maroons by arguing their cultures were limited by being "completely outside of the colonial world." He insists that "flight from the world does not change the world." See Ferdinand, *Decolonial Ecology: Thinking from the Caribbean World* (Cambridge: Polity, 2022), 157.

4 I have retained the spelling and punctuation of the original manuscript. "History of the Revolted Negroes in Jamaica." Long Papers, Add. Manuscripts 12431, ca. 1733–39, folio 69, British Library. Although this chapter limits its discussion to travel narratives, Barbara Lalla argues that, during the Romantic period, "the maroon as a fictional type (not necessarily

tied to the Maroon as a sociohistorical entity) begins to take form, growing in independence, a speaker awaiting a discourse." See Lalla, *Defining Jamaican Fiction: Marronage and the Discourse of Survival* (Tuscaloosa: University of Alabama Press, 1996), 54–5. Frances Botkin also discusses fictional and nonfictional representations of the Maroons. See Botkin, *Thieving Three-Fingered Jack: Transatlantic Tales of a Jamaican Outlaw, 1780–2015* (New Brunswick, NJ: Rutgers University Press, 2017).

5 Alex A. Moulton, "Towards the Arboreal Side-Effects of Marronage: Black Geographies and Ecologies of the Jamaican Forest," *Environment and Planning E: Nature and Space*, 2022: 4, 6. Along similar lines, John Favini suggests, "in stark contrast to the settler presupposition that nature was a realm separate from humanity, Maroons here enact an embodied merging of people and place, human and plant." See Favini, "Caring for Nature: Anonymity, Conservation, and the Jamaican Maroons," *Social and Economic Studies* 67.1 (2018): 22. Mario Nisbett argues that the Jamaican Maroons "presented a radical break from some of the most exploitative regimes in the early modern Americas." See *The Workings of Diaspora: Jamaican Maroons and the Claims to Sovereignty* (Lanham, MD: Lexington Books, 2021), 21.

6 R. C. Dallas, *The History of the Maroons, from Their Origin to the Establishment of Their Chief Tribe at Sierra Leone* (London: Longman and Rees, 1803), 106.

7 This chapter focuses only on Nanny of the Maroons. In British Caribbean history, the name Nanny has revolutionary significance because, as Hilary McD. Beckles points out, there is a "Nanny of the Maroons, Jamaica's sole official national heroine, and Nanny Grigg who is described in the literature of the 1816 Barbados slave rebellion as a revolutionary ideologue." See Beckles, "Historicizing Slavery in West Indian Feminisms," *Feminist Review* 59 (1998): 46. Both figures were revolutionary because "both Nanny of the Maroons and Nanny Grigg constituted matriarchal leadership within the revolutionary tradition of antislavery. They organised men and minds for violent anti-slavery warfare." See Hilary McD. Beckles, *Centering Woman: Gender Discourses in Caribbean Slave Society* (Kingston: Ian Randle Publishers, 1999), 163.

8 Philip Thicknesse, *Memoirs and Anecdotes of Philip Thicknesse* (Dublin: Graisberry and Campbell, 1788), 74.

9 Jack P. Green explains the origin of the 1763 map: "During the early 1760s, Thomas Craskell and James Simpson published three large maps, one for each of Jamaica's three counties, based upon surveys they had conducted in 1756–61. Together, these maps provided the most detailed cartographical representation of the island yet produced." See Green, *Settler Jamaica in the 1750s: A Social Portrait* (Charlottesville: University of Virginia Press, 2016), 4. Trevor Burnard and John Garrigus note that the Craskell map is significant because it established the new "plantation machine" of large plantations and slavery. Yet, it also emphasized the permanence of the counter-plantations of the Maroon towns. See Burnard and Garrigus, *The Plantation Machine:*

Atlantic Capitalism in French Saint-Domingue and British Jamaica (Philadelphia: University of Pennsylvania Press, 2016), 31.

10 Moulton, "Towards the Arboreal Side-Effects of Marronage," 4.

11 Kamau Brathwaite, *Wars of Respect: Nanny and Sam Sharpe* (Kingston: API, 1977), 16. Brathwaite argues that Nanny is significant in a separate publication because "the culture & cultural skills that went into marronage were very much part of her personality and achievement." See Brathwaite, "Nanny, Palmares, and the Caribbean Maroon Connection." In *Maroon Heritage: Archaeological, Ethnographic, and Historical Perspectives*, edited by E. Kofi Agorsah, 119–38 (Mona: University of West Indies Press, 2000), 120. Barbara Klamon Kopytoff also notes the significance of Nanny in Jamaican history: "The single truly outstanding figure among the Windward Maroons was not a headman, but Nanny, a formidable obeah woman, after whom two successive settlements were named. Though she seems to have had considerable political influence, she did not displace the headmen in the settlements that bore her name; but it is she who is remembered, not they." See Kopytoff, "The Early Political Development of Jamaican Maroon Societies," *The William and Mary Quarterly* 35.2 (1978): 300. For more on Nanny's significance, see also Alan Tuelon, "Nanny – Maroon Chieftainess," *Caribbean Quarterly* 19.4 (1973): 20–7.

12 Sharpe, *Ghosts of Slavery: A Literary Archeology of Black Women's Lives* (Minneapolis: University of Minnesota Press, 2003), 2.

13 Botkin, *Thieving Three-Fingered Jack*, 21. Although Jack was not a Maroon, Botkin argues, "the inextricable relationship between Jack and the Maroons who killed him creates a critical space to think about the different ways to practice marronage, to fight or resist dominant cultures. Maroons today continue to grapple with Jamaican mainstream culture, struggling with the issue of land rights, representation, and cultural heritage in a developing country where tourism heralds the new colonialism" (8).

14 C. L. G. Harris, "The 'Spirit of Nanny,'" *Jamaica Gleaner*. August 6, 1967, 11. I discovered references to these articles in Sharpe's analysis of Nanny in *Ghosts of Slavery*. Bev Carey, a Maroon who has researched oral histories of Nanny, relates a similar story of Nanny's pumpkin provisions: "Nanny called on Nayankypon (Yankypon), the Creator God, to save her people from sure extinction. The Maroons said that she prayed with fervour and was rewarded with a vision, a dream in which she was directed to plant the pumpkin seeds in her pocket. These seeds, miraculously, in a time far shorter than it had ever been known to happen, almost overnight, germinated, grew long vines which bore an extremely heavy crop of pumpkins, on which her people were able to subsist, until they were able to reap from their old cultivations." See Carey, *The Maroon Story: The Authentic and Original History of the Maroons in the History of Jamaica, 1490–1880* (St. Andrew: Agouti Press, 1997), 288.

15 Although stories of Nanny emphasize that she grew pumpkins, B. W. Higman points out that the term "pumpkin" can mean many varieties of winter squash. See Higman, *Jamaican Food: History, Biology, Culture*

(Kingston: University of West Indies Press, 2008), 209. Moreover, pumpkins and squash were grown alongside the diverse food cultures of the Windward Maroons, as Harris outlines: "It should be understood, however, that the chief source of food was the preserved flesh of the wild boar, thatch-head (the succulent section of the thatch palm revealed when the boughs are properly peeled off), shrimps or black crawfish or janga with which the springs teemed, and cacoon, the fruit of the cacoon withes." See Harris, "Spirit of Nanny," 11.

16 Kenneth M. Bilby, *True-Born Maroons* (Gainesville: University Press of Florida, 2005), 247–60. Lucille Mathurin also argues that Nanny's story resides in "strong oral traditions of her descendants who still occupy the towns which she established in the Portland mountains." See Mathurin, *The Rebel Woman in the British West Indies during Slavery* (Kingston: Institute of Jamaica, 1975), 34.

17 Sylvia Wynter, "Novel and History, Plot and Plantation," *Savacou* 5 (1971): 95–102. Evelyn O'Callaghan provides a helpful analysis of this aspect of Wynter's argument: "In other words, Caribbean people came into being as adjuncts to the product (sugar cane) which they produced." See O'Callaghan, "Caribbean Picturesque from William Beckford to Contemporary Tourism." In *Caribbean Literature in Transition, 1800–1920*, edited by Evelyn O'Callaghan and Tim Watson, 67–84 (Cambridge: Cambridge University Press, 2021), 68.

18 Sophie Chao, "Plantation," *Environmental Humanities* 14.2 (2022): 362.

19 Nicholas Blomley, "Making Private Property: Enclosure Common Right and the Work of Hedges," *Rural History* 18 (2007): 8.

20 Carey, *The Maroon Story*, 171. Carey's assessment of Maroon agricultural expertise in Jamaica has also been noted by Nicholas Rosomoff and Judith Carney in their larger study of the Caribbean marronage. They argue, "liberated from the ceaseless toil of chattel slavery, maroons hunted and farmed for themselves. Survival and liberty crucially depended on diverse cultural knowledge systems that would make tropical soils yield. Maroons could plant food staples presumably of their own choosing – even labor-intensive crops such as rice and cassava (manioc)." See Rosomoff and Carney, *In the Shadow of Slavery: Africa's Botanical Legacy in the Atlantic World* (Berkeley: University of California Press, 2011), 81.

21 In his life narrative, *Horrors of Slavery*, Wedderburn represented his powerful grandmother, Talkee Amy, as an obeah woman, as discussed in Chapter 3. It is impossible to know what exactly Nanny's obeah practices might have been because, as Diana Paton argues, "obeah is a creation of colonialism as much as it is a construction of Africans in the Caribbean." See Paton, *The Cultural Politics of Obeah: Religion, Colonialism and Modernity in the Caribbean World* (Cambridge: Cambridge University Press, 2015), 48. Various definitions fail to capture obeah entirely because, as Michelle Burham adds, "obeah will not stay still, and writings about obeah have historically struggled and failed to fix it. Its restlessness has only been enhanced by the dream of stasis that characterizes the language and conceptual

systems with which Westerners have described and attempted to make sense of it." See Burham, "Obeah's Unproductive Bodies: A Response to 'Obeah: Knowledge, Power, and Writing in the Early Atlantic World,'" *Atlantic Studies* 12, no. 2 (2015): 237. Teresa N. Washington differently argues that Nanny can be understood, instead of as an obeah woman, as an Àjé, a witch figure in African Diasporic traditions. See Washington, *Our Mothers, Our Powers, Our Texts: Manifestations of Àjé in Africana Literature* (Bloomington: Indiana University Press, 2005), 74–5.

22 Alan Richardson, "Romantic Voodoo: Obeah and British Culture, 1797–1807," *Studies in Romanticism* 32.1 (1993): 28.

23 Mavis Campbell, *The Maroons of Jamaica, 1655–1796: A History of Resistance, Collaboration and Betrayal* (Grandby, MA: Bergin and Garvey, 1988), 51. Jenny Sharpe also explains that within the Maroon's storytelling, they prefer "to use the term *science* for designating the ability to command and communicate with dead ancestors, and to draw on their powers for healing the sick and for determining the outcome of events." See Sharpe, *Ghosts of Slavery*, 80.

24 Dipesh Charkrbarty, *Provincializing Europe: Postcolonial Thought and Historical Difference* (Princeton, NJ: Princeton University Press, 2008), 103. Allowing for gaps in knowledge about the Maroons' subaltern pasts, such as Nanny's pumpkin growing, attends to SJ Zhang's suggestion that scholars "practice unlearning extractive reading methods and instead try out a way of reading that leaves space for what was withheld or what should not have been taken to begin with." See Zhang, "*Simarrona*: Beyond Etymologies toward a Practice of Unlearning," *Small Axe: A Caribbean Journal of Criticism* 27.2 (2023): 126.

25 Karla Gottlieb, *The Mother of Us All: The History of Queen Nanny* (London: Africa World Press, 2000), 55.

26 Angelita Reyes, *Mothering across Cultures: Postcolonial Representations* (Minneapolis: University of Minnesota Press, 2001), 82. Reyes also notes that Nanny's obeah has been used to discredit her history: "In fact, because these empowerment stories arise from the Maroon belief in obeah, early historians denied that such a figure as Nanny actually existed."

27 Multiple scholars have argued that Goodison's poetry performs Caribbean women's empowerment, so it should not be read as personal but rather as political and collective. This further testifies to the enduring significance of Nanny's ecologies. For example, Christine Pagnoulle argues that Goodison's poetry outlines a "pilgrimage out of dispossession" and "a trip back into collective memory and a trip out into new possibilities." See Pagnoulle, "Pilgrimage out of Dispossession," *Commonwealth* 17.1 (1994): 100. Similarly, Hugh Hodges argues that Goodison uses the "public function of poetry as healing rite." See Hodges, "Start-Over: Possession Rites and Healing Rituals in the Poetry of Lorna Goodison," *Research in African Literatures* 36.2 (2005): 19.

28 Lorna Goodison, "Nanny," in *Guinea Woman: New and Selected Poems* (Manchester: Carcanet, 2000), 24–5.

29 Jahan Ramazani, *A Transnational Poetics* (Chicago: University of Chicago Press, 2015), 562.

30 Ronald Cummings, "Jamaican Female Masculinities: Nanny of the Maroons and the Genealogy of the Man-Royal," *Journal of West Indian Literature* 21.1/2 (2012): 129–54.

31 Stella Dadzie, *A Kick in the Belly: Women, Slavery and Resistance* (London: Verso, 2020), 159.

32 Dani Burlison, "Paul Lewin Continues Storytelling Tradition through Painting." KQED, August 4, 2015. www.kqed.org/arts/10872336/paul-lewins-roots-of-the-cotton-tree-opens-august-7-in-oakland. I am grateful to Paul Lewin for generously allowing me to reproduce his painting, *Nanny and the Pumpkin Seeds*. More information about Paul Lewin's work can be found at Art House SF: www.arthousesf.com/collections/paul-lewin. Additional work is available on his website www.paullewinartshop.com.

33 Michael Craton, *Testing the Chains: Resistance to Slavery in the British West Indies* (Ithaca, NY: Cornell University Press, 2009), 94. Craton also notes that Nanny was granted land legally: "The original land grant of 500 acres at New Nanny Town in 1741 had been issued to the redoubtable Nanny herself, as if she and her followers had been ordinary settlers."

34 Kimberly John, Colin L. G. Harris, and Susan Otuokon. "Seeking and Securing Sacred Natural Sites among Jamaica's Windward Maroons." In *Sacred Natural Sites: Conserving Nature and Culture*, edited by Bas Verschuuren, Robert Wild, Jeffrey A. McNeely, and Gonzalo Oviedo, 146–55 (London: Earthscan, 2010). While the fight for communal land protection is ongoing, the legality of Maroons making collective decisions about land use has been challenged by the Jamaican government. Kenneth M. Bilby points out that in negotiations about sovereignty, the "Maroons are not willing to separate the question of land rights from the larger issue of self-determination." See Bilby, "Maroon Autonomy in Jamaica," *Cultural Survival Quarterly* 25.4 (2002): 7. Robert Connell would agree that the Maroons' collective approach to land use has increasing relevance for conservation. He argues that in the face of Bauxite mining that now threatens their lands with exploitation, Jamaican Maroons continue "pressing forward with their visions of land tenure and ecological sustainability." See Connell, "Maroon Ecology: Land, Sovereignty, and Environmental Justice," *The Journal of Latin American and Caribbean Anthropology* 25.2 (2020): 229.

35 Dallas was born in Jamaica, and for a short time, he managed his Scottish father's plantation, which included ninety-one enslaved people. Otherwise, there is little information about Dallas's life. While implicated in slavery through his father's plantation, Dallas wrote an anonymous two-volume critique of slavery, *A Short Journey in the West Indies* (1790). He is perhaps best known for his relationship with Lord Byron. He corresponded with and edited his poetry from 1808–11. Dallas published his account of their relationship in *Recollections of the Life of Lord Bryon* (London: Charles Knight, 1824). For more information about Dallas's life, see Jean D'Costa

and Barbara Lalla, *Voices in Exile: Jamaican Texts of the 18th and 19th Centuries* (Birmingham: University of Alabama Press, 2009), 17; and Matthew Parker, *The Sugar Barons: Family, Corruption, Empire, and War in the West Indies* (New York: Bloomsbury Publishing, 2011), 336. For data about the enslaved people on Dallas's estate, see "Robert Charles Dallas." *Legacies of British Slavery database*, University College London. www.ucl.ac.uk/lbs/person/view/2146651103.

36 R. C. Dallas, *The History of the Maroons, from Their Origin to the Establishment of Their Chief Tribe at Sierra Leone* (London: Longman and Rees, 1803), Vol. 2, 392–93. Dallas also equivocates on the issue of slavery. Near the conclusion of *History of the Maroons*, he insisted he has "an ardent tendency in my heart to disapprove the slave trade" before assuring readers that he also sees both sides of the issue.

37 The dogs brought in to subdue the Maroons demonstrate, according to Paul Youngquist, that "the Maroons as a group are distinctive for their proximity to the animal" in the European imagination. See Youngquist, "The Cujo Effect." In *Gorgeous Beasts: Animal Bodies in Historical Perspective*, edited by Joan B. Landes, Paula Young Lee, and Paul Youngquist, 57–72 (University Park: Pennsylvania State University Press, 2015), 59.

38 Ruma Chopra has outlined the complex history of the transport of Maroons to Nova Scotia. She argues, "in Nova Scotia, well-meaning abolitionists transformed Jamaica's dangerous enemies into 'helpless and injured subjects,' exiled from their homeland by Jamaican tyrants." See Chopra, *Almost Home: Maroons between Slavery and Freedom in Jamaica, Nova Scotia, and Sierra Leone* (New Haven, CT: Yale University Press, 2018), 7.

39 Dallas, *History of the Maroons*, 1. 1–3.

40 *The Edinburgh Review* Vol. 2 (4), 1803: 378, 390. Mark Schoenfeld notes the "dehumanizing tendency" of the review. Dallas wrote a rebuttal in the *Anti-Jacobin Review*, and Brougham was outraged that the rebuttal suggested he approved of the use of dogs to hunt the Maroons. Dallas also retaliated by joining Lord Byron to criticize *Edinburgh Review* in *English Bards and Scotch Reviewers*. See Schoenfeld, *British Periodicals and Romantic Identity: The "Literary Lower Empire"* (Basingstoke: Palgrave Macmillan, 2008), 80–1.

41 Craton, *Testing the Chains*, 219.

42 Mavis Campbell argues that "Dallas displayed less of the ethnocentricity – not to say racial bias – typical of the European attitude of the period to colonial people." See Campbell, *The Maroons of Jamaica*, 10.

43 Bryan Edwards, *The Proceedings of the Governor and Assembly of Jamaica, in Regard to the Maroon Negroes* (London: John Stockdale, 1796), 29.

44 Craton, *Testing the Chains*, 64.

45 Dallas, *History of the Maroons*, 106–7. At another point, Dallas referred to Maroon delicacies as an "Epicurian list" of delights (90).

46 Anna Tsing, *The Mushroom at the End of the World: On the Possibility of Life in Capitalist Ruins* (Princeton, NJ: Princeton University Press, 2015), 255.

47 Edwards, *Proceedings of the Governor and Assembly of Jamaica*, 30.

48 Dallas, *History of the Maroons*, 107–8.
49 Alex A. Moulton, "Plotting a New Course for Environmental Humanities: Provision Grounds, Race, and the Future," *Environmental Humanities* 16.2 (2024): 276.
50 In Chapter 3, Shauna J. Sweeney's concept of "market marronage" was used to analyze higgling in *Horrors of Slavery* and *History of Mary Prince*. See Sweeney, "Market Marronage: Fugitive Women and the Internal Marketing System in Jamaica, 1781–1834," *The William and Mary Quarterly* 76.2 (2019): 197–222. On the subversive potential of market-based rumors, see Julius S. Scott, *The Common Wind: Afro-American Currents in the Age of the Haitian Revolution* (London: Verso, 2018), 118.
51 Dallas, *History of the Maroons*, 35.
52 Kathryn Benjamin Golden, "'Armed in the Great Swamp': Fear, Maroon Insurrection, and the Insurgent Ecology of the Great Dismal Swamp," *Journal of African American History* 106.1 (2021): 21. Golden is writing about the Maroon communities in Great Dismal Swamp in Virginia, but her insights can also be applied to the Jamaican internal markets.
53 "History of the Revolted Negroes in Jamaica." Long Papers, British Library. Add.MS 12431, ca. 1733–39, folio 71.
54 Willie Jamaal Wright, "The Morphology of Marronage," *Annals of the American Association of Geographers* 110.4 (2020): 1135. This also demonstrates how, during colonization, the land itself resisted extraction. Rob Nixon contends, "whether the target is an immobile resource such as forests, a mobile resource such as water, of a fugitive resource such as wildlife, the environment itself is not a predictably quiescent victim. Resistance may assume not just human forms but also arise from an unanticipated recalcitrance on the part of the targeted resource." See Nixon, *Slow Violence and the Environmentalism of the Poor* (Cambridge, MA: Harvard University Press, 2011) 20–1.
55 Dallas, *The History of the Maroons*, 50.
56 *History of the Maroons* is also the first written use of the term "Cockpit Country": See B. W. Higman and B. J. Hudson, *Jamaican Place Names* (Jamaica: University of West Indies Press, 2009), 100.
57 An exception can be found on an 1842 map of Jamaica for the Colonial Office, which recorded "The Maroon Old Path" between Old Nanny Town and Charles Town, a legacy of Nanny's early eighteenth-century abolitionist ecologies. Arrowsmith, John. "Map of Jamaica ... By J. Arrowsmith." London, 1842. Located in the British Library.
58 Vincent Brown, *Tacky's Revolt: The Story of an Atlantic Slave War* (Cambridge, MA: Harvard University Press, 2020), 107.
59 Turnpike roads were also used by the colonial government to control access to food and markets, especially after emancipation, as Tim Barringer notes: "Toll roads were often built on the routes to markets, with the support of the Jamaica Assembly, as a means of retarding the developing agrarian production on peasant smallholdings, whose success would potentially compromise the profitability of remaining plantations." See Barringer, "Land, Labor,

Landscape: Views of the Plantation in Victorian Jamaica." In *Victorian Jamaica*, edited by Tim Barringer and Wayne Modest, 263–78. Durham, NC: Duke University Press, 2018), 290.

60 Kopytoff explains the "unusual limestone formation called the Cockpit Country": "This wilderness consists of a succession of sinkholes whose sides rise to form low but steep hills; jagged rocks are interspersed with dense vegetation; surface water is scarce." See Kopytoff, "Early Political Development of Jamaican Maroon Societies," 290.

61 Dallas, *History of the Maroons*, 89.

62 James Knight, *Manuscript of the Natural, Moral, and Political History of Jamaica*. Add MS 12415, Vol. 2, 1742, 94. The anonymous "History of the Revolted Negroes in Jamaica" similarly notes the Maroon's ecological warfare: "Their knowledge of the woods & Mountains and their Robust Hardinness and activity, screened them continually from the pursuits of our parties." Long Papers, Add. Manuscripts 12431, ca. 1733–39, folio 71, British Library.

63 John Favini "Caring for Nature: Anonymity, Conservation, and the Jamaican Maroons," *Social and Economic Studies* 67.1 (2018): 21. Favini further elaborates, "this non-separation from local ecology is embodied in traditional Maroon 'ambush' – a ritually donned form of camouflage in which a Maroon totally covers their body with vines until they are undifferentiable from the surrounding forest. An innovative battle technique during the war with the British, ambush continues to be used at certain ritual moments or during important celebrations" (22).

64 Rinaldo Walcott, *The Long Emancipation: Moving toward Black Freedom* (Durham, NC: Duke University Press, 2021), 108, 107. Quilumbos are subsistence communities organized by formerly enslaved people. Case Watkins has outlined the connection between quilumbos polycultures and cultural autonomy in Brazil. See Watkins, "Landscapes and Resistance in the African Diaspora: Five Centuries of Palm Oil on Bahia's Dendê Coast," *Journal of Rural Studies* 61 (2018): 137–54.

65 Chopra, *Almost Home*, 21. However, the Maroons may have secretly assisted enslaved plantation workers, as C. L. G. Harris argues, "being natural tacticians then, they did not make an outright attack on the ignominious clause because it presented a perfect facade behind which operations could be carried out for the benefit of their 'brethren' in distress." Harris goes on to state that beyond potential assistance, the Maroon example was a significant factor that contributed to the abolition of slavery: "The exploits of these people [Maroons] against the superior arms of the British soldiers fired the imagination of Wilberforce and crystallized his determination to seek no respite from the exacting and dangerous task until slavery – the great open sore of the world – was no more." See Harris, "The Maroons-Praised and Condemned," *Jamaica Gleaner* (July 23, 1967), 7.

66 Morris, *Scotland and the Caribbean*, 183.

67 George Beckford and Michael Witter argue that the Maroon treaty was "another example of the tactics of divide and rule." See *Small Garden …*

Bitter Weed: Struggle and Change in Jamaica (Jamaica: Maroon Publishing, 1982), 20. Paul Youngquist reads the Maroon treaty as "a bold declaration of indigenous rights, an act of anti-colonial countermapping that lays claim not merely to a represented territory but more completely to a whole way of life, grounded in that Maroon common and sustained by collective ownership without deed." See "Maps without Territory: Disappearing Trelawney Town." In *Romantic Cartographies: Mapping, Literature, Culture, 1789–1832*, edited by Sally Bushell, Julia S. Carlson, and Damian Walford Davies, 271–91 (Cambridge: Cambridge University Press, 2020), 272.

68 For a full account of Stedman's biography, see Richard and Sally Price, "Introduction," in *Stedman's Surinam: Life in an Eighteenth-Century Slave Society* (Baltimore: Johns Hopkins University Press, 1992), xi–lxxv.

69 Richard and Sally Price explain that Joseph Johnson hired a proslavery writer, William Thomson, to edit Stedman's text. While the 1796 version minimized the "coarseness" of Stedman's style, it also, unfortunately, excised his harsh judgment of the violent excesses of Surinam planter society. Ibid., xlv.

70 Debbie Lee, *Slavery and the Romantic Imagination* (Philadelphia: University of Pennsylvania Press, 2002): 116; Saree Makdisi, *William Blake and the Impossible History of the 1790s* (Chicago: University of Chicago Press, 2003), 252.

71 Nicole N. Aljoe, *Creole Testimonies: Slave Narratives from the British West Indies, 1709–1838* (New York: Palgrave, 2012), 33. Helen Thomas has written about Stedman's relationship with Joanna and the "dynamics of miscegenation." See Thomas, *Romanticism and Slave Narratives: Transatlantic Testimonies* (Cambridge: Cambridge University Press, 2000), 125–32. Most significant for the popularity and distribution of Joanna's story was Lydia Maria Child's republication of it in the United States in *Narrative of Joanna, an Emancipated Slave of Surinam* (Boston: Isaac Knapp, 1838).

72 Price, "Introduction," xiv.

73 Elizabeth Bohls, *Slavery and the Politics of Place: Representing the Colonial Caribbean, 1770–1833* (Cambridge: Cambridge University Press, 2014), 55. Bohls also notes an oscillation in Stedman's text in which he "alternately praises incompatible ways of living in and from tropical nature: the stripped down self-sufficiency of the itinerant Maroons and the slave-driven commodity production of the colonial machine" (66).

74 Rachel B. Herrmann, *No Useless Mouth: Waging War and Fighting Hunger in the American Revolution* (Ithaca, NY: Cornell University Press, 2019), 13. I also discuss Herrmann's concept of "victual warfare" in Chapter 1.

75 J. G. Stedman, *Narrative of a Five Years' Expedition against the Revolted Negroes of Surinam*, edited by Richard Price and Sally Price (Baltimore: Johns Hopkins University Press, 1988), 449. The quotations analyzed in the following section are taken from J. G. Stedman's 1791 draft version of *Narrative* that he originally submitted to Joseph Johnson. The draft is unedited, and my quotations retain Stedman's nonstandard spelling and punctuation.

76 Ibid., 404. Stedman expresses surprise at finding the Maroons growing rice, a staple from plantations, in their settlements. Yet this evidence coincides with oral stories that have been told by generations of Saramaka Maroons. One example is: "Paánza is a female slave, who one day decides to flee as she is harvesting rice on a plantation. But before she runs, Paánza scoops up some grains of ripened rice and stuffs this seed rice in her hair. She escapes, and brings the grains to the maroons living in the forest. This, Saramaka descendants recount, is how they came to grow rice." Rice cultivation then amounts to evidence of the forethought and planning that went into creating Maroon communities in Surinam. See Richard Rosomoff and Judith Carney, *In the Shadow of Slavery: Africa's Botanical Legacy in the Atlantic World* (Berkeley: University of California Press, 2011), 92.
77 Stedman, *Narrative of a Five Years' Expedition*, 449.
78 Rosomoff and Carney, *The Shadow of Slavery*, 97. What Stedman documented is also similar to what, in the Haitian context, Jean Casimir calls counter-plantations: "Their emancipation-knowledge moved them beyond the absolute disorder into which they had arrived, carrying them toward a response to slavery: the counter-plantation order." See Casimir, *The Haitians: A Decolonial History*. Translated by Laurent Dubois (Chapel Hill: University of North Carolina Press, 2020), 328.
79 Alan Bewell, *Romanticism and Colonial Disease* (Baltimore: Johns Hopkins University Press, 1999), 93.
80 Emily Senior, *The Caribbean and the Medical Imagination, 1764–1834: Slavery, Disease, and Colonial Modernity* (Cambridge: Cambridge University Press, 2018), 92.
81 Stedman, *Narrative of a Five Years' Expedition*, 409. In keeping with the theme of the Maroons' health, the frontispiece to Stedman's *Narrative*, engraved by Franceso Bartolozzi, depicted the health of a Maroon who has been murdered. Marcus Wood reads this image as pornographic, since it "sentimentalizes, sexualizes, and trans-sexualizes the body of the black victim at the moment of death." Indeed, the naked Maroon alongside the phallic imagery of Stedman's pistol, sword, and rifle suggested a violent, racist homoeroticism. At the same time, Stedman's image stands out not just because of his whiteness, but also because of the way he gazes vacantly forward, leaning on his rifle and standing on one foot. Stedman dominates the scene, but he bears the marks of ill health. See Wood, *Slavery, Empathy, and Pornography* (Oxford: Oxford University Press, 2002), 98.
82 Stedman, *Narrative of a Five Years' Expedition*, 412.
83 Bohls, *Slavery and the Politics of Place*, 62.
84 Often discussed are the torture scenes in *A Negro Hung Alive by the Ribs to the Gallows* or *Flagellation of a Female Samboe Slave*, for example. See David V. Erdman, *Prophet against Empire* (New York: Dover Publications, 1991) 233; and Anne K. Mellor, "Sex, Violence, and Slavery: Blake and Wollstonecraft," *Huntington Library Quarterly* 58.3/4 (1995): 345–70.

85 Susan Scott Parrish, "Embodying African Knowledge in Colonial Surinam: Two William Blake Engravings in Stedman's 1796 Narrative." In *Slave Portraiture in the Atlantic World*, edited by Agnes Lugo-Ortiz and Angela Rosenthal, 257–82 (Cambridge: Cambridge University Press, 2013), 259. Parrish also contends that, together, Blake and Stedman "fashioned a portrait of African optical and territorial mastery that challenged their viewers' habits of identification" (277). Similarly, Monique Allewaert notes that colonists were startled by their lack of knowledge and skill to traverse Surinam's landscape: "Anglo-European colonists, unfamiliar with this ecology, were at a significant disadvantage against the Africans, Indians, and poor whites who were forced to labor there and who used the knowledge and skills they had gained from this labor to disrupt the order of the plantation." See Allewaert, *Ariel's Ecology: Plantations, Personhood, and Colonialism in the American Tropics* (Minneapolis: University of Minnesota Press, 2013), 47.

86 Stedman, *Narrative of a Five Years' Expedition*, 534.

87 Blake altered Stedman's design based on an engraving he had done previously for John Hunter's *An Historical Journal of the Transactions at Port Jackson and Norfolk Island* (1793). Robert Essick notes of the engraving: "The family is a scruffy little group in the drawing [received from Hunter], and faces seem more like simplified caricatures than careful representations. Not only has Blake altered the disposition of the figures, but he has transformed the poor and naked aborigines into noble savages." See Essick, *William Blake, Printmaker* (Princeton, NJ: Princeton University Press, 1980), 53. Essick's reproductions of both engravings expose several similarities between *Family of Negro Slaves* and the Aboriginal people in *A Family of New South Wales*. Both families are depicted as parents with two children, and they represent food sovereignty with a line of freshly caught fish.

88 Lily Gurton-Wachter, "Blake's 'Little Black Thing': Happiness and Injury in the Age of Slavery," *ELH* 87.2 (2020): 539. Gurton-Wachter also argues that by focusing on happiness, Stedman and Blake usefully "turn away from the numbing repetition of sentimental clichés of suffering and an interest instead in the power of opaque and unnamable modes of feeling."

89 Stedman, *Narrative of a Five Years' Expedition*, 534.

90 Although Blake developed a long-term friendship with Stedman during his work for the *Narrative*, they did not meet until 1792, well after Stedman had written the draft for Joseph Johnson, so Blake could not have influenced Stedman's writing. See Price, "Introduction," xxxviii. G. E. Bentley details the intricacies of Blake and Stedman's friendship. See Bentley, *The Stranger from Paradise: A Biography of William Blake* (New Haven, CT: Yale University Press, 2001), 111–17. However, the question remains as to what extent Stedman might have influenced Blake's views on slavery. David V. Erdman persuasively argues, "the persons and problems of Stedman's *Narrative* reappear, modified, in the texts and illustrations of Blake's *Visions [of the Daughters of Albion (1793)].*" Erdman, *Prophet against Empire*, 233.

91 Moulton, "Plotting a New Course," 275.

92 Stedman, *Narrative of a Five Years' Expedition*, 410.
93 Ferdinand, *Decolonial Ecology*, 148.

Chapter 6

1 Incidentally, Lord Holland's Friendship Estate was located just a few miles from both James Wedderburn and Matthew Lewis's plantations.
2 I have retained the grammatical errors of the original. Letter from Thomas McNeil to Lord Holland, February 15, 1839, Holland House Papers at the British Library (Add Ms. 51816, ff. 169–70). Quoted in B. W. Higman, *Jamaica Surveyed: Plantation Maps and Plans of the Eighteenth and Nineteenth Centuries* (Kingston: Institute of Jamaica Publications Limited, 1988), 108.
3 Ryan Hanley discovered *An Address to the Right Honourable Lord Brougham and Vaux* (1831) in the Rhodes House collections of the Bodleian Libraries. I have not read the original text of the newly discovered *Address*. I am instead relying on the pamphlet's reproduction in full by Hanley in his article, "A Radical Change of Heart: Robert Wedderburn's Last Word on Slavery," *Slavery & Abolition* 37. 2 (2016): 423–45. The quotation is from page 438. My Conclusion explores the pamphlet in depth.
4 Quoted in Higman, *Jamaica Surveyed*, 108. The laborers argued for what anthropologist Jean Besson identifies as Caribbean "family land." She explains, "minuscule plots of land are regarded as the inalienable property of all descendants of an ancestor who obtained the land." These plots were "a strategy for maximizing freehold rights." See Besson, "Land Tenure in the Free Villages of Trelawny, Jamaica: A Case Study in the Caribbean Peasant Response to Emancipation," *Slavery & Abolition* 5.1 (1984): 4. Furthermore, by evoking the ultimate authority of the British Queen, this quotation also resonates with Hilary McD. Beckles' observation that "most enslaved Africans were extracted from societies ruled by monarchs, and were socialized to read political environments by privileging the ideas and actions of kings." See Beckles, "The Wilberforce Song: How Enslaved Caribbean Blacks Heard British Abolitionists," *Parliamentary History* 26.4 (2007): 117.
5 Thomas C. Holt, *The Problem of Freedom: Race, Labor, and Politics in Jamaica and Britain, 1832–1938* (Baltimore: Johns Hopkins University Press, 1992), 168. Holt also points out that "drafters of the apprenticeship system did regard the slaves as children needing to be reeducated as wage laborers and resocialized as citizens" (56).
6 Malcom Ferdinand, *Decolonial Ecology: Thinking from the Caribbean World* (Cambridge: Polity, 2022), 121, 117.
7 Ruth Wilson Gilmore, *Abolitionist Geography: Essays towards Liberation* (London: Verso, 2022), 481.
8 McNeil's letters outline a localized conflict. However, they are representative of the larger experience of newly freed Black people in the Caribbean. The amount of unoccupied land in Jamaica enabled formerly enslaved people to leave plantations instead of paying rent. Richard S. Dunn documents, "in

Jamaica – and also in Trinidad and British Guiana – there was a great deal of unoccupied, uncultivated land, so the ex-slaves would be able to desert the sugar estates and set up independent settlements in the bush." Dunn's extensive historical research about Jamaica's Westmoreland parish found that from 1838 to 1860, the parish went from 150 to 750 small freeholds held by Black laborers. By 1861, two-thirds of Black people residing in Westmoreland were independent peasant farmers. See Dunn, *A Tale of Two Plantations: Slave Life and Labor in Jamaica and Virginia* (Cambridge, MA: Harvard University Press, 2014), 370–1, 382–84.

9 Catherine Hall, *Civilising Subjects: Metropole and Colony in the English Imagination, 1830–1867* (Chicago: University of Chicago Press, 2002), 121.

10 Tim Barringer, "Land, Labor, Landscape: Views of the Plantation in Victorian Jamaica." In *Victorian Jamaica*, edited by Tim Barringer and Wayne Modest, 263–78 (Durham, NC: Duke University Press, 2018), 294.

11 George Beckford and Michael Witter, *Small Garden ... Bitter Weed: Struggle and Change in Jamaica* (Jamaica: Maroon Publishing, 1982), 40. Shauna J. Sweeney also documents that "emancipation was defined by pitched battles over access to provision grounds, many of which were technically located on plantation property, and a surge in the number of 'free villages' organized around subsistence cultivation and the informal economy." See Sweeney, "Market Marronage: Fugitive Women and the Internal Marketing System in Jamaica, 1781–1834," *The William and Mary Quarterly* 76.2 (2019): 222.

12 J. M. Neeson, *Commoners: Common Right, Enclosure, and Social Change in England, 1700–1820* (Cambridge: Cambridge University Press, 1993), 34.

13 Joseph Sturge and Thomas Harvey, *The West Indies in 1837* (London: Hamilton, Adams, and Co, 1838), 358. This text is an example of the post-abolition hybrid text that Martha Schoolman describes: "Those who weren't satisfied with mere data traveled to the British Caribbean to see for themselves, often contributing to the growing, oddly hybrid genre of the West Indian travelogue-cum-agricultural report, in which the authors would provide traveler's recommendations about accommodations, health, and hygiene, along with descriptions of life on the now free-labor plantations, and transcriptions of interviews with planters and the formerly enslaved." See Schoolman, "West Indian Emancipation and the Time of Regionalism in the Hemispheric 1850s." In *Mapping Region in Early American Writing*, edited by Edward Watts, Keri Holt, and John Funchion, 81–96 (Athens: University of Georgia Press, 2015), 86–7.

14 Hall, *Civilising Subjects*, 136.

15 Ibid., 108.

16 Richard Huzzey, "Concepts of Liberty: Freedom, Laissez-Faire and the State after Britain's Abolition of Slavery." In *Emancipation and the Remaking of the British Imperial World*, edited by Catherine Hall, Nicholas Draper, and Keith McClelland, 149–72 (Manchester: Manchester University Press, 2014), 156.

17 Quoted in ibid., 157.

18 Christopher Taylor, *Empire of Neglect: The West Indies in the Wake of British Liberalism* (Durham, NC: Duke University Press, 2018), 104.
19 Sturge and Harvey, *West Indies in 1837*, 378.
20 The biopolitical control of free labor was already well underway in Great Britain. As Ron Broglio argues, "food is a way in which the biopower of the masses, the swinish multitude, resists quantification." See Broglio, *Beasts of Burden: Biopolitics, Labor, and Animal Life in British Romanticism* (Albany: State University of New York Press, 2017), 27.
21 Sturge and Harvey, *West Indies in 1837*, 379.
22 Raj Patel and Jason W. Moore, *A History of the World in Seven Cheap Things: A Guide to Capitalism, Nature, and the Future of the Planet* (Berkeley: University of California Press, 2017), 22. Patel and Moore further argue, "capitalism's practices of cheap nature would define whose lives and whose work mattered – and whose did not." Thus, in plantation capitalism, "care for young and old, for the sick and those with special needs, agricultural work, and the work of extrahuman natures (animals, soils, forests, fuels) was rendered largely invisible" (24–5).
23 Sturge and Harvey, *West Indies in 1837*, 378–79.
24 Ibid., 380.
25 Catherine Hall documents that Sturge was in conversation with other advocates for free villages. She notes that these men formed a discourse of speaking for Black Jamaicans, by, paradoxically, excluding their voices: "The authors quoted each other, were reviewed favourably in the same journals and newspapers, provided reference points for the same section of the public. Their particular version of colonial discourse, their strategic creation of a space for subject peoples through the production of knowledge and exercise of power and surveillance, was abolitionist discourse, organized around the notion of 'negroes' (their terminology) as younger brothers and sisters." See Hall, *White, Male and Middle Class: Explorations in Feminism and History* (Cambridge: Polity, 2013), 211.
26 Phillippo's humanitarian efforts arose from the belief that "the Jamaican slave community was filled with degenerates desperately in need of his guiding hand." Colleen A. Vasconcellos, *Slavery, Childhood, and Abolition in Jamaica, 1788–1838* (Athens: University of Georgia Press, 2015), 72.
27 Marcus Wood, *The Horrible Gift of Freedom: Atlantic Slavery and the Representation of Emancipation* (Athens: University of Georgia Press, 2010), 119.
28 Most antislavery proponents advocated for "the vision of the West Indies as a successful business environment where formerly enslaved people would provide labor for up-to-date capitalist enterprises that respected humanitarian principles." Alex Tyrrell, "A Business of Philanthropy: The Montserrat Company, 1856–1961," *The Journal of Caribbean History* 38.2 (2004): 186.
29 Thomas Carlyle, "Occasional Discourse on the Negro Question" *Fraser's Magazine*, 40 (December 1849), 671. The essay discussed here was first published in *Fraser's Magazine*; Carlyle expanded and retitled the essay,

"Occasional Discourse on the N*** Question," which Thomas Bosworth reissued in pamphlet form in 1853. For information about the publication history of "Occasional Discourse," including differences between the two versions, see Rodger L. Tarr, "Emendation as Challenge: Carlyle's 'Negro Question' from Journal to Pamphlet," *Papers of the Bibliographical Society of America* 75. 3 (1981): 341–45.

30 Sturge and Harvey, *West Indies in 1837*, 378.

31 Tarr, "Emendation as Challenge," 342; Helen Small, *The Function of Cynicism at the Present Time* (Oxford: Oxford University Press, 2020), 96. While Tarr's article helpfully outlines the publication history, I disagree with Tarr's assessment that "it should be remembered that Carlyle's concern was for the immediate 'black Irishman' and not for the remote, and to him, metaphorical 'Quashee.'" Along these lines, David Theo Goldberg suggests, "Carlyle's negrophobia was tied up with a critique of laissez faire capitalist political economy prevailing at the time. The failure of the potato crop due to extended drought had devastated Irish peasants (which he witnessed first-hand), and the mid-century recession had caused massive unemployment among the English working classes, represented in Carlyle's discourse in the forlorn figure of the 'Distressed Needlewoman.'" See Goldberg, "Liberalism's Limits: Carlyle and Mill on 'The Negro Question,'" *Nineteenth-Century Contexts* 22 (2000): 205.

32 Gretchen Gerzina, *Black London: Life before Emancipation* (New Brunswick, NJ: Rutgers University Press, 1995), 7. Verene A. Shepherd agrees that Carlyle's essay was part of a larger intellectual movement: "Freed from slavery, entrapped within white supremacist economic, legal, and political systems, blacks were now the target of a major intellectual effort to demonstrate, using methods of the social and natural sciences, that they were mentally inferior to whites." See Shepherd, "Work, Culture, and Creolization: Slavery and Emancipation in Eighteenth and Nineteeth-Century Jamaica." In *Art and Emancipation in Jamaica: Isaac Mendes Belisario and His Worlds*, edited by T. J. Barringer, Gillian Forrester, and Barbaro Martinez-Ruiz, 27–39 (New Haven, CT: Yale Center for British Art in association with Yale University Press, 2007), 38.

33 See Orlando Patterson, *The Sociology of Slavery: An Analysis of the Origins, Development and Structure of Negro Slave Society in Jamaica* (London: Fairleigh Dickenson University Press, 1969), 175. Susan Scott Parrish notes that the stereotype was sometimes used by enslaved people to their advantage: "On Jamaican plantations, slaves developed the practice of Quashee, playing into their masters' stereotypes of incompetence to stall the exaction of labor or expertise." See Parrish, *American Curiosity: Cultures of Natural History in the Colonial British Atlantic World* (Chapel Hill: University of North Carolina Press, 2006), 263. Another context for using the name can be found in the 1821 trial of maroons named Quashie and Cudjoe. More information about this trial can be found in Diana Paton, *The Cultural Politics of Obeah: Religion, Colonialism and Modernity in the Caribbean World* (Cambridge: Cambridge University Press, 2015), 88–9.

34 Carlyle, "Occasional Discourse," 671.

35 I would like to thank Nihad Farooq for noticing this connection. After emancipation, white Southerners strategically animalized growing or eating watermelon. The powerful trope of African Americans growing and eating watermelon is wielded to this day to dehumanize them. After the election of President Barack Obama, numerous references to watermelon were deployed to critique his leadership. For more on the history of watermelons in the United States, see William R. Black, "How Watermelons Became Black: Emancipation and the Origins of a Racist Trope," *Journal of the Civil War Era* 8.1 (2018): 64–86. Black argues, "the watermelon had a potentially subversive power. This was demonstrated when enslaved people boasted of their watermelon crops or paraded their produce throughout town" (68).

36 Jean Casimir, *The Haitians: A Decolonial History*. Translated by Laurent Dubois (Chapel Hill: University of North Carolina Press, 2020), 332.

37 J. T. Roane, "Plotting the Black Commons," *Souls: A Critical Journal of Black Politics, Culture, and Society* 20.3 (2018): 242. Kathryn Yusoff similarly argues that "the relation of slave to provision ground was a relation to a contingent earth, a material relation forged in resistance to the dehumanizing of colonialism that opened a carceral geography." See Yusoff, *A Billion Black Anthropocenes or None* (Minneapolis: University of Minnesota Press, 2018), 36.

38 Carlyle, "Occasional Discourse," 674.

39 Alan Rice, *Radical Narratives of the Black Atlantic* (London: Continuum, 2003), 155.

40 Wendell Berry, *The Art of the Commonplace: The Agrarian Essays of Wendell Berry* (Berkeley: Counterpoint, 2002), 130.

41 Walden Bello, *The Food Wars* (London: Verso, 2009), 35.

42 As a thinker who valorized the past, Carlyle's model of Black servitude came from the British medieval manor and not from Caribbean slavery, which he knew very little about. Alice Chandler argues that this medievalism was a "dream of order," that was constructed by arguing for "the superiority of medieval civilization by exaggerating the wealth of England in the Middle Ages." See Chandler, *A Dream of Order: The Medieval Ideal in Nineteenth-Century English Literature* (Lincoln: University of Nebraska Press, 1970), 68.

43 Carlyle, "Occasional Discourse," 675.

44 Hall, *Civilising Subjects*, 48.

45 Wood, *Slavery, Empathy, and Pornography*, 373. Wood further clarifies that Carlyle "defends chattel slavery because of its contractual basis, which is seen as long term, as compared with the temporary contract systems of laissez-faire, which are wholly contingent on the vagaries of the marketplace" (358). Vanessa D. Dickerson argues that Carlyle did not even attempt to imagine the perspective of African Jamaicans because "he most probably did not credit poor Quashee with enough intelligence to evince any rhetorical skills." See Dickerson, *Dark Victorians* (Urbana-Champaign: University of Illinois Press, 2008), 78.

46 Carlyle, "Occasional Discourse," 672.

47 James Steuart, for example, also argued that tropical climates were hostile to the work ethic: "If the soil be vastly rich, situated in a warm climate, and naturally watered, the productions of the earth will be almost spontaneous; this will make the inhabitants lazy." See Steuart, *An Inquiry into the Principles of Political Oeconomy* (Dublin: James Williams, 1770), 34. The connection between Carlyle and Steuart is discussed in Catherine Hall, *Civilizing Subjects*, 48–9.

48 Bryan Edwards, *The History, Civil and Commercial, of the British Colonies in the West Indies* (London: John Stockdale, 1793), II, 162).

49 Matthew Lewis, *Journal of a West-India Proprietor* (London: J. Murray, 1834), 101.

50 Raymond Williams, "Ideas of Nature" in *Problems in Materialism and Culture: Selected Essays* (London: Verso, 1980), 76. Williams refers to Locke's argument that human beings created private property by working and improving the land: "Whatsoever then he removes out of the state that nature hath provided, and left it in, he hath mixed his labour with, and joined to it something that is his own, and thereby makes it his property." See John Locke, *Two Treatises of Government and A Letter concerning Toleration*, edited by Ian Shapiro (New Haven, CT: Yale University Press, 2003), 111.

51 Holt, *The Problem of Freedom*, 279.

52 Carlyle, "Occasional Discourse," 675, 676. However, Carlyle was no uncritical proponent of capitalism. Marcus Wood argues that Carlyle "defends chattel slavery because of its contractual basis which is seen as long term, as compared with the temporary contract systems of laissez-faire, which are wholly contingent on the vagaries of the market place." See Wood, *Slavery, Empathy, and Pornography* (Oxford: Oxford University Press, 2002), 373. Similarly, Susan Kingsley Kent argues, "Carlyle saw in slavery, or its preferred alternative, a system of 'servants hired for life,' the proper and divinely ordered relationship of 'wise men' to foolish others." See Kent, *Gender and Power in Britain 1640–1990* (New York: Routledge, 2002), 221.

53 Thomas Malthus, *An Essay on the Principle of Population* (London: Joseph Johnson, 1803), 250. In England, Malthusian biopolitical theories of scarcity and the enclosure laws worked together to repress long-established common rights. These repressive apparatuses not only made private property legal and criminalized commoning, but they also naturalized private property to repress the cultural memory of the commons.

54 David Collings, *Monstrous Society: Reciprocity, Discipline, and the Political Uncanny, c. 1780–1848* (Lewisburg, PA: Bucknell University Press, 2009), 163. Mitchell Dean similarly argues that the movement into a capitalist economy was accompanied by a shift from government as a patriarchal benefactor to a government that disciplines the poor simply by removing institutional barriers to the Malthusian "*bioeconomic* laws of population and subsistence." See Dean, *The Constitution of Poverty: Toward a Genealogy of Liberal Governance* (London: Routledge, 1991), 120.

55 Robert Wedderburn, *The Forlorn Hope, or a Call to the Supine to Rouse from Indolence and Assert Public Rights* (London: C Jennison, 1817), 15. Wedderburn's sentiments on Malthus are unsurprising because the Spencean Philanthropists openly opposed Malthus. Malcolm Chase argues, "'Malthusianism' was perhaps the central social issue preoccupying radicalism in these decades. More than any other body of ideas, Malthusian economics was an affront to the belief system prevalent in the early industrial working class. Agrarian concepts of nature and society lay at the core of this system." See Chase, *The People's Farm: English Radical Agrarianism, 1775–1840* (Oxford: Clarendon Press, 1988), 132.

56 Sturge and Harvey, *West Indies in 1837*, 360.

57 Malthusian concepts of nature, however, ultimately fail, and Robert Mitchell argues, "as a consequence, nature – pace Malthus – can never dictate regulatory relationships; rather, humans must create and choose among forms of self-regulation by channeling and linking various forms of natural movements." See Mitchell, "Regulating Life: Romanticism, Science, and the Liberal Imagination," *European Romantic Review* 29.3 (2018): 275–93. Catherine Gallagher notes that difficult work for delayed gratification is a necessary part of capitalist culture: "Capitalism must define labor as unpleasurable, because we seek the reward at the end (wages). If we delighted in labor itself – as for example, a mode of self-expression, an experience of mastery, or a means of self-realization – we would not be counting the hours and trying to make them pay." See Gallagher, *The Body Economic: Life, Death, and Sensation in Political Economy and the Victorian Novel* (Princeton, NJ: Princeton University Press, 2006), 58.

58 Carlyle, "Occasional Discourse," 676.

59 Ibid., 675.

60 Beckford and Witter, *Small Garden*, 43.

61 J. S. Mill, "The Negro Question." *Fraser's Magazine for Town and Country*, 40 (January 1850), 29.

62 Ibid., 30. Anthony Bogues argues that Mill's "vision was not a fixed racial and colonial order but one in which imperial polity should be geared toward training the colonial child-subject and eventually allowing him or her some degree of political equality." See Bogues, "John Stuart Mill and 'The Negro Question': Race, Colonialism, and the Ladder of Civilization." In *Race and Racism in Modern Philosophy*, 217–34 (Ithaca, NY: Cornell University Press, 2005), 229.

63 Lisa Lowe, *The Intimacies of Four Continents* (Durham, NC: Duke University Press, 2015), 15.

64 Kenneth M. Bilby, *True-Born Maroons* (Gainesville: University Press of Florida, 2005), 3. Mario Nisbett further notes that post-emancipation "the British increasingly attempted to curtail Maroon autonomy." See Nisbett, *The Workings of Diaspora: Jamaican Maroons and the Claims to Sovereignty* (Lanham, MD: Lexington Books, 2021), 22.

65 Alex A. Moulton, "Towards the Arboreal Side-Effects of Marronage: Black Geographies and Ecologies of the Jamaican Forest," *Environment and Planning E: Nature and Space* 6.1 (2023): 6.

Conclusion

1 Catherine Hall, *Civilising Subjects: Metropole and Colony in the English Imagination, 1830–1867* (Chicago: University of Chicago Press, 2002), 108, 24.

2 Michael Craton, *Testing the Chains: Resistance to Slavery in the British West Indies* (Ithaca, NY: Cornell University Press, 2009), 252. Diana Paton also argues that in response to emancipation, formerly enslaved people "removed themselves as far as possible from the subordination inherent in wage labor in plantation societies, a form of subordination that in fact echoed, rather than stood apart from, slavery." See Paton, *No Bond but the Law: Punishment, Race, and Gender in Jamaican State Formation, 1780–1870* (Durham, NC: Duke University Press, 2004), 9.

3 Ruth Wilson Gilmore, *Abolitionist Geography: Essays towards Liberation* (London: Verso, 2022), 474. The continuing resonance of this issue in the twenty-first century seems to bear out Thomas C. Holt's insight: "The emancipation of slaves helps to frame freedom as problematic for us all. Paradoxically, it is from ex-slaves that we may well learn much of what it means to be free." See Holt, *The Problem of Freedom Race, Labor, and Politics in Jamaica and Britain, 1832–1938* (Baltimore: Johns Hopkins University Press, 1992), 9.

4 Ryan Hanley, "A Radical Change of Heart: Robert Wedderburn's Last Word on Slavery," *Slavery & Abolition* 37.2 (2016): 433. Hanley discovered *An Address to the Right Honourable Lord Brougham and Vaux* (1831) in the Rhodes House collections of the Bodleian Libraries.

5 I have not read the original text of the newly discovered *Address*. Instead, I am relying on its full reproduction by Hanley in ibid., 436.

6 In another article, Hanley usefully draws out the connections between the emergence of racism and working-class discourse. For many working-class writers, "the money and attention being poured into the abolitionist movement would have been better spent on the equally exploited, but inherently more deserving, white British workers." See Hanley, "Slavery and the Birth of the Working-Class Racism in England, 1814–1833," *Transactions of the Royal Historical Society* 26 (2016): 104.

7 Lisa Lowe, *The Intimacies of Four Continents* (Durham, NC: Duke University Press, 2015), 13.

8 Malcom Ferdinand, *Decolonial Ecology: Thinking from the Caribbean World* (Cambridge: Polity, 2022), 12. My reading of Wedderburn here is also informed by Stefan M. Wheelock's argument that when scholars read Black writers only within the ideals of white radical abolitionism or heroic violent resistance, they neglect their more nuanced prophetic and speculative intellectual projects. See Wheelock, *Barbaric Culture and Black Critique: Black Antislavery Writers, Religion, and the Slaveholding Atlantic* (Charlottesville: University of Virginia Press, 2016), 20–1.

9 Wedderburn, *An Address*, 435.

10 Paton, *No Bond but the Law*, 7–8. Rinaldo Walcott further points out, "it is precisely because of Black people's intimate relationship to property as both an idea and an actual practice as a result of having been property ourselves, that we understand the entire carceral network and the innumerable problems that afflict it are intimately bound up with modern conceptions of property." See Walcott, *On Property* (Windsor: Canadiana, 2021), 27.
11 Katherine McKittrick, "Plantation Futures," *Small Axe: A Caribbean Journal of Criticism* 17.3 (2013): 1–15.
12 I discussed Lewis's plan for emancipation through land reparations in Chapter 4. The extract from Lewis's letter to Wilberforce is quoted from D. L. Macdonald, *Monk Lewis: A Critical Biography* (Toronto: University of Toronto Press, 2000), 53. Padraic X. Scanlan also argues that Wedderburn believed that "if freed people held land in common, then no missionaries could hector, no landlords could gouge, and no police could overawe." See Scanlan, *Slave Empire: How Slavery Built Modern Britain* (London: Robinson, 2022), 290.
13 Sylvia Wynter, "Novel and History, Plot and Plantation," *Savacou* 5 (1971): 100–1.
14 Joseph Sturge suggested limited and controlling formerly enslaved people's independent food production in *The West Indies in 1837* (London: Hamilton, Adams, and Co., 1838). This text is discussed at length in Chapter 6.
15 Elizabeth DeLoughry argues "although the plantation complex greatly impacted the environmental history of the region, sites outside the Euclidean grids of the plantocracy provided vital alternative communities and continuities with African and indigenous traditions. Accordingly, these spaces have become integral to the Caribbean historical imagination in the wake of decolonization." She traces Black ecologies in contemporary decolonial Caribbean literature, such as Sylvia Wynter's *Hills of Hebron*, Michelle Cliff's *No Telephone to Heaven*, and Edna Brodber's *The Rainmaker's Mistake*. See DeLoughrey, "Ecocriticism: The Politics of Place." In *Routledge Companion to Anglophone Caribbean Literature*, edited by Michael A. Bucknor and Alison Donnell, 265–75 (New York: Routledge, 2011), 26.
16 Édouard Glissant, *Poetics of Relation*. Translated by Betsy Wing (Ann Arbor: University of Michigan Press, 2010), 144.
17 George Boulukos, *The Grateful Slave: The Emergence of Race in Eighteenth-Century British and American Culture* (Cambridge: Cambridge University Press, 2008), 21.
18 Wedderburn, *Address*, 437–38.
19 Letter from Thomas McNeil to Lord Holland, quoted in B. W. Higman, *Jamaica Surveyed: Plantation Maps and Plans of the Eighteenth and Nineteenth Centuries* (Kingston: Institute of Jamaica Publications Limited, 1988), 108.
20 Michel-Rolph Trouillot, *Haiti: State against Nation* (New York: New York University Press, 1990), 39–40.
21 Jean Casimir, *The Haitians: A Decolonial History*. Translated by Laurent Dubois (Chapel Hill: University of North Carolina Press, 2020), 351.

22 Wedderburn points to a counter-modernity that is still relevant. Walden Bello argues, "the 'peasant way' has relevance not only to peasants but to everyone threatened by the catastrophic consequences of global capital's vision for organizing production, community, and life itself." See Bello, *The Food Wars* (London: Verso, 2009), 15.

23 For work along these lines, see Joseph Albernaz, "Abolition, Ultra-Radicalism, and the Generation of the General Strike," *Critical Times: Interventions in Global Critical Theory* 5.3 (2022): 538–69.

24 For more on the transatlantic dimensions of Owen's utopian thought, see Michael Morris, "The Problem of Slavery in the Age of Improvement: David Dale, Robert Owen and New Lanark Cotton." In *Cultures of Improvement in Scottish Romanticism, 1707–1840*, edited by Alex Benchimol and Gerard Lee McKeever, 111–31 (London: Routledge, 2018).

25 Stefano Harney and Fred Moten, *The Undercommons: Fugitive Planning and Black Study* (Brooklyn: Autonomedia, 2013), 17.

26 In a previous project, I argued that William Cobbett's calls for a "cottage economy" suggested that producing and consuming one's own food, especially bread, beer, and bacon, was a site of self-identification and communal identity. Yet that identity was only for native Englishmen, thus excluding the global reach of England's plantation systems and workers oppressed by them. See Katey Castellano, "Subsistence as Resistance: William Cobbett's Food Politics" in *The Ecology of British Romantic Conservatism, 1790–1837* (Basingstoke: Palgrave Macmillan, 2013), 113–40.

Bibliography

Albernaz, Joseph. "Abolition, Ultra-Radicalism, and the Generation of the General Strike." *Critical Times: Interventions in Global Critical Theory* 5.3 (2022): 538–69.

Alcalá, Roberto del Valle. "Class Antagonism and the Limits of Utopia in Matthew Lewis and Robert Owen." *Nineteenth-Century Contexts* 43.4 (2021): 465–77.

Aljoe, Nicole N. *Creole Testimonies: Slave Narratives from the British West Indies, 1709–1838*. New York: Palgrave Macmillan, 2012.

Allewaert, Monique. *Ariel's Ecology: Plantations, Personhood, and Colonialism in the American Tropics*. Minneapolis: University of Minnesota Press, 2013.

Altick, Richard D. *The English Common Reader: A Social History of the Mass Reading Public 1800–1900*. Chicago: University of Chicago Press, 1957.

Anonymous. "History of the Revolted Negroes in Jamaica." Long Papers, British Library. Add.MS 12431, ca 1733–39.

Aravamudan, Srinivas. *Tropicopolitans: Colonialism and Agency, 1688–1804*. Durham, NC: Duke University Press, 1999.

Barrell, John. *The Idea of Landscape and the Sense of Place 1730–1840: An Approach to the Poetry of John Clare*. Cambridge: Cambridge University Press, 1972.

Barringer, Tim. "Land, Labor, Landscape: Views of the Plantation in Victorian Jamaica." In *Victorian Jamaica*, edited by Tim Barringer and Wayne Modest, 263–78. Durham, NC: Duke University Press, 2018.

"Picturesque Prospects and the Labor of the Enslaved." In *Art and Emancipation in Jamaica: Isaac Mendes Belisario and His Worlds*, edited by T. J. Barringer, Gillian Forrester, and Barbaro Martinez-Ruiz, 41–63. New Haven, CT: Yale University Press, 2007.

Beckford, George and Michael Witter. *Small Garden ... Bitter Weed: Struggle and Change in Jamaica*. Jamaica: Maroon Publishing, 1982.

Beckford, William. *A Descriptive Account of the Island of Jamaica*. London: T. and J. Egerton, 1790.

Beckles, Hilary McD. *Centering Woman: Gender Discourses in Caribbean Slave Society*. Kingston: Ian Randle Publishers, 1999.

"Historicizing Slavery in West Indian Feminisms." *Feminist Review* 59 (1998): 34–56.

"The Wilberforce Song: How Enslaved Caribbean Blacks Heard British Abolitionists." *Parliamentary History* 26.4 (2007): 113–26.

Bello, Walden. *The Food Wars*. London: Verso, 2009.

Bell's Life in London and Sporting Chronicle 3.103–9 (1824).

Bentley, G. E. *The Stranger from Paradise: A Biography of William Blake*. New Haven, CT: Yale University Press, 2001.

Bermingham, Ann. *Landscape and Ideology: The English Rustic Tradition, 1760–1860*. Berkeley: University of California Press, 1986.

Berry, Wendell. *The Art of the Commonplace: The Agrarian Essays of Wendell Berry*. Berkeley: Counterpoint, 2002.

Besson, Jean. "Land Tenure in the Free Villages of Trelawny, Jamaica: A Case Study in the Caribbean Peasant Response to Emancipation." *Slavery & Abolition* 5.1 (1984): 3–23.

Bewell, Alan. *Romanticism and Colonial Disease*. Baltimore: Johns Hopkins University Press, 1999.

"'The Stranger and the Exile Who Is in Our Land within Our Gates': Mary Prince as a Black British Immigrant." *Modern Philology* 118.2 (2020): 234–51.

Bilby, Kenneth M. "Maroon Autonomy In Jamaica." *Cultural Survival Quarterly* 25.4 (2002): 1–8.

True-Born Maroons. Gainesville: University of Florida Press, 2005.

Black, William R. "How Watermelons Became Black: Emancipation and the Origins of a Racist Trope." *Journal of the Civil War Era* 8.1 (2018): 64–86.

Blake, William. *The Complete Poetry and Prose of William Blake*. New York: Anchor Books, 1988.

Blomley, Nicholas. "Making Private Property: Enclosure, Common Right, and the Work of Hedges." *Rural History* 18 (2007): 1–21.

Bogues, Anthony. *Black Heretics, Black Prophets: Radical Political Intellectuals*. New York: Routledge, 2003.

"John Stuart Mill and 'The Negro Question': Race, Colonialism, and the Ladder of Civilization." In *Race and Racism in Modern Philosophy*, 217–34. Ithaca, NY: Cornell University Press, 2005.

Bohls, Elizabeth. *Romantic Literature and Postcolonial Studies*. Edinburgh: Edinburgh University Press, 2013.

Slavery and the Politics of Place: Representing the Colonial Caribbean, 1770–1833. Cambridge: Cambridge University Press, 2014.

Botkin, Frances R. "Questioning the 'Necessary Order of Things': Maria Edgeworth's 'The Grateful Negro,' Plantation Slavery, and the Abolition of the Slave Trade." In *Discourses of Slavery and Abolition: Britain and Its Colonies, 1760–1838*, edited by Brycchan Carey, Markman Ellis, and Sara Salih, 194–208. Basingstoke: Palgrave Macmillan, 2004.

Thieving Three-Fingered Jack: Transatlantic Tales of a Jamaican Outlaw, 1780–2015. New Brunswick, NJ: Rutgers University Press, 2017.

Boulukos, George. *The Grateful Slave: The Emergence of Race in Eighteenth-Century British and American Culture*. Cambridge: Cambridge University Press, 2008.

Brathwaite, E. Kamau. "Creative Literature of the British West Indies during the Period of Slavery." *Savacou* 1.1 (1970): 46–73.

"Nanny, Palmares, and the Caribbean Maroon Connection." In *Maroon Heritage: Archaeological, Ethnographic, and Historical Perspectives*, edited by E. Kofi Agorsah, 119–38. Mona: University of West Indies Press, 2000.

Wars of Respect: Nanny and Sam Sharpe. Kingston: API for the National Heritage Week Committee, 1977.

Broglio, Ron. *Animal Revolution*. Minneapolis: University of Minnesota Press, 2022.

Beasts of Burden: Biopolitics, Labor, and Animal Life in British Romanticism. Albany: State University of New York Press, 2017.

Brougham, Henry. "Dallas's *History of the Maroons*." *The Edinburgh Review* 2.4 (1803): 376–91.

Brown, Vincent. *The Reaper's Garden: Death and Power in the World of Atlantic Slavery*. Cambridge, MA: Harvard University Press, 2008.

Tacky's Revolt: The Story of an Atlantic Slave War. Cambridge, MA: Harvard University Press, 2020.

Brown-Glaude, Winnifred R. *Higglers in Kingston: Women's Informal Work in Jamaica*. Nashville: Vanderbilt University Press, 2011.

Bulamah, Rodrigo C. "From Marrons to Kreyòl: Human-Animal Relations in the Early Caribbean." In *Global Plantations in the Modern World: Sovereignties, Ecologies, Afterlives*, edited by Colette Le Petitcorps, Marta Macedo, and Irene Peano, 35–58. Basingstoke: Palgrave Macmillan, 2023.

Burlison, Dani. "Paul Lewin Continues Storytelling Tradition through Painting." KQED, August 4, 2015. www.kqed.org/arts/10872336/paul-lewins-roots-of-the-cotton-tree-opens-august-7-in-oakland.

Burnard, Trevor, and John Garrigus. *The Plantation Machine: Atlantic Capitalism in French Saint-Domingue and British Jamaica*. Philadelphia: University of Pennsylvania Press, 2016.

Burnham, Michelle. "Obeah's Unproductive Bodies: A Response to 'Obeah: Knowledge, Power, and Writing in the Early Atlantic World.'" *Atlantic Studies* 12.2 (2015): 235–43.

Bush, Barbara. *Slave Women in Caribbean Society, 1650–1838*. Bloomington: Indiana University Press, 1990.

Byron, George Gordon. "Letter to Thomas Moore." January 2, 1821. *Lord Byron and His Times*. https://lordbyron.org.

Camp, Stephanie M. H. *Closer to Freedom: Enslaved Women and Everyday Resistance in the Plantation South*. Chapel Hill: University of North Carolina Press, 2004.

Campbell, Mavis C. *The Maroons of Jamaica, 1655–1796: A History of Resistance, Collaboration and Betrayal*. Grandby, MA: Bergin and Garvey, 1988.

Carey, Bev. *The Maroon Story: The Authentic and Original History of the Maroons in the History of Jamaica, 1490–1880*. St. Andrew: Agouti Press, 1997.

Carey, Brycchan. "Abolishing Cruelty: The Concurrent Growth of Anti-slavery and Animal Welfare Sentiment in British and Colonial Literature." *Journal for Eighteenth-Century Studies* 43.2 (2020): 203–20.

Carlile, Richard. "To the Christian Judge Bailey." *The Republican* 18.5 (1822): 548–56.

Carlyle, Thomas. "Occasional Discourse on the Negro Question." *Fraser's Magazine for Town and Country*, 40 (December 1849): 670–79.

Carney, Judith Ann, and Richard Nicholas Rosomoff. *In the Shadow of Slavery: Africa's Botanical Legacy in the Atlantic World*. Berkeley: University of California Press, 2011.

Casid, Jill H. *Sowing Empire: Landscape and Colonization*. Minneapolis: University of Minnesota Press, 2005.

Casimir, Jean. *The Haitians: A Decolonial History*. Translated by Laurent Dubois. Chapel Hill: University of North Carolina Press, 2020.

Castellano, Katey. *The Ecology of British Romantic Conservatism, 1790–1837*. Basingstoke: Palgrave Macmillan, 2013.

"Provision Grounds against the Plantation: Robert Wedderburn's *The Axe Laid to the Root* (1817)." *Small Axe: A Caribbean Journal of Criticism* 25.1 (2021): 15–27.

"'She Trafficked on Her Own Account': Black Women's Abolitionist Geographies in Robert Wedderburn's *Horrors of Slavery* (1824) and *History of Mary Prince* (1831)." *European Romantic Review* 35.2 (2024), 321–39.

Chakrabarty, Dipesh. *Provincializing Europe: Postcolonial Thought and Historical Difference*. Princeton, NJ: Princeton University Press, 2008.

Chander, Manu Samriti. *Brown Romantics: Poetry and Nationalism in the Global Nineteenth Century*. Lewisburg, PA: Bucknell University Press, 2017.

"Romantic Diversitarianism: Problems and Promises." *European Romantic Review* 31.3 (2020): 295–300.

Chander, Manu Samriti, and Patricia A. Matthew. "Abolitionist Interruptions: Romanticism, Slavery, and Genre." *European Romantic Review* 29.4 (2018): 431–34.

Chandler, Alice. *A Dream of Order: The Medieval Ideal in Nineteenth-Century English Literature*. Lincoln: University of Nebraska Press, 1970.

Chandler, James. *England in 1819: The Politics of Literary Culture and the Case of Romantic Historicism*. Chicago: University of Chicago Press, 1998.

Chao, Sophie. "Plantation." *Environmental Humanities* 14.2 (2022): 361–66.

Chase, Malcolm. *The People's Farm: English Radical Agrarianism, 1775–1840*. Oxford: Clarendon Press, 1988.

Chopra, Ruma. *Almost Home: Maroons between Slavery and Freedom in Jamaica, Nova Scotia, and Sierra Leone*. New Haven, CT: Yale University Press, 2018.

Clare, John. *Poems of the Middle Period, 1822–1837*, vols. 1–5. Edited by Eric Robinson, David Powell, and P. M. S. Dawson. Oxford: Clarendon Press, 1996.

Cobbett, William. *Cottage Economy*. London: Peter Davies, Ltd., 1926.

"To the Journeymen and Labourers of England, Wales, Scotland and Ireland." *Political Register* 31.18 (1816).

"To the Radicals." *Political Register* 39.4 (1821).

Collings, David. *Monstrous Society: Reciprocity, Discipline, and the Political Uncanny, c. 1780–1848*. Lewisburg, PA: Bucknell University Press, 2009.

"Colvile, Andrew." *Hudson's Bay Company Archives*, Archives of Manitoba, 2002. www.gov.mb.ca/chc/archives/_docs/hbca/biographical/c/colvile_andrew.pdf.

"Colvile, Andrew." *Legacies of British Slavery database*, University College London. www.ucl.ac.uk/lbs/person/view/24188.

Connell, Robert. "Maroon Ecology: Land, Sovereignty, and Environmental Justice." *The Journal of Latin American and Caribbean Anthropology* 25.2 (2020): 218–35.

Cottrell, Jeffrey. "At the End of the Trade: Obeah and Black Women in the Colonial Imaginary." *Atlantic Studies* 12.2 (2015): 200–18.

Cowan, Yuri. "Sporting Periodicals." In *The Routledge Handbook to Nineteenth-Century British Periodicals and Newspapers*, edited by Andrew King, Alexis Easley, and John Morton, 307–17. London: Routledge, 2016.

Craton, Michael. *Testing the Chains: Resistance to Slavery in the British West Indies*. Ithaca, NY: Cornell University Press, 2009.

Cugoano, Quobna Ottobah. *Thoughts and Sentiments on the Evil of Slavery*. Edited by Vincent Carretta. New York: Penguin, 1999.

Cummings, Ronald. "Jamaican Female Masculinities: Nanny of the Maroons and the Genealogy of the Man-Royal." *Journal of West Indian Literature* 21.1/2 (2012): 129–54.

Dadzie, Stella. *A Kick in the Belly: Women, Slavery and Resistance*. London: Verso, 2020.

Dallas, R. C. *The History of the Maroons: From Their Origin to the Establishment of Their Chief Tribe at Sierra Leone*. London: Longman and Rees, 1803.

Recollections of the Life of Lord Bryon. London: Charles Knight, 1824.

"Dallas, Robert Charles." *Legacies of British Slavery database*, University College London. www.ucl.ac.uk/lbs/person/view/2146651103.

Davis, Janae, Alex Moulton, Levi Van Sant, and Brian Williams. "Anthropocene, Capitalocene, . . . Plantationocene? A Manifesto for Ecological Justice in an Age of Global Crisis." *Geography Compass* 13.5 (2019): 1–15.

D'Costa, Jean, and Barbara Lalla. *Voices in Exile: Jamaican Texts of the 18th and 19th Centuries*. Birmingham: University of Alabama Press, 2009.

Dean, Mitchell. *The Constitution of Poverty: Toward a Genealogy of Liberal Governance*. London: Routledge, 1991.

DeLoughrey, Elizabeth. "Ecocriticism: The Politics of Place." In *Routledge Companion to Anglophone Caribbean Literature*, edited by Michael A. Bucknor and Allison Donnell, 265–75. New York: Routledge, 2011.

"Yams, Roots, and Rot: Allegories of the Provision Grounds." *Small Axe: A Caribbean Journal of Criticism* 15.1 (2011): 58–75.

Diaby, Bakary. "Black Women and/in the Shadow of Romanticism." *European Romantic Review* 30.3 (2019): 249–54.

"Feeling Black, Feeling Back: Fragility and Romanticism." *Symbiosis* 23.1 (2019): 117–38.

Dickerson, Vanessa D. *Dark Victorians*. Urbana-Champaign: University of Illinois Press, 2008.

Dillon, Elizabeth Maddock. "The Plantationocene and the Performative Commons: A Brief History of Uncommoning." *The Minnesota Review* 93 (2019): 83–93.

Dinius, Marcy J. "'Look!! Look!!! At This!!!!': The Radical Typography of David Walker's 'Appeal.'" *PMLA:Publications of the Modern Language Association of America* 126.1 (2011): 55–72.

Dirks, Robert. *The Black Saturnalia: Conflict and Its Ritual Expression on British West Indian Slave Plantations*. Gainesville: University Presses of Florida, 1987.

Dunn, Richard S. *A Tale of Two Plantations: Slave Life and Labor in Jamaica and Virginia*. Cambridge, MA: Harvard University Press, 2014.

Edgeworth, Maria. *Popular Tales*, 3 vols. London: Joseph Johnson, 1804.

Edwards, Bryan. *The History, Civil and Commercial, of the British Colonies in the West Indies*. London: John Stockdale, 1793.

The Proceedings of the Governor and Assembly of Jamaica, in Regard to the Maroon Negroes. London: John Stockdale, 1796.

Equiano, Olaudah. *The Interesting Narrative*. Edited by Brycchan Carey. Oxford: Oxford University Press, 2018.

Erdman, David V. *Blake: Prophet against Empire*. New York: Dover Publications, 1991.

Essick, Robert N. *William Blake, Printmaker*. Princeton, NJ: Princeton University Press, 1980.

Evans, Thomas. *Christian Policy, the Salvation of the Empire*. London, 1816.

Farooq, Nihad M. "'A Useful Delusion': Valentine Farm and the Flight for Freedom." *Utopian Studies* 30.1 (2019): 87–110.

Favini, John. "Caring for Nature: Anonymity, Conservation, and the Jamaican Maroons." *Social and Economic Studies* 67.1 (2018): 7–31.

Federici, Silvia. *Caliban and the Witch: Women, the Body, and Primitive Accumulation*. Brooklyn, NY: Autonomedia, 2004.

Ferdinand, Malcom. *Decolonial Ecology: Thinking from the Caribbean World*. Translated by Anthony Paul Smith. Cambridge: Polity, 2022.

Ferguson, Moira. *Subject to Others: British Women Writers and Colonial Slavery, 1670–1834*. New York: Routledge, 1992.

Fuentes, Marisa J. *Dispossessed Lives: Enslaved Women, Violence, and the Archive*. Philadelphia: University of Pennsylvania Press, 2016.

Gallagher, Catherine. *The Body Economic: Life, Death, and Sensation in Political Economy and the Victorian Novel*. Princeton, NJ: Princeton University Press, 2006.

Gallagher, Catherine, and Stephen Greenblatt. "The Potato in the Materialist Imagination." In *Practicing New Historicism*, 110–35. Chicago: University of Chicago Press, 2000.

Gerzina, Gretchen. *Black London: Life before Emancipation*. New Brunswick, NJ: Rutgers University Press, 1995.

Gibbs, Jenna M. *Performing the Temple of Liberty: Slavery, Theater, and Popular Culture in London and Philadelphia, 1760–1850*. Baltimore: Johns Hopkins University Press, 2014.

Gikandi, Simon. *Slavery and the Culture of Taste*. Princeton, NJ: Princeton University Press, 2014.

Gilmartin, Kevin. *Print Politics: The Press and Radical Opposition in Early Nineteenth-Century England*. Cambridge: Cambridge University Press, 1997.

Gilmore, Ruth Wilson. *Abolitionist Geography: Essays towards Liberation*. London: Verso, 2022.

Gilroy, Paul. *The Black Atlantic: Modernity and Double-Consciousness*. Cambridge, MA: Harvard University Press, 1993.

Glissant, Édouard. *Poetics of Relation*. Translated by Betsy Wing. Ann Arbor: University of Michigan Press, 2010.

Goffe, Rachel. "Reproducing the Plot: Making Life in the Shadow of Premature Death." *Antipode* 55.4 (2023): 1024–46.

Goldberg, David Theo. "Liberalism's Limits: Carlyle and Mill on 'The Negro Question.'" *Nineteenth-Century Contexts* 22 (2000): 203–16.

Golden, Kathryn Benjamin. "'Armed in the Great Swamp': Fear, Maroon Insurrection, and the Insurgent Ecology of the Great Dismal Swamp." *Journal of African American History* 106.1 (2021): 1–26.

Goodison, Lorna. *Guinea Woman: New and Selected Poems*. Manchester: Carcanet, 2000.

Gottlieb, Karla. *The Mother of Us All: The History of Queen Nanny*. London: Africa World Press, 2000.

Greene, Jack P. *Settler Jamaica in the 1750s: A Social Portrait*. Charlottesville: University of Virginia Press, 2016.

Gurton-Wachter, Lily. "Blake's 'Little Black Thing': Happiness and Injury in the Age of Slavery." *ELH* 87.2 (2020): 519–52.

Hakewill, James. *A Picturesque Tour of the Island of Jamaica; from Drawings Made in the Years 1820 and 1821*. London: Hurst and Robinson, 1825.

Hall, Catherine. *Civilising Subjects: Metropole and Colony in the English Imagination, 1830–1867*. Chicago: University of Chicago Press, 2002.

"Rewriting the Past: Imperial Histories of the Antislavery Nation." In *Victorian Jamaica*, edited by Tim Barringer and Wayne Modest, 263–78. Durham, NC: Duke University Press, 2018.

White, Male and Middle Class: Explorations in Feminism and History. Cambridge: Polity, 2013.

Hanley, Ryan. *Beyond Slavery and Abolition: Black British Writing, c.1770–1830*. Cambridge: Cambridge University Press, 2018.

"Cato Street and the Caribbean." In *The Cato Street Conspiracy: Plotting, Counter-Intelligence, and the Revolutionary Tradition in Britain and Ireland*, edited by Jason McElligott and Martin Conboy, 81–100. Manchester: Manchester University Press, 2020.

"A Radical Change of Heart: Robert Wedderburn's Last Word on Slavery." *Slavery & Abolition* 37. 2 (2016): 423–45.

"Slavery and the Birth of the Working Class Racism in England, 1814–1833." *Transactions of the Royal Historical Society* 26 (2016): 103–23.

Harkin, Maureen. "Matthew Lewis's *Journal of a West India Proprietor*: Surveillance and Space on the Plantation." *Nineteenth-Century Contexts* 24.2 (2002): 139–50.

Harney, Stefano, and Fred Moten. *The Undercommons: Fugitive Planning and Black Study*. Brooklyn, NY: Autonomedia, 2013.

Harris, C. L. G. "The Maroons-Praised and Condemned." *Jamaica Gleaner*, July 23, 1967.

"The 'Spirit of Nanny.'" *Jamaica Gleaner*, August 6, 1967.

Hartman, Saidiya. "The Belly of the World: A Note on Black Women's Labors." *Souls: A Critical Journal of Black Politics, Culture, and Society* 18.1 (2016): 166–73.

Scenes of Subjection: Terror, Slavery, and Self-Making in Nineteenth-Century America. Oxford: Oxford University Press, 1997.

"Venus in Two Acts." *Small Axe: A Caribbean Journal of Criticism* 12.2 (2008): 1–14.

Haywood, Ian. *Romanticism and Caricature*. Cambridge: Cambridge University Press, 2013.

The Revolution in Popular Literature: Print, Politics, and the People, 1790–1860. Cambridge: Cambridge University Press, 2004.

Hensley, Nathan K. "Landscape with Storm (Unfinished)." *Victorian Review* 47.1 (2021): 34–40.

Herrmann, Rachel B. *No Useless Mouth: Waging War and Fighting Hunger in the American Revolution*. Ithaca, NY: Cornell University Press, 2019.

Hess, Scott. *William Wordsworth and the Ecology of Authorship: The Roots of Environmentalism in Nineteenth-Century Culture*. Charlottesville: University of Virginia Press, 2012.

Higgins, David. "Stewardship and Plenitude: William Bartram, the Lake Poets, and Romantic Ecology." In *Transatlantic Literary Ecologies*, edited by Kevin Hutchings and John Miller, 42–57. London: Routledge, 2016.

Higman, B. W. *Jamaica Surveyed: Plantation Maps and Plans of the Eighteenth and Nineteenth Centuries*. Kingston: Institute of Jamaica Publications Limited, 1988.

Jamaican Food: History, Biology, Culture. Kingston: University of West Indies Press, 2008.

Higman, B. W., and B. J. Hudson. *Jamaican Place Names*. Jamaica: University of West Indies Press, 2009.

Hodges, Hugh. "Start-Over: Possession Rites and Healing Rituals in the Poetry of Lorna Goodison." *Research in African Literatures* 36.2 (2005): 19–32.

Hoermann, Raphael. "'A Very Hell of Horrors?' The Haitian Revolution and the Early Transatlantic Haitian Gothic." *Slavery & Abolition* 37.1 (2015): 183–205.

"'Fermentation Will Be Universal': Intersections of Race and Class in Robert Wedderburn's Black Atlantic Discourse of the Transatlantic Revolution." In *Britain's Black Past*, edited by Gretchen H. Gerzina, 295–314. Liverpool: Liverpool University Press, 2020.

Holt, Thomas C. *The Problem of Freedom Race, Labor, and Politics in Jamaica and Britain, 1832–1938*. Baltimore: Johns Hopkins University Press, 1992.

Hone, J. Ann. *For the Cause of Truth: Radicalism in London, 1796–1821*. Oxford: Clarendon Press, 1982.

Hunt, Nadine. "Remembering Africans in Diaspora: Robert Wedderburn's 'Freedom Narrative.'" In *Slavery in Africa and the Caribbean: A History of Enslavement and Identity since the 18th Century*, edited by Olatunji Ojo and Nadine Hunt, 175–98. London: New York: I. B. Tauris, 2012.

Huzzey, Richard. "Concepts of Liberty: Freedom, Laissez-Faire and the State after Britain's Abolition of Slavery." In *Emancipation and the Remaking of the British Imperial World*, edited by Catherine Hall, Nicholas Draper, and Keith McClelland, 149–72. Manchester: Manchester University Press, 2014.

Jackson, Lee. *Dirty Old London: The Victorian Fight against Filth*. New Haven, CT: Yale University Press, 2014.

James, C. L. R. *The Black Jacobins: Toussaint L'Ouverture and the San Domingo Revolution*. New York: Vintage, 1989.

John, Kimberly, Colin L.G. Harris, and Susan Otuokon. "Seeking and Securing Sacred Natural Sites among Jamaica's Windward Maroons." In *Sacred Natural Sites: Conserving Nature and Culture*, edited by Bas Verschuuren, Robert Wild, Jeffrey A. McNeely, and Gonzalo Oviedo, 146–55. London: Earthscan, 2010.

Johnson, Shelby. "'The Fate of St. Domingo Awaits You': Robert Wedderburn's Unfinished Revolution." *The Eighteenth Century* 61.4 (2020): 373–90.

"Plotting the Plantationocene with *The History of Mary Prince*." *ABO: Interactive Journal for Women in the Arts, 1640–1830* 13.1 (2023): 1–14.

Kent, Susan Kingsley. *Gender and Power in Britain 1640–1990*. New York: Routledge, 2002.

Klancher, Jon P. *The Making of English Reading Audiences, 1790–1832*. Madison: University of Wisconsin Press, 1987.

Knight, James. *Manuscript of the Natural, Moral, and Political History of Jamaica*. British Library. ADD MS 12415, Vol. 2, 1742.

Kopytoff, Barbara Klamon. "The Early Political Development of Jamaican Maroon Societies." *The William and Mary Quarterly* 35.2 (1978): 287–307.

Lalla, Barbara. *Defining Jamaican Fiction: Marronage and the Discourse of Survival*. Tuscaloosa: University of Alabama Press, 1996.

"Dungeons of the Soul: Frustrated Romanticism in Eighteenth and Nineteenth Century Literature of Jamaica." *MELUS* 21.3 (1996): 3–23.

Landry, Donna. *The Invention of the Countryside: Hunting, Walking, and Ecology in English Literature, 1671–1831*. Basingstoke: Palgrave Macmillan, 2001.

Laqueur, Thomas W. *The Work of the Dead: A Cultural History of Mortal Remains*. Princeton, NJ: Princeton University Press, 2015.

Lee, Debbie. "Black Single Mothers in Romantic History and Literature." In *Race, Romanticism and the Atlantic*, edited by Paul Youngquist, 165–81. London: Routledge, 2013.

Slavery and the Romantic Imagination. Philadelphia: University of Pennsylvania Press, 2002.

Lewis, Matthew. *Journal of a West-India Proprietor*. London: J. Murray, 1834.

Linebaugh, Peter. *The Magna Carta Manifesto: Liberties and Commons for All*. Berkeley: University of California Press, 2008.

Stop, Thief! The Commons, Enclosures, and Resistance. Oakland, CA: PM Press, 2014.

Linebaugh, Peter, and Marcus Rediker. *The Many-Headed Hydra: Sailors, Slaves, Commoners, and the Hidden History of the Revolutionary Atlantic*. Boston: Beacon Press, 2000.

Livesay, Daniel. *Children of Uncertain Fortune: Mixed-Race Jamaicans in Britain and the Atlantic Family, 1733–1833*. Chapel Hill: University of North Carolina Press, 2018.

Locke, John. *Two Treatises of Government and A Letter concerning Toleration*. Edited by Ian Shapiro. New Haven, CT: Yale University Press, 2003.

Lowe, Lisa. *The Intimacies of Four Continents*. Durham, NC: Duke University Press, 2015.

Macaulay, Zachary. *Negro Slavery, or a View of Some of the More Prominent Features of That State of Society as It Exists in the United States of America and in the Colonies of the West Indies*. London: Richard Taylor, 1823.

Macdonald, D. L. *Monk Lewis: A Critical Biography*. Toronto: University of Toronto Press, 2000.

Madera, Judith. *Black Atlas: Geography and Flow in Nineteenth-Century African American Literature*. Durham, NC: Duke University Press, 2015.

Makdisi, Saree. *Making England Western: Occidentalism, Race, and Imperial Culture*. Chicago: University of Chicago Press, 2013.

William Blake and the Impossible History of the 1790s. Chicago: University of Chicago Press, 2003.

Malthus, T. R. *An Essay on the Principle of Population*. London: Joseph Johnson, 1803.

Marx, Karl. *The Marx-Engles Reader*, edited by Robert C. Tucker. New York: W. W. Norton, 1978.

Mathurin, Lucille. *The Rebel Woman in the British West Indies during Slavery*. Kingston: Institute of Jamaica, 1975.

Matthew, Patricia A. "Quilt 5: Race, Blackness, and Romanticism." *Studies in Romanticism* 61. 1 (2022): 1–10.

"A Report on 'Race, Blackness, and Romanticism: Dialogues.'" *Studies in Romanticism* 61.1 (2022): 137–50.

McCallum, Shara. *No Ruined Stone*. Farmington, ME: Alice James Books, 2021.

McCalman, Iain. "Anti-slavery and Ultra-Radicalism in Early Nineteenth-Century England: The Case of Robert Wedderburn." *Slavery & Abolition* 7.2 (1986): 99–117.

"Introduction." In *The Horrors of Slavery and Other Writings by Robert Wedderburn*, edited by Iain McCalman, 1–40. Princeton, NJ: Marcus Wiener, 1991.

Radical Underworld: Prophets, Revolutionaries, and Pornographers in London, 1795–1840. Cambridge: Cambridge University Press, 1988.

McGhee, J. Alexandra. "Fever Dreams: Obeah, Tropical Disease, and Cultural Contamination in Colonial Jamaica and the Metropole." *Atlantic Studies* 12.2 (2015): 179–99.

McKittrick, Katherine. *Demonic Grounds: Black Women and the Cartographies of Struggle*. Minneapolis: University of Minnesota Press, 2006.

"Plantation Futures." *Small Axe: A Caribbean Journal of Criticism* 17.3 (2013): 1–15.

Mee, Jon. *Dangerous Enthusiasm: William Blake and Culture of Radicalism in the 1790s*. Oxford: Clarendon Press, 1992.

Mellor, Anne K. "Sex, Violence, and Slavery: Blake and Wollstonecraft." *Huntington Library Quarterly* 58.3/4 (1995): 345–70.

Mintz, Sidney. "The Origins of the Jamaican Market System." In *The Slavery Reader*, edited by Gad J. Heuman and James Walvin, 521–44. London: Routledge, 2003.

"Reflections on Caribbean Peasantries." *New West Indian Guide* 57.1/2 (1983): 1–17.

Sweetness and Power: The Place of Sugar in Modern History. New York: Penguin Books, 1986.

Tasting Food, Tasting Freedom: Excursions into Eating, Culture, and the Past. Boston: Beacon Press, 1997.

Mill, John Stuart. "The Negro Question." *Fraser's Magazine for Town and Country*, 41 (January 1850): 25–31.

Mitchell, Robert. "Regulating Life: Romanticism, Science, and the Liberal Imagination." *European Romantic Review* 29.3 (2018): 275–93.

Morison, Stanley. *The English Newspaper, 1622–1932: An Account of the Physical Development of Journals Printed in London*. Cambridge: Cambridge University Press, 2009.

Morris, Michael. "The Problem of Slavery in the Age of Improvement: David Dale, Robert Owen and New Lanark Cotton." In *Cultures of Improvement in Scottish Romanticism, 1707–1840*, edited by Alex Benchimol and Gerard Lee McKeever, 111–31. London: Routledge, 2018.

Scotland and the Caribbean, c.1740–1833: Atlantic Archipelagos. New York: Routledge, 2015.

"Yonder Awa: Slavery and Distancing Strategies in Scottish Literature." In *Recovering Scotland's Slavery Past: The Caribbean Connection*, edited by Tom M. Devine, 41–61. Edinburgh: Edinburgh University Press, 2015.

Moulton, Alex A. "Plotting a New Course for Environmental Humanities: Provision Grounds, Race, and the Future." *Environmental Humanities* 16.2 (2024): 271–90.

"Towards the Arboreal Side-Effects of Marronage: Black Geographies and Ecologies of the Jamaican Forest." *Environment and Planning E: Nature and Space* 6.1 (2023): 3–23.

Moulton, Alex A. and Inge Salo. "Black Geographies and Black Ecologies as Insurgent Ecocriticism." *Environment and Society: Advances in Research* 13.1 (2022): 156–174.

Mullen, Stephen. *The Glasgow Sugar Aristocracy: Scotland and Caribbean Slavery, 1775–1838*. London: University of London Press, 2022.

Neeson, J. M. *Commoners: Common Right, Enclosure, and Social Change in England, 1700–1820*. Cambridge: Cambridge University Press, 1993.

Niblett, Michael. "'The Landscape Heaved with Unspeakable Terror': The Weird Presence of the World-Food-System in the Cultural Imaginaries of England and the Caribbean." In *Literary and Cultural Production, World-Ecology, and the Global Food System*, edited by Chris Campbell, Michael Niblett, and Kerstin Oloff, 65–92. Basingstoke: Palgrave Macmillan, 2021.

Nisbett, Mario. *The Workings of Diaspora: Jamaican Maroons and the Claims to Sovereignty*. Lanham, MD: Lexington Books, 2021.

Nixon, Rob. *Slow Violence and the Environmentalism of the Poor*. Cambridge, MA: Harvard University Press, 2011.

O'Callaghan, Evelyn. "Caribbean Picturesque from William Beckford to Contemporary Tourism." In *Caribbean Literature in Transition, 1800–1920*, edited by Evelyn O'Callaghan and Tim Watson, 67–84. Cambridge: Cambridge University Press, 2021.

"Early Colonial Narratives of the West Indies: Lady Nugent, Eliza Fenwick, Matthew Lewis and Frieda Cassin." In *Routledge Companion to Anglophone Caribbean Literature*, edited by Michael A. Bucknor and Alison Donnell, 149–56. New York: Routledge, 2011.

Ogborn, Miles. *The Freedom of Speech: Talk and Slavery in the Anglo-Caribbean World*. Chicago: University of Chicago Press, 2019.

Olney, James. "'I Was Born': Slave Narratives, Their Status as Autobiography and as Literature." In *The Slave's Narrative*, edited by Charles T. Davis and Henry Louis Gates Jr., 148–75. Oxford: Oxford University Press, 1991.

Paine, Thomas. *The Paine Reader*, edited by Michael Foot and Isaac Kramnick. New York: Penguin Books, 1987.

Pagnoulle, Christine. "Pilgrimage out of Dispossession." *Commonwealth* 17.1 (1994): 100–5.

Paravisini-Gebert, Lizabeth. "Colonial and Postcolonial Gothic: The Caribbean." In *The Cambridge Companion to Gothic Fiction*, edited by Jerrold E. Hogle, 229–57. Cambridge: Cambridge University Press, 2006.

Parker, Matthew. *The Sugar Barons: Family, Corruption, Empire, and War in the West Indies*. New York: Bloomsbury Publishing, 2011.

Parrish, Susan Scott. *American Curiosity: Cultures of Natural History in the Colonial British Atlantic World*. Chapel Hill: University of North Carolina Press, 2006.

"Embodying African Knowledge in Colonial Surinam: Two William Blake Engravings in Stedman's 1796 *Narrative*." In *Slave Portraiture in the Atlantic World*, edited by Agnes Lugo-Ortiz and Angela Rosenthal, 257–82. Cambridge: Cambridge University Press, 2013.

Parry, John H. "Plantation and Provision Ground: An Historical Sketch of the Introduction of Food Crops into Jamaica." *Revista de Historia de América* 39 (1955): 1–20.

Patel, Raj and Jason A. Moore. *A History of the World in Seven Cheap Things: A Guide to Capitalism, Nature, and the Future of the Planet*. Berkeley: University of California Press, 2017.

Paton, Diana. *The Cultural Politics of Obeah: Religion, Colonialism and Modernity in the Caribbean World.* Cambridge: Cambridge University Press, 2015.

No Bond but the Law: Punishment, Race, and Gender in Jamaican State Formation, 1780–1870. Durham, NC: Duke University Press, 2004.

"Witchcraft, Poison, Law, and Atlantic Slavery." *William and Mary Quarterly* 69.2 (2012): 235–64.

Patterson, Orlando. *Slavery and Social Death: A Comparative Study*. Cambridge, MA: Harvard University Press, 1982.

The Sociology of Slavery: An Analysis of the Origins, Development and Structure of Negro Slave Society in Jamaica. London: Fairleigh Dickenson University Press, 1969.

Pencek, Eric. "Intolerable Anonymity: Robert Wedderburn and the Discourse of Ultra-Radicalism." *Nineteenth-Century Contexts* 37.1 (2015): 61–77.

Picken, Cassidy. "Annihilated Property: Slavery and Reproduction after Abolition." *European Romantic Review* 28.5 (2017): 601–24.

Plasa, Carl. *Slaves to Sweetness: British and Caribbean Literatures of Sugar*. Liverpool: Liverpool University Press, 2011.

Posmentier, Sonya. *Cultivation and Catastrophe: The Lyric Ecology of Modern Black Literature*. Baltimore: Johns Hopkins University Press, 2017.

Pratt, Mary Louise. *Imperial Eyes: Travel Writing and Transculturation*. London: Routledge, 1992.

Price, Richard, and Sally Price. "Introduction." In *Stedman's Surinam: Life in an Eighteenth-Century Slave Society*, xi–lxxv. Baltimore: Johns Hopkins University Press, 1992.

Prince, Mary. *The History of Mary Prince*. Edited by Sara Salih. New York: Penguin, 2000.

Ramazani, Jahan. *A Transnational Poetics*. Chicago: University of Chicago Press, 2015.

Reyes, Angelita. *Mothering across Cultures: Postcolonial Representations*. Minneapolis: University of Minnesota Press, 2001.

Rice, Alan. *Radical Narratives of the Black Atlantic*. London: Continuum, 2003.

Richards, Leah, and Maurice Milne. "Bell's Life in London." In *Dictionary of Nineteenth-Century Journalism in Great Britain and Ireland*, edited by Laurel Brake and Marysa Demoor, 46–47. London: British Library, 2009.

Richardson, Alan. "Romantic Voodoo: Obeah and British Culture, 1797–1807." *Studies in Romanticism* 32.1 (1993): 3–28.

Roane, J. T. "Plotting the Black Commons." *Souls: A Critical Journal of Black Politics, Culture, and Society* 20.3 (2018): 239–66.

Roberts, Neil. *Freedom as Marronage*. Chicago: University of Chicago Press, 2015.

Robertson, James. *Joseph Knight*. London: Fourth Estate, 2004.

Rodriques, Janelle. "Obeah, Religion, and Nineteenth-Century Literature." In *Caribbean Literature in Transition: 1800–1920*, edited by Evelyn O'Callaghan and Tim Watson, 198–212. Cambridge: Cambridge University Press, 2020.

Rowney, Matthew. *In Common Things: Commerce, Culture, and Ecology in British Romantic Literature*. Toronto: University of Toronto Press, 2022.

Salih, Sara. "Introduction." In *The History of Mary Prince*, vii–xxxiv. London: Penguin Books, 2000.

Sandiford, Keith A. *The Cultural Politics of Sugar: Caribbean Slavery and Narratives of Colonialism*. Cambridge University Press, 2000.

Scanlan, Padraic X. *Slave Empire: How Slavery Built Modern Britain*. London: Robinson, 2022.

Schoenfield, Mark. *British Periodicals and Romantic Identity: The "Literary Lower Empire."* Basingstoke: Palgrave Macmillan, 2008.

Schoolman, Martha. "West Indian Emancipation and the Time of Regionalism in the Hemispheric 1850s." In *Mapping Region in Early American Writing*, edited by Edward Watts, Keri Holt, and John Funchion, 81–96. Athens: University of Georgia Press, 2015, 86–7.

Scott, David. *Conscripts of Modernity: The Tragedy of Colonial Enlightenment*. Durham, NC: Duke University Press, 2004.

Scott, Julius S. *The Common Wind: Afro-American Currents in the Age of the Haitian Revolution*. London: Verso, 2018.

Scrivener, Michael. *Seditious Allegories: John Thelwall and Jacobin Writing*. University Park: Pennsylvania State University Press, 2001.

Seacole, Mary. *Wonderful Adventures of Mrs. Seacole in Many Lands*. Edited by Sara Salih. London: Penguin Classics, 2005.

Senior, Emily. *The Caribbean and the Medical Imagination, 1764–1834: Slavery, Disease and Colonial Modernity*. Cambridge: Cambridge University Press, 2018.

Sharpe, Jenny. *Ghosts of Slavery: A Literary Archeology of Black Women's Lives*. Minneapolis: University of Minnesota Press, 2003.

Shepherd, Verene A. "Work, Culture, and Creolization: Slavery and Emancipation in Eighteenth and Nineteeth-Century Jamaica." In *Art and Emancipation in Jamaica: Isaac Mendes Belisario and His Worlds*, edited by T. J. Barringer, Gillian Forrester, and Barbaro Martinez-Ruiz, 27–39. New Haven, CT: Yale Center for British Art in association with Yale University Press, 2007.

Shiva, Vandana. *The Enclosure and Recovery of the Commons: Biodiversity, Indigenous Knowledge, and Intellectual Property Rights*. New Delhi: Research Foundation for Science, Technology, and Ecology, 1997.

Sinanan, Kerry. "Mary Prince's Back and Her Critique of Anti-slavery Sympathy." *Studies in Romanticism* 61.1 (2022): 67–78.

"The 'Slave' as Cultural Artifact: The Case of Mary Prince." *Studies in Eighteenth-Century Culture* 49 (2020): 67–87.

Sinha, Manisha. *The Slave's Cause: A History of Abolition*. New Haven, CT: Yale University Press, 2016.

Small, Helen. *The Function of Cynicism at the Present Time*. Oxford: Oxford University Press, 2020.

Smith, Olivia. *The Politics of Language, 1791–1819*. Oxford: Clarendon Press, 1986.

Snell, K. D. M. *Annals of the Labouring Poor: Social Change and Agrarian England, 1660–1900*. Cambridge: Cambridge University Press, 1987.

Spence, Thomas. *The Giant-Killer; or Anti-landlord.* London, 1814.

The Restorer of Society to Its Natural State. London: J. Smith, 1801.

The Rights of Infants. London, 1797.

Spillers, Hortense. *Black, White, and in Color: Essays on American Literature and Culture.* Chicago: University of Chicago Press, 2003.

Stedman, John Gabriel. *Narrative of a Five Years Expedition against the Revolted Negroes of Surinam.* Edited by Richard Price and Sally Price. Baltimore: Johns Hopkins University Press, 1988.

Narrative of Joanna, an Emancipated Slave of Surinam. Edited by Lydia Maria Child. Boston: Isaac Knapp, 1838.

Steuart, James. *An Inquiry Into the Principles of Political Oeconomy.* Dublin: James Williams, 1770.

Sturge, Joseph, and Thomas Harvey. *The West Indies in 1837.* London: Hamilton, Adams, and Co, 1838.

Sweeney, Shauna J. "Market Marronage: Fugitive Women and the Internal Marketing System in Jamaica, 1781–1834." *The William and Mary Quarterly* 76.2 (2019): 197–222.

Tarr, Rodger L. "Emendation as Challenge: Carlyle's 'Negro Question' from Journal to Pamphlet." *Papers of the Bibliographical Society of America* 75. 3 (1981): 341–45.

Taylor, Christopher. *Empire of Neglect: The West Indies in the Wake of British Liberalism.* Durham, NC: Duke University Press, 2018.

Terry, Judith. "Introduction." In *Journal of a West India Proprietor, by Matthew Lewis,* ix–xxxiv. Oxford: Oxford University Press, 1999.

Thicknesse, Philip. *Memoirs and Anecdotes of Philip Thicknesse.* Dublin: Graisberry and Campbell, 1788.

Thomas, Helen. *Romanticism and Slave Narratives: Transatlantic Testimonies.* Cambridge: Cambridge University Press, 2000.

Thomas, Sue. *Telling West Indian Lives: Life Narrative and the Reform of Plantation Slavery Cultures 1804–1834.* New York: Palgrave Macmillan, 2014.

Thompson, Carl. *The Suffering Traveller and the Romantic Imagination.* Oxford: Clarendon Press, 2007.

Thompson, E. P. *Customs in Common.* New York: The New Press, 1993.

The Making of the English Working Class. New York: Vintage, 1966.

Trouillot, Michel-Rolph. *Haiti: State against Nation.* New York: New York University Press, 1990.

Tsing, Anna Lowenhaupt. *The Mushroom at the End of the World: On the Possibility of Life in Capitalist Ruins.* Princeton, NJ: Princeton University Press, 2015.

Tuelon, Alan. "Nanny – Maroon Chieftainess." *Caribbean Quarterly* 19.4 (1973): 20–7.

Turner, Mary. *Slaves and Missionaries: The Disintegration of Jamaican Slave Society, 1787–1834.* Urbana: University of Illinois Press, 1982.

Turner, Sasha. *Contested Bodies: Pregnancy, Childrearing, and Slavery in Jamaica.* Philadelphia: University of Pennsylvania Press, 2017.

Tyrrell, Alex. "A Business of Philanthropy: The Montserrat Company, 1856–1961." *The Journal of Caribbean History* 38.2 (2004): 184–212.

Vasconcellos, Colleen A. *Slavery, Childhood, and Abolition in Jamaica, 1788–1838*. Athens: University of Georgia Press, 2015.

Walcott, Rinaldo. *The Long Emancipation: Moving toward Black Freedom*. Durham: Duke University Press, 2021.

On Property. Windsor, Ontario: Canadiana, 2021.

Washington, Teresa N. *Our Mothers, Our Powers, Our Texts: Manifestations of Àjé in Africana Literature*. Bloomington: Indiana University Press, 2005.

Waqif, Ajmal. "Cato Street and the Spencean Politics of Transnational Insurrection." In *The Cato Street Conspiracy: Plotting, Counter-Intelligence and the Revolutionary Tradition in Britain and Ireland*, edited by Jason McElligott and Martin Conboy, 101–17. Manchester: Manchester University Press, 2019.

Warner, Ashton. *Negro Slavery Described by a Negro*. Edited by Susanna Strickland. London, 1831.

Watkins, Case. "Landscapes and Resistance in the African Diaspora: Five Centuries of Palm Oil on Bahia's Dende Coast." *Journal of Rural Studies* 61 (2018): 137–54.

Watson, Tim. *Caribbean Culture and British Fiction in the Atlantic World, 1780–1870*. Cambridge: Cambridge University Press, 2008.

Wedderburn, Robert. *An Address to the Right Honourable Lord Brougham and Vaux* (1831), reprinted in Ryan Hanley's "A Radical Change of Heart: Robert Wedderburn's Last Word on Slavery." *Slavery & Abolition* 37. 2 (2016): 423–445.

The Axe Laid to the Root, or a Fatal Blow to Oppressors, Being an Address to the Planters and Negroes on the Island of Jamaica. London: A Seale, 1817.

The Forlorn Hope, or a Call to the Supine to Rouse from Indolence and Assert Public Rights. London: C Jennison, 1817.

"The Holy Liturgy." *Lion* 1:12 (1828): 359–61.

The Horrors of Slavery and Other Writings by Robert Wedderburn. Edited by Iain McCalman. Princeton, NJ: Marcus Wiener, 1991.

The Horrors of Slavery. London, 1824.

The Trial of the Rev. Robt Wedderburn for Blasphemy. Edited by Erasmus Perkins. London, 1820.

Truth Self-Supported, or, a Refutation of Certain Doctrinal Errors, Generally Adopted in the Christian Church. London, ca.1802.

Wheelock, Stefan M. *Barbaric Culture and Black Critique: Black Antislavery Writers, Religion, and the Slaveholding Atlantic*. Charlottesville: University of Virginia Press, 2016.

Williams, Eric. *Capitalism and Slavery*, 3rd edition. Chapel Hill: University of North Carolina Press, 2014.

Williams, Raymond. *Problems in Materialism and Culture: Selected Essays*. London: Verso, 1980.

"Radical and/or Respectable." In *The Press We Deserve*, edited by Richard Boston, 14–26. London: Routledge & Kegan Paul, 1970.

Winter, Kari J. *Subjects of Slavery, Agents of Change: Women and Power in Gothic Novels and Slave Narratives, 1790–1865*. Athens: University of Georgia Press, 2010.

Wisecup, Kelly, and Toni Wall Jaudon. "On Knowing and Not Knowing about Obeah." *Atlantic Studies* 12.2 (2015): 129–43.

Wright, Willie Jamaal. "The Morphology of Marronage." *Annals of the American Association of Geographers* 110.4 (2020): 1134–49.

Wong, Edlie L. *Neither Fugitive nor Free: Atlantic Slavery, Freedom Suits, and the Legal Culture of Travel*. New York: New York University Press, 2009.

Wood, Marcus. *Blind Memory: Visual Representations of Slavery in England and America, 1780–1865*. New York: Routledge, 2000.

The Horrible Gift of Freedom: Atlantic Slavery and the Representation of Emancipation. Athens: University of Georgia Press, 2010.

Slavery, Empathy, and Pornography. Oxford: Oxford University Press, 2002.

"William Cobbett, John Thelwall, Radicalism, Racism and Slavery: A Study in Burkean Parodics." *Romanticism on the Net* 15 (1999).

Worrall, David. *Radical Culture: Discourse, Resistance and Surveillance, 1790–1820*. Detroit: Wayne State University Press, 1992.

Wynter, Sylvia. "Novel and History, Plot and Plantation." *Savacou* 5 (1971): 95–102.

Yekani, Elahe Haschemi. *Familial Feeling: Entangled Tonalities in Early Black Atlantic Writing and the Rise of the British Novel*. Basingstoke: Palgrave Macmillan, 2020.

Youngquist, Paul. "Black Romanticism: A Manifesto." *Studies in Romanticism* 56.1 (2017): 1–14.

"The Cujo Effect." In *Gorgeous Beasts: Animal Bodies in Historical Perspective*, edited by Joan B. Landes, Paula Young Lee, and Paul Youngquist, 57–72. University Park: Pennsylvania State University Press, 2015.

"Introduction." In *Race, Romanticism, and the Atlantic*, edited by Paul Youngquist, 1–22. Farnham: Ashgate, 2013.

"Maps without Territory: Disappearing Trelawney Town." In *Romantic Cartographies: Mapping, Literature, Culture, 1789–1832*, edited by Sally Bushell, Julia S. Carlson, and Damian Walford Davies, 271–91. Cambridge: Cambridge University Press, 2020.

Yusoff, Kathryn. *A Billion Black Anthropocenes or None*. Minneapolis: University of Minnesota Press, 2018.

Zhang, SJ. "*Simarrona*: Beyond Etymologies toward a Practice of Unlearning." *Small Axe: A Caribbean Journal of Criticism* 27.2 (2023): 122–27.

Index

Page numbers for illustrations are in *italics*.

CAMBRIDGE STUDIES IN ROMANTICISM

General Editor
JAMES CHANDLER, University of Chicago

1 *Romantic Correspondence: Women, Politics and the Fiction of Letters*
MARY A. FAVRET

2 *British Romantic Writers and the East: Anxieties of Empire*
NIGEL LEASK

3 *Poetry as an Occupation and an Art in Britain, 1760–1830*
PETER MURPHY

4 *Edmund Burke's Aesthetic Ideology: Language, Gender and Political Economy in Revolution*
TOM FURNISS

5 *In the Theatre of Romanticism: Coleridge, Nationalism, Women*
JULIE A. CARLSON

6 *Keats, Narrative and Audience*
ANDREW BENNETT

7 *Romance and Revolution: Shelley and the Politics of a Genre*
DAVID DUFF

8 *Literature, Education, and Romanticism: Reading as Social Practice, 1780–1832*
ALAN RICHARDSON

9 *Women Writing about Money: Women's Fiction in England, 1790–1820*
EDWARD COPELAND

10 *Shelley and the Revolution in Taste: The Body and the Natural World*
TIMOTHY MORTON

11 *William Cobbett: The Politics of Style*
LEONORA NATTRASS

12 *The Rise of Supernatural Fiction, 1762–1800*
E. J. CLERY

13 *Women Travel Writers and the Language of Aesthetics, 1716–1818*
ELIZABETH A. BOHLS

14 *Napoleon and English Romanticism*
SIMON BAINBRIDGE

15 *Romantic Vagrancy: Wordsworth and the Simulation of Freedom*
CELESTE LANGAN

16 *Wordsworth and the Geologists*
JOHN WYATT

17 *Wordsworth's Pope: A Study in Literary Historiography*
ROBERT J. GRIFFIN

18 *The Politics of Sensibility: Race, Gender and Commerce in the Sentimental Novel*
MARKMAN ELLIS

19 *Reading Daughters' Fictions, 1709–1834: Novels and Society from Manley to Edgeworth*
CAROLINE GONDA

20 *Romantic Identities: Varieties of Subjectivity, 1774–1830*
ANDREA K. HENDERSON

21 *Print Politics: The Press and Radical Opposition in Early Nineteenth-Century England*
KEVIN GILMARTIN

22 *Reinventing Allegory*
THERESA M. KELLEY

23 *British Satire and the Politics of Style, 1789–1832*
GARY DYER

24 *The Romantic Reformation: Religious Politics in English Literature, 1789–1824*
ROBERT M. RYAN

25 *De Quincey's Romanticism: Canonical Minority and the Forms of Transmission*
MARGARET RUSSETT

26 *Coleridge on Dreaming: Romanticism, Dreams and the Medical Imagination*
JENNIFER FORD

27 *Romantic Imperialism: Universal Empire and the Culture of Modernity*
SAREE MAKDISI

28 *Ideology and Utopia in the Poetry of William Blake*
NICHOLAS M. WILLIAMS

29 *Sexual Politics and the Romantic Author*
SONIA HOFKOSH

30 *Lyric and Labour in the Romantic Tradition*
ANNE JANOWITZ

31 *Poetry and Politics in the Cockney School: Keats, Shelley, Hunt and Their Circle*
JEFFREY N. COX

32 *Rousseau, Robespierre and English Romanticism*
GREGORY DART

33 *Contesting the Gothic: Fiction, Genre and Cultural Conflict, 1764–1832*
JAMES WATT

34 *Romanticism, Aesthetics, and Nationalism*
DAVID ARAM KAISER

35 *Romantic Poets and the Culture of Posterity*
ANDREW BENNETT

36 *The Crisis of Literature in the 1790s: Print Culture and the Public Sphere*
PAUL KEEN

37 *Romantic Atheism: Poetry and Freethought, 1780–1830*
MARTIN PRIESTMAN

38 *Romanticism and Slave Narratives: Transatlantic Testimonies*
HELEN THOMAS

39 *Imagination under Pressure, 1789–1832: Aesthetics, Politics, and Utility*
JOHN WHALE

40 *Romanticism and the Gothic: Genre, Reception, and Canon Formation, 1790–1820*
MICHAEL GAMER

41 *Romanticism and the Human Sciences: Poetry, Population, and the Discourse of the Species*
MAUREEN N. MCLANE

42 *The Poetics of Spice: Romantic Consumerism and the Exotic*
TIMOTHY MORTON

43 *British Fiction and the Production of Social Order, 1740–1830*
MIRANDA J. BURGESS

44 *Women Writers and the English Nation in the 1790s*
ANGELA KEANE

45 *Literary Magazines and British Romanticism*
MARK PARKER

46 *Women, Nationalism and the Romantic Stage: Theatre and Politics in Britain, 1780–1800*
BETSY BOLTON

47 *British Romanticism and the Science of the Mind*
ALAN RICHARDSON

48 *The Anti-Jacobin Novel: British Conservatism and the French Revolution*
M. O. GRENBY

49 *Romantic Austen: Sexual Politics and the Literary Canon*
CLARA TUITE

50 *Byron and Romanticism*
JEROME MCGANN and
JAMES SODERHOLM

51 *The Romantic National Tale and the Question of Ireland*
INA FERRIS

52 *Byron, Poetics and History*
JANE STABLER

53 *Religion, Toleration, and British Writing, 1790–1830*
MARK CANUEL

54 *Fatal Women of Romanticism*
ADRIANA CRACIUN

55 *Knowledge and Indifference in English Romantic Prose*
TIM MILNES

56 *Mary Wollstonecraft and the Feminist Imagination*
BARBARA TAYLOR

57 *Romanticism, Maternity and the Body Politic*
JULIE KIPP

58 *Romanticism and Animal Rights*
DAVID PERKINS

59 *Georgic Modernity and British Romanticism: Poetry and the Mediation of History*
KEVIS GOODMAN

60 *Literature, Science and Exploration in the Romantic Era: Bodies of Knowledge*
TIMOTHY FULFORD,
DEBBIE LEE, and
PETER J. KITSON

61 *Romantic Colonization and British Anti-slavery*
DEIRDRE COLEMAN

62 *Anger, Revolution, and Romanticism*
ANDREW M. STAUFFER

63 *Shelley and the Revolutionary Sublime*
CIAN DUFFY

64 *Fictions and Fakes: Forging Romantic Authenticity, 1760–1845*
MARGARET RUSSETT

65 *Early Romanticism and Religious Dissent*
DANIEL E. WHITE

66 *The Invention of Evening: Perception and Time in Romantic Poetry*
CHRISTOPHER R. MILLER

67 *Wordsworth's Philosophic Song*
SIMON JARVIS

68 *Romanticism and the Rise of the Mass Public*
ANDREW FRANTA

69 *Writing against Revolution: Literary Conservatism in Britain, 1790–1832*
KEVIN GILMARTIN

70 *Women, Sociability and Theatre in Georgian London*
GILLIAN RUSSELL

71 *The Lake Poets and Professional Identity*
BRIAN GOLDBERG

72 *Wordsworth Writing*
ANDREW BENNETT

73 *Science and Sensation in Romantic Poetry*
NOEL JACKSON

74 *Advertising and Satirical Culture in the Romantic Period*
JOHN STRACHAN

75 *Romanticism and the Painful Pleasures of Modern Life*
ANDREA K. HENDERSON

76 *Balladeering, Minstrelsy, and the Making of British Romantic Poetry*
MAUREEN N. MCLANE

77 *Romanticism and Improvisation, 1750–1850*
ANGELA ESTERHAMMER

78 *Scotland and the Fictions of Geography: North Britain, 1760–1830*
PENNY FIELDING

79 *Wordsworth, Commodification and Social Concern: The Poetics of Modernity*
DAVID SIMPSON

80 *Sentimental Masculinity and the Rise of History, 1790–1890*
MIKE GOODE

98 *Romantic Women Writers, Revolution and Prophecy*
ORIANNE SMITH

99 *Britain, France and the Gothic, 1764–1820*
ANGELA WRIGHT

100 *Transfiguring the Arts and Sciences*
JON KLANCHER

101 *Shelley and the Apprehension of Life*
ROSS WILSON

102 *Poetics of Character: Transatlantic Encounters 1700–1900*
SUSAN MANNING

103 *Romanticism and Caricature*
IAN HAYWOOD

104 *The Late Poetry of the Lake Poets: Romanticism Revised*
TIM FULFORD

105 *Forging Romantic China: Sino-British Cultural Exchange 1760–1840*
PETER J. KITSON

106 *Coleridge and the Philosophy of Poetic Form*
EWAN JAMES JONES

107 *Romanticism in the Shadow of War: Literary Culture in the Napoleonic War Years*
JEFFREY N. COX

108 *Slavery and the Politics of Place: Representing the Colonial Caribbean, 1770–1833*
ELIZABETH A. BOHLS

109 *The Orient and the Young Romantics*
ANDREW WARREN

110 *Lord Byron and Scandalous Celebrity*
CLARA TUITE

111 *Radical Orientalism: Rights, Reform, and Romanticism*
GERARD COHEN-VRIGNAUD

112 *Print, Publicity, and Popular Radicalism in the 1790s*
JON MEE

113 *Wordsworth and the Art of Philosophical Travel*
MARK OFFORD

114 *Romanticism, Self-Canonization, and the Business of Poetry*
MICHAEL GAMER

115 *Women Wanderers and the Writing of Mobility, 1784–1814*
INGRID HORROCKS

116 *Eighteen Hundred and Eleven: Poetry, Protest and Economic Crisis*
E. J. CLERY

117 *Urbanization and English Romantic Poetry*
STEPHEN TEDESCHI

118 *The Poetics of Decline in British Romanticism*
JONATHAN SACHS

119 *The Caribbean and the Medical Imagination, 1764–1834: Slavery, Disease and Colonial Modernity*
EMILY SENIOR

120 *Science, Form, and the Problem of Induction in British Romanticism*
DAHLIA PORTER

121 *Wordsworth and the Poetics of Air*
THOMAS H. FORD

122 *Romantic Art in Practice: Cultural Work and the Sister Arts, 1760–1820*
THORA BRYLOWE

123 *European Literatures in Britain, 1815–1832: Romantic Translations*
DIEGO SIGALIA

124 *Romanticism and Theatrical Experience: Kean, Hazlitt and Keats in the Age of Theatrical News*
JONATHAN MULROONEY

125 *The Romantic Tavern: Literature and Conviviality in the Age of Revolution*
IAN NEWMAN

126 *British Orientalisms, 1759–1835*
JAMES WATT

127 *Print and Performance in the 1820s: Improvisation, Speculation, Identity*
ANGELA ESTERHAMMER

128 *The Italian Idea: Anglo-Italian Radical Literary Culture, 1815–1823*
WILL BOWERS

129 *The Ephemeral Eighteenth Century: Print, Sociability, and the Cultures of Collecting*
GILLIAN RUSSELL

130 *Physical Disability in British Romantic Literature*
ESSAKA JOSHUA

www.ingramcontent.com/pod-product-compliance
Ingram Content Group UK Ltd.
Pitfield, Milton Keynes, MK11 3LW, UK
UKHW020705160125
453751UK00007B/40

9 781009 523905